CASTLES IN WALES AND THE MARCHES

D. J. CATHCART KING AT CHEPSTOW CASTLE ADDRESSING THE 1983 EASTER
CONFERENCE OF THE SOCIETY FOR MEDIEVAL ARCHAEOLOGY

CASTLES IN WALES
AND THE MARCHES

ESSAYS IN HONOUR OF
D. J. CATHCART KING

Edited by
John R. Kenyon and Richard Avent

CARDIFF
UNIVERSITY OF WALES PRESS
1987

© University of Wales, 1987

British Library Cataloguing in Publication Data

Castles in Wales and the Marches: essays
  in honour of D. J. Cathcart King.
  1. Castles——Wales——History
  I. King, D. J. Cathcart   II. Kenyon, John R.
  III. Avent, Richard
  942.9   DA737

ISBN 0-7083-0948-8

Printed by The Bath Press, Avon

Contents

Plates

Figures

Tables

Preface

Over thirty years have elapsed since David King published his first paper on a Welsh castle. Since then (and often working in collaboration with Judge Clifford Perks) he has stripped the ivy from the walls of our knowledge of many of both the better and the lesser known castles of Wales and the Welsh March. However, although his detailed studies of individual castles have concentrated on this area, he has, at the same time, been compiling a corpus of castles covering the whole of England and Wales and this, his *magnum opus*, was published as the two-volume *Castellarium Anglicanum* in 1983. It is, and will remain, a standard work of reference for as long as castles continue to be studied.

We felt that our debt to David King should be recognized in the form of a collection of essays on the same theme as his own particular area of research. The following papers are thus offered in gratitude and as a measure of our respect for a scholar who is truly 'King of the Castle'.

JOHN R. KENYON
RICHARD AVENT
Cardiff, 1985

The Contributors

L. ALCOCK, Professor of Archaeology, University of Glasgow.

R. AVENT, Principal Inspector of Ancient Monuments and Historic Buildings, Cadw: Welsh Historic Monuments.

P. A. BARKER, Reader in British Archaeology, Department of Extra-Mural Studies, University of Birmingham.

L. A. S. BUTLER, Senior Lecturer in Medieval Archaeology, University of Leeds.

J. R. KENYON, Librarian, National Museum of Wales.

J. K. KNIGHT, Inspector of Ancient Monuments and Historic Buildings, Cadw: Welsh Historic Monuments.

J. M. LEWIS, Assistant Keeper, Department of Archaeology and Numismatics, National Museum of Wales.

J. C. PERKS, Circuit Judge.

D. F. RENN, Senior Actuary (4), Government Actuary's Department.

C. J. SPURGEON, Senior Investigator, Royal Commission on Ancient and Historical Monuments in Wales.

A. J. TAYLOR, formerly Chief Inspector of Ancient Monuments and Historic Buildings, Department of the Environment.

M. W. THOMPSON, formerly Principal Inspector of Ancient Monuments and Historic Buildings, Welsh Office.

P. V. WEBSTER, Senior Lecturer, Department of Extra-Mural Studies, University College, Cardiff.

G. WILLIAMS, Professor Emeritus of History, University College of Swansea.

Acknowledgements

This volume of essays was conceived in the spring of 1982; the fact that the typescript was completed by the end of the following year is a reflection of the generous co-operation which the editors received, at all stages, from the contributors: we thank them all.

The editors and the University of Wales Press are grateful to the following for permission to use their material in this book:

British Library, Pls. IV and V; National Library of Wales, Pl, VI. National Museum of Wales, cover illustration; Ordnance Survey, Pl. XV; Public Record Office, Pl. VII; Royal Commission on Ancient and Historical Monuments in Wales, Pls. I–III, X–XIV; Welsh Office, Cadw: Welsh Historic Monuments, Pls. IX, XVI and Tab. 5; Welsh Office, Cartographic Services (reproduced from Ordnance Survey maps SN21 SE and SN31 SW), Fig. 32.

Finally, we would like to thank John Rhys and Anne Howells, of the University of Wales Press, for their assistance in seeing this book through to publication.

Welsh Counties

Local government re-organization in 1974 resulted in the creation of eight new counties in Wales based, with the exception of the three new Glamorgans, on the amalgamation of the old shire counties into larger administrative units. Both are used in this book and the following list provides an approximate concordance between the two.

Since 1974	Before 1974
Clwyd	Denbighshire Flintshire north-eastern Merioneth
Gwynedd	Anglesey Caernarfonshire Merioneth (apart from north-eastern corner)
Powys	Brechonshire Montgomeryshire Radnorshire
Dyfed	Cardiganshire Carmarthenshire Pembrokeshire
Gwent	Monmouthshire
West Glamorgan Mid Glamorgan South Glamorgan	Glamorgan

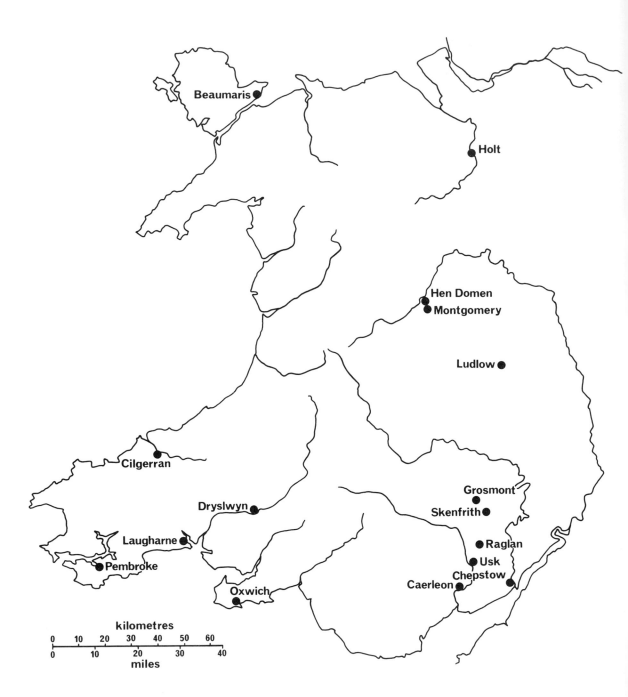

Location Map of Castles Described in the Text

David James Cathcart King: a memoir

J. C. PERKS

D AVID KING was born in Coombe Dingle near Bristol in 1913, and was educated at Clifton College and at Bristol University where he read law and took the degrees of Bachelor of Laws and Master of Laws, being the first person to receive the latter degree.

I met him for the first time shortly before the outbreak of the 1939–45 war, when we were both members of the Clifton Rowing Club, and displaying a maximum of keenness with a minimum of skill in the same clinker-built coxed four. David was also a keen sculler and had the distinction of being the worst sculler who raced under the club colours, a distinction he held only because I was so clumsy that I was not allowed out in a sculler.

It took a long time for us to discover that we shared an interest in castles as well as an interest in rowing and beer, each of us assuming that our particular form of lunacy was unlikely to be shared by anyone else in a rowing club. But in some way that I cannot now remember the discovery was made, and made in time for one short castle-hunting holiday before the outbreak of war compelled us to transfer our immediate interest from medieval to modern fortification. Our holiday was, however, a memorable one, including a visit to Richard's Castle in Herefordshire. I suppose one's first visit to Richard's Castle must always leave a deep impression, but ours was made unforgettable by the atmosphere of the place which made us both very uncomfortable when we were together and, after the first few moments, unwilling to be alone.

The war separated us except for one very short meeting in Kent, so that I can only speak of David's activities during those years from scraps of information which I picked up from him later. His service with the Royal Artillery took him to Syria, Iraq and Italy. Italy saw his most effective military service. It was there that he lost a leg and gained the Military Cross, and it was there also that he was recommended for the award of the Military Cross instead of being court-martialled when the full circumstances under which he returned to his regiment without his pistol after an engagement with the enemy were revealed.

It was in Syria, however, that he was able to pursue his castle studies, studies that resulted in two valuable papers, one giving for the first time an acceptable account of the great siege of Krak des Chevaliers, a task which required a scholar who was also a soldier, and the other giving the first account in English, and the best in any language, of the citadel of Damascus.

His visit to Krak was made even more memorable than such a visit must be because the French insisted that the place was so dangerous that an officer must have a military escort. The fact was that whereas a French officer would very likely have had his throat cut by one of the many Arabs in the castle, a British officer was perfectly safe, and David was able to leave his escort sitting in the shade and get on with his inspection without being hindered.

In Damascus things were not so easy. The trouble arose from the fact that the citadel stood in part of the city that was out-of-bounds to all ranks of the British Army. No doubt his fellow gunner, Brigadier Mortimer Wheeler, had he been stationed nearby, would have had no difficulty in obtaining the necessary permission to enter the forbidden area, but things were not so easy for Lieutenant King. That he overcame the difficulties we know because his paper in *Archaeologia* puts the matter beyond dispute. How he overcame these difficulties is not so widely known, and since to disclose his method would even now probably involve breaches of the Official Secrets Act I shall not disclose it. Suffice it to say that it was highly ingenious and quite unscrupulous, and if the Military Police had realised what this apparently guileless subaltern was doing they would have been anything but amused.

In time he obtained the permission he needed and could proceed to and from the citadel without the use of stratagems. This was not, however, the end of his embarrassments. The citadel at that time was used by the French as a military prison, and a room in one of the towers that David wanted to plan was used as a class-room for some form of instruction. To measure a room of complex shape in intense heat and without a companion to hold one end of the tape or to note down the measurements must always be less than enjoyable, but to undertake it, as David had to do, with a class of military criminals standing rigidly to attention under the orders of their most punctilious sergeant must have been nightmarish.

On leaving the army he chose teaching as his profession and for many years, until his retirement, taught in first one and then a second preparatory school in north Somerset where his infectious passion for medieval history, reinforced by his high technical skill in model-making, must have been an inspiration to generations of small boys. In fact it was one of his former pupils, Mark Cheshire, who collaborated with him in his paper on the town walls of Pembroke. It was, I believe, the experience that he gained in directing the model-making of his pupils that led to his own outstanding work in producing working models of siege-engines.

We had been demobilised within a short time of each other in February 1946 and had planned to celebrate our freedom by a second foray into the Marches of Wales, but ice and snow frustrated us and it was not until that summer that we were to make the first of many visits of varying duration to south Wales. This part of Wales was chosen because it was conveniently close to Bristol where we both then lived, and partly because it was liberally supplied with castles, many of which were almost unknown and very few of which had ever been adequately examined or published.

David planned these trips with all the care appropriate to an operation of war, even providing beautifully drawn maps showing the sites we hoped to find. He also did all the driving whenever we had any petrol. My only major contributions consisted of making reconnaissances on foot in difficult country (a task I could do better than he could since I had twice as many legs as he had) and holding one end of the tape when measurements were taken.

In this way we spent many happy days and learnt a good deal about the castles of south Wales, knowledge which we used in the production of papers on a number of castles, large and small, including the huge and little known castle of Llangibby. In every case the heavy work of writing, illustrating and dealing with editors fell on David's shoulders, my role being little more than that of *advocatus diaboli* on questions of dating.

As years went by my family and professional commitments made our joint expeditions no longer possible, and I was reduced to watching from the touchline. As late as 1981, however, he proposed to me that we should go to Criccieth and try and solve the problems posed by that most enigmatic of castles; unfortunately this was not possible, but I hope that it will not be long before he goes either alone or with some younger companion and solves the problems as he is so well able to do, especially now that his masterpiece has at last been published.

Looking back over an association lasting almost half a century, I account myself a very lucky man to have been privileged to play Watson to such a Holmes.

Castle-studies and the archaeological sciences: some possibilities and problems

LESLIE ALCOCK

I first met David Cathcart King in the late 1950s, when my Dinas Powys excavation led me to investigate the ringwork castles of south-east Wales. Our only formal collaboration was in this field, in which he was very definitely the senior partner,[1] but over the years, I have continued to enjoy his friendship, and to benefit from his attitude to scholarly research. That attitude might best be described as an irreverence, often robust, but sometimes puckish, towards Authority and authorities. It is well expressed by a phrase which, I believe, we coined together: *nescio ergo sum*. I would emphasize that we draw a careful distinction between scholarly nescience and mere porcine ignorance. I hope that the essay which follows may reflect something, at least, of this attitude.

Because of my long-standing admiration for DJCK, I was pleased to be invited to contribute to the present tribute volume; but I had difficulty in choosing a suitable topic, since my involvement in castle-excavations has been intermittent, and largely incidental to the examination of earlier periods. I remembered, however, that he had taught not only history but also mathematics, and that he had made a notable contribution to experimental archaeology. It seemed fitting, therefore, to present him with a brief survey of the potential which the archaeological sciences have for the specific field of castle-studies.

The first systematic survey of the topic was the symposium *Scientific Methods in Medieval Archaeology*,[2] itself the outcome of a conference held in the University of California at Los Angeles in 1967, at which scientists and medieval archaeologists had discussed mutual interests and problems. The resulting volume was a pioneering study in interdisciplinary scholarship, sometimes definitive in its conclusions, but in other areas tentative, because of the undeveloped state of the relevant scientific techniques. (In the present context, it should be mentioned that only two castles—Leicester and Sully-sur-Loire (Loiret)—featured in the discussion.) At the time, it was agreed to hold a further conference to review the state of the art after techniques had been developed and improved; but this proposal was never implemented, and Berger's volume remains unique.

Indeed, little systematic application of the archaeological sciences to medieval

[1] King and Alcock (1969).
[2] Berger (1970).

archaeology, including castle-studies, can be found in the literature. On the part of the scientists themselves, most effort is devoted to research in prehistoric periods, no doubt for readily understandable reasons. In the archaeological literature, a search through the Château Gaillard proceedings and other relevant journals reveals only a slight exploitation of a narrow range of scientific techniques except in the field of artefact analysis. Nor will much discussion be found of possible relationships between science and medieval archaeology in textbooks on archaeological methods. A brief, but none the less praiseworthy exception is Barker's exposition of the convergence of scientific, documentary and archaeological evidence at Hen Domen.[3] More recently, Higham has set out the possibilities of science-based chronologies in his survey of dating methods in medieval archaeology.[4] He rounds this off with case studies from the castles of Okehampton and Hen Domen; and it is significant that he can quote only a single science-derived date from each site.

It will be obvious that, within the scope of a tribute-essay (and, be it said, the limitations of my own ignorance), I cannot offer any broad or thorough conspectus of the field. I have tried to keep two distinct groups of scholars in mind. For scientists, I hope to foster awareness of the value of castle-excavations in providing evidence relevant to their own research interests. For castle-students, I aim to demonstrate areas where collaboration with scientists seems likely to be particularly fruitful or exciting. At the same time, I wish to point out certain limitations in the available archaeological techniques which, as experience shows, have not been adequately appreciated by historians.

I have concentrated on the three areas of chronology, environmental studies, and experimental archaeology, and I have deliberately omitted any account of artefact analysis or prospecting. I am also particularly aware of the absence of any consideration of mathematical approaches, computer (and other) modelling, and spatial analysis: all potentially fruitful techniques which have been largely ignored in castle-studies.[5] Finally, I make no apology for the eclectic nature of my specific examples. In an essay which cannot hope to be comprehensive, I have aimed instead at vivid and concrete detail.

A. Chronology

The development of methods of dating based on natural processes, and independent of archaeological criteria, has always been a principal aim of archaeological science. Consequently, discussion of chronological techniques formed a major part of the Los Angeles proceedings in 1967. It should be said at the outset that mutual benefits often accrue from the collaboration that is involved between scientists and archaeologists. For instance, the use of radioactive carbon to date artefacts arose from the wish of physicists to use archaeologically-derived dates

---

[3] Barker (1977), 216–17.

[4] Higham (1982).

[5] For readers who wish to explore this field, a good introduction is Orton (1980). See also Jope (1972). Occurring as they do in large numbers, earthwork castles would be particularly suitable for mathematical analysis.

to test hypotheses about radioactive decay; and much of the work in magnetic dating has told us more about secular changes in the earth's magnetic field than about archaeological chronology.

In this paper, I shall largely confine myself to the two principal scientific techniques applicable to the dating of castles—radiocarbon assay, and tree-ring dating—with only a passing mention of two other potential techniques, those based on thermoremanent magnetism and on thermoluminescence.

1. *Radiocarbon dating*[6]

Since Willard Libby first recognized the value of radioactive carbon (carbon-14) for estimating the age of organic materials, radiocarbon dating has been widely acclaimed by archaeologists as providing an accurate chronology that is independent of archaeological dating methods such as association and typology or seriation. It is not necessary here to describe the basic principles or methodology that are involved; but it may be as well to stress that the method is only applicable to organic materials such as wood or bone; and that what it dates is the death of the organism, for instance the cutting down of a tree or the killing of an animal: and emphatically not the burning down of a building.

My purpose here is to concentrate on the specific problems which arise when radiocarbon age estimates are used in a historically datable period. If this seems a limited and negative approach, its value will be appreciated by anyone who, for instance, has had to refuse requests for funds for dates intended to discriminate between two structural periods on a motte-top that were less than a century apart.

In a historical period, the first problem is posed by the divergence which has been noticed between estimated radiocarbon years or time, and calendar years or real time, to use the customary shorthand expressions. The reasons for the discrepancy are unclear, but its reality has been demonstrated by a large body of comparisons between calculated radiocarbon dates and tree-ring dates; the latter, as we shall see (pp. 10–13), do indeed correspond exactly to solar or calendar years. In the historical context of castle-studies, it is axiomatic that we need dates in calendar years; so before it can be used, a carbon-14 age estimate must be converted into calendar years by means of a calibration chart.[7] Such charts are, indeed, readily available; but except for the special case of wiggle-matching, discussed below, they represent not exact statements but estimates of statistical probability. In no way can a calibrated radiocarbon date achieve the status of absolute accuracy and precision that is inherent in a historical date.

The reasons for this, in fact, lie deeper than the discrepancy between carbon years and calendar years, in the very nature of the original age-estimate. This should always be correctly quoted in a form such as 1315 ± 30, where the first

---

[6] Good account in Aitken (1974); briefer survey in Burleigh (1980). Major discussion of archaeological applications in Allibone *et al.* (1970).

[7] Clark (1975); Stuiver (1982).

element is conventionally referred to as the 'central date' and the second element is the error term or standard deviation (sigma): an estimate of the uncertainty involved in each individual date. Now at first sight, the medieval historian is well used to dates of this kind. A charter, for instance, might be dated 1266 × 1272, because one of its signatories is known, on other evidence, to have come to office in 1266 and to have died by 1272. These two years then provide absolute limits to the charter. It would be natural to think that 1315 ± 30 is the equivalent of 1285 × 1345: an unhelpfully wide bracket, it is true, but still an absolute one. Such a belief would be wholly erroneous.

The standard deviation arises because what is being measured in a radiocarbon age estimate is a number of events which are individually random but which can be expressed as a statistical average; namely beta-particle emissions. It is from the measured frequency of these that the radioactivity of a sample, and hence its age, are calculated.[8] On average, a gramme of carbon in equilibrium with the atmosphere emits fourteen or fifteen particles per minute; but because of the random nature of the emissions, there is no certainty that fourteen or fifteen emissions would be counted in any individual minute. It follows that the actual radioactivity of a sample—and hence its age—cannot be measured absolutely, but only approximately. The standard deviation expresses the statistical limits of the approximation. These limits are such that there is a 68 per cent chance that the true date falls within a bracket of 1-sigma either side of the central date: in the case quoted, in the bracket 1285–1345. But it is better practice to use a 2-sigma bracket, which increases the probability of accuracy to 95 per cent: in this case 1255–1375. With present techniques of measurement it is unusual to see a sigma as low as thirty years, and sixty or seventy years is more normal, giving a 2-sigma bracket of 240 or 280 years. It will be readily apparent that, as a result of the statistically-derived error term alone, it is futile to think of comparing radiocarbon dates within limits of less than several centuries.

This point must be further emphasized from the evidence of other studies. Recently, for instance, a series of eight replicate samples from a single tree were dated by twenty different laboratories. In general terms, the results compared well from one laboratory to another. None the less, the observed discrepancies were such as to suggest that the quoted counting errors, of the kind already discussed, should be multiplied by a factor of between two and three if accuracy is desired.[9] Beyond this, it is recognized that there is a wide range of potential sources of error which are not readily calculable. A comparison between ten carbon-14 dates for samples derived from a historically datable event at Cadbury Castle, and the historical date itself,[10] led to the conclusion that 'it is normally beyond the scope of radiocarbon dating to define absolute archaeological time-scales to better than within several centuries.'[11]

---

[8] This account does not apply to carbon-14 measurement by high energy, mass spectroscopy; but I see no early possibility of this technique being made available for medieval dating.

[9] International Study Group (1982).

[10] Alcock (1980), 708–12.

[11] Campbell *et al.* (1979), 37.

After this pessimistic appraisal we should recognize that there are, neverthe-less, circumstances where the medievalist might welcome dates of low precision if their accuracy were guaranteed. A startling instance of this is Piboule's demonstration, on the evidence of radiocarbon dates, that some French souter-rains are works of the eleventh to fifteenth centuries AD, and must therefore take their place in the medieval history of *les structures de défense*; previously, these underground chambers would have been regarded very firmly as works of the last millennium BC and the first millennium AD.[12] Another case might arise in the excavation of a small circular earthwork which, on surface morpho-logy alone, might be pre-Roman, or might be a medieval ringwork castle. In a region of ceramic poverty, the typology of excavated artefacts might totally fail to distinguish between one possibility or the other, whereas radiocarbon dates from structural timbers or an associated hearth would put the period beyond doubt.

The moral of all this is that excavators of castles need to be fully aware that a radiocarbon age estimate is unlikely to give them the kind of precision which they require; but there will nevertheless be circumstances in which it is the most accurate date available.

2. *Dating by thermoremanent magnetism and thermoluminescence*[13]

Whereas radiocarbon dating depends on measuring the decaying radioactivity of organic substances such as wood and bone, two other methods are based on the properties of baked clay, such as that in ovens, hearths and kilns.[14]

a) Thermoremanent magnetism

When clay is heated, some of the minerals present in it align themselves to the direction of the local magnetic field. This direction varies with time on a cyclical, but irregular curve. It has therefore been necessary to establish the curve empirically on the evidence of magnetic measurements from kilns and ovens with known dates, which have been established initially on historical or archaeological grounds. In other words, the technique is not independent of historical or archaeological chronologies. Once a satisfactory curve has been established, it is possible to compare the magnetic direction of a newly excavated oven or hearth, and to read off its date.

In the 1960s, samples from Hen Domen, Ludgershall, Northampton and San-dal castles were among those used to establish the medieval curve.[15] As yet, however, no magnetic dates relevant to castle-dating have been published in detail.[16] Nevertheless, the technique has considerable potential for medieval chronology-building, because the curve from *c.* AD 900 is now considered to be

---

[12] Piboule (1982).

[13] Basic statement in Aitken (1970); also Burleigh (1980).

[14] Both are also applicable to pottery, but this is expressly omitted here.

[15] Aitken and Hawley (1966); Aitken and Hawley (1967); Hurst (1966).

[16] For problematic dates from Stamford and Okehampton, see Mahany (1977), 232; Higham (1982), 103.

well established. A bracket of ± 25 years is claimed; considerably more precise, that is, than a conventional radiocarbon date.

b) Thermoluminescence

Many elements, such as some forms of potassium and uranium, undergo spontaneous radioactive decay, and the radiation that this generates can produce 'radiation damage' in materials in the local environment: for instance, in a body of clay. A second result of firing clay is that the 'radiation damage' which has been incurred over geological time is wiped out, and in effect, an internal 'clock' is set to zero. Subsequently, further 'radiation damage' accumulates with the passage of time; and if this is measured, then the lapse of time since the firing of the clay can be calculated. The measurement is achieved by heating the clay, and recording the energy which is emitted in the form of light: hence the term thermoluminescence. The method has considerable potential for castle-dating, especially because dates within ± 10 per cent of the age of the sample may be expected; but despite this, I can find no instance of it being used to date castle hearths or ovens.

3. *Dendrochronology*

Although dendrochronology, or tree-ring dating, was primarily developed in order to date prehistoric timbers which had been preserved in extremely arid conditions in America, its applicability to standing buildings of medieval origin has been recognized for some decades. Consequently, two of the papers of the Los Angeles conference are devoted respectively to general dendrochronology, and to central European dendrochronology for the middle ages.[17] Slight reference was also made in the published papers of the conference to the use of tree-ring dates as a check on radiocarbon dates.[18] There are no specific examples, however, of dates from castles. Apart from the timbers of standing buildings, waterlogged wood from excavated medieval sites also provides good samples for the technique. Examples of dates derived from such timbers can be found occasionally in the Château Gaillard proceedings.[19] The method is not without problems and difficulties, including discrepancies between tree-ring dates and those derived from ceramic typology. Some of these may result from either the re-use of old timbers, or the insertion of replacement timbers, in any one building.[20] A singular triumph has been the precise dating of the Danish geometrical fortress of Trelleborg to the autumn of 980 or the spring of 981.[21]

In simple terms, the method itself is based on the fact that each year a tree puts on a new growth ring, so that, in the case of a newly felled tree, it is possible to determine its age simply by counting rings inward from the bark to the core. Secondly, in normal conditions, the individual rings differ in their

[17] Ferguson (1970); Huber and Giertz (1970).
[18] Horn (1970).
[19] Hertz (1973); Janssen (1972); Leboutet (1972); Lutz (1977); Stiesdal (1982).
[20] Hinz (1975).
[21] Roesdahl (1982).

width in response to climatic variations, which are likely to occur uniformly over a fairly wide region. By plotting, on a graph, the annual variations in ring width, it is possible to correlate the earlier rings on a newly felled tree with the later rings on an ancient tree, or, in archaeological applications, a beam from such a tree. The width-pattern of the earlier rings on the ancient beam may be compared in turn with the outer rings from a yet older timber. In this way, a master curve, extending over centuries or millennia, may be constructed. It should be added that the comparison of ring-width plots is nowadays done both by eye and by computer-matching.

Elegantly simple though it is in principle, the method has certain snags in archaeological practice. There is uncertainty over the size of the area within which climatic variations, and therefore ring-width patterns, are likely to be homogeneous.[22] In some environmental circumstances, the width variation within a particular tree may be too slight to measure: the rings are then described as complacent. For precise dating, it is obviously necessary to have the very latest rings preserved, but these sapwood rings are frequently removed from building timbers. This is especially the case where a beam has been squared off from the heartwood of a tree. Fortunately, in medieval carpentry, planks and staves were often cleft radially from the trunk, and even if the bark and sapwood were trimmed off, it is possible to make a close estimate of the number of rings that have been lost. (At the Trelleborg, sapwood and even bark were preserved: hence the precise date.) Despite these snags, once the master curve has been established for an area and a species—in medieval Europe, usually oak—it is possible to date any individual ring to a precise year, and to establish the felling date of a building-timber within a twenty-year bracket or less if any sapwood is present. There can be no doubt that this is the most precise dating technique which the archaeological scientist can at present offer to the castle-student.

It is worth considering at this point what suitable timbers might be found in a castle. Roof-structures would appear to be an obvious source; but given the possibility of the replacement of individual timbers, or even of whole roof-structures—a possibility well exemplified by the unresolved controversy over the dating of the hall roof at Leicester Castle[23]—it is evident that they must be used with caution. The intra-mural timbers used as reinforcement in the walls of some castles would be ideal, because, of course, they are intimately linked to the construction itself: but unfortunately we are normally presented only with the empty chases, the timber itself having perished.[24] Far more promising are the timbers used for bridges, which were often of large scantling, and, in the case of sites with wet ditches, are likely to be preserved by waterlogging. This likelihood is increased by the structural characteristic that the posts of bridges were often not earthfast but were tenoned into transverse sole-plates.[25] We shall shortly see the importance of the bridge-timbers at Caerlaverock, but

---

[22] Berger *et al.* (1971).
[23] Horn (1970), 56–66.
[24] Wilcox (1972); Binding (1977).
[25] Rigold (1973); Rigold (1975).

we may note in passing the dendrochronological date of *c.* 1360 for a bridge built of oak and elm at Waltham Abbey.[26]

Turning now to the establishment of master curves for Britain and Ireland: a pioneering survey was published by Schove and Lowther in 1957.[27] At that time, they could only present 'floating chronologies' for the Anglo-Saxon and medieval periods—that is, curves that were not firmly tied to absolute dates. A major reason for this was the shortage of oak timbers for years around 1700, so that it was impossible to link medieval timbers with modern ones. Attempts were made therefore to fix the medieval chronology by correlating particularly wide or narrow rings with climatic events recorded in contemporary documents. It was two decades before Baillie was able to announce the establishment of an oak chronology for Ulster covering a span of 966 years before the present.[28] Other landmarks were the development of reference curves for oaks from southern England, and for Yorkshire, covering respectively the years 1230–1546 and 1350–1590.[29] In 1977, a major symposium at the National Maritime Museum, Greenwich, surveyed the development of dendrochronology, its methods, results and applications, on a European-wide basis.[30] Finally, to bring this outline down to the time of writing, in 1982 Baillie produced a comprehensive account of tree-ring dating, with particular reference to the establishment of a Belfast chronology that was fixed over the past two millennia and which could be applied to the whole of Ireland, and to Scotland as well.[31]

It is at this point that we can return to the relevance of dendrochronology to castle-studies. Among the timbers used by Baillie in demonstrating the medieval dendrochronology of Scotland were some from successive phases of the bridge at Caerlaverock Castle.[32] These were large squared beams, and in some cases sapwood was still present at the arrises. Consequently it was possible to establish a felling date of 1277, or shortly thereafter, for the first phase bridge of a castle that was known to have been besieged in 1300. A group of timbers felled in the late spring of 1333 may refer to a refurbishment shortly before Edward III's victory at Halidon Hill. The second phase of the bridge could be dated to 1371 or shortly thereafter. This precise dating of the Caerlaverock bridges may be contrasted with the case of the Eynsford Castle bridge where four possible tree-ring dates were offered—1035, 1221, 1138 and 1046 in order of preference—and the excavator was left to choose 1138 on archaeological grounds.[33] This, of course, violates the principle that 'a match [of ring-widths] is or is not correct—there are no alternatives'; or the dendrochronologist's advice to the archaeologist: 'Do not accept multiple-choice dates.'[34]

[26] Huggins (1970).
[27] Schove and Lowther (1957).
[28] Baillie (1976).
[29] Fletcher *et al.* (1974); Morgan (1977).
[30] Fletcher (1978).
[31] Baillie (1982).
[32] Baillie (1982), 160–63; Baillie forthcoming.
[33] Rigold (1975), 91.
[34] Morgan (1980); Baillie (1982), 263.

To sum up: given, on the one hand, large oak timbers, with marked ring-width variation and some preserved sapwood, and, on the other hand, a well constructed regional master curve, dendrochronology provides the most precise and accurate method of dating which archaeological science can at present offer to the excavators of castles. Moreover, further refinements can be expected. One is the filling up of gaps in the master curve. Another is the use of tree-ring dates, in association with three or more high precision radiocarbon dates (that is, with a standard deviation of $\pm$ 15 years or less), spread across a single timber, to produce a high precision calibration. This is the technique known as wiggle-matching, because of the sinuosity of the curves involved. The technique has been applied at Caerlaverock, and an account is promised in the full report on the tree-ring dates from that site.[35]

B. Environmental and biological studies

Another major field of archaeological science is constituted by biological and environmental studies. It is true that most research has been concentrated on prehistoric periods, and the study of the environment in more recent centuries has been largely, but not entirely, neglected.[36] It is, nevertheless, the case that castles can provide suitable contexts for the recovery of environmental and biological evidence; and that such evidence can provide information about the setting of a castle, and about the way of life of its inhabitants, which cannot be obtained from other sources. In response to these opportunities, there is now a marked trend towards the appearance of specialist appendices by biologists and soil scientists in major excavation reports.

In simple terms, a castle may provide three broad types of context for environmental and biological evidence:[37]

1. pre-castle surfaces, buried under earthworks, or pre-castle soils incorporated in their make-up, are a major source of information about the environment upon which the castle was imposed.
2. peripheral areas, such as silting ditches, may contain evidence for climatic and botanical changes during the period of a castle's use.
3. internal structures, such as floors (especially kitchen floors), latrine-pits and drains, may incorporate more intimate evidence of the way of life of the inhabitants.

We may look at each of these in turn.

1. *The pre-castle environment*

At Lismahon (Co. Down), where a motte had been raised over an early medieval rath, it was possible, by comparing the soil beneath the rath with the modern

[35] Baillie forthcoming.
[36] Evans (1975), 158–87.
[37] Limbrey (1975); Evans (1978), especially 112–29.

plough soil outside it, to show that the area had not been cultivated before the rath was built.[38] Likewise at Middleton Stoney (Oxon.), the ditch of the inner bailey of the castle had been cut through a soil which had not been cultivated for some centuries; it may have been pasture, or even woodland.[39] In complete contrast was the discovery of field systems beneath the earthworks at Hen Domen and Sandal. At Hen Domen, the evidence came partly through archaeological techniques—the discovery of ridge and furrow cut by the bailey ditch and underlying the bailey bank. Incidentally, the results of primary field survey were then enhanced by computer modelling. The major scientific input, however, came from an analysis of pollen grains and bracken spores from the soil beneath the bailey bank. These suggested that an area formerly used for arable cultivation had been abandoned for that purpose, but had possibly been used as rough grazing, for a decade or so before the castle was built.[40] At Sandal, it was again the analysis of pollen from the pre-castle cultivation ridges which revealed arable farming, with grassland in the vicinity. The evidence allowed Jones to infer the character of the field system, and to assess its implications for pre-Norman territorial organization.[41]

2. *Silting ditches*

The ditch of a castle is likely to provide a damp, if not actually waterlogged, context, with anaerobic conditions ideal for the preservation of organic material: that is to say, botanical and zoological specimens. These might include both microscopic (pollen grains) and macroscopic (seeds, fruits, leaves, branches) vegetable remains, which have blown into the ditch; small, even microscopic animals which lived and died in the ditch, or fell into it; and human detritus, such as food refuse, or discarded wooden, straw, leather, or textile artefacts deliberately thrown in. Unless the ditch is periodically cleared out, the material will accumulate in regular stratified order, except, of course, that heavy items may tend to sink. A promising instance is the moat of Barnard Castle. Cut through unstable clay and shale, it must rapidly have silted to a depth of 2 m, preserving in the process leather and wooden objects, and much environmental evidence.[42] At Hen Domen there is a similar promise of environmental evidence of all kinds from the waterlogged filling of the bailey ditch.[43] At Sandal, analysis of both macro- and micro-fossils from the outer ditch and from garderobes, in conjunction with charcoal samples, presented a picture of some cereal cultivation in the vicinity of the castle. During its occupation, an oak-dominated woodland was reduced to mixed oak woodland; subsequently, the outer ditch was

---

[38] Proudfoot (1959).

[39] Evans (1972).

[40] Barker and Lawson (1971). Pollen report by P. M. Moore, 69–70; computer graphics by S. Laflin, 71–72.

[41] Rees and Bartley (1983b); Jones (1983).

[42] Austin (1979).

[43] Barker and Higham (1982), 95.

colonized by shrubs, especially willow, and ultimately by oak trees.[44] Occasionally environmental evidence can even be obtained from a dry context, as has been shown by a study of slugs and snails from the inner bailey ditch at Middleton Stoney.[45]

Despite the promise of these and other ditches, little has yet been published in detail. At present, the outstanding account of biological material from a military ditch in Britain comes not from a castle but from the Roman auxiliary fort at Bearsden on the Antonine Wall.[46] It is mentioned here, not because of its chronological relevance, but because it shows the kind of information which will become available, in fullness of time, from castle-excavations as well. Chemical and biological analysis—including the identification of intestinal parasites—showed that the Bearsden ditch had served in part as a sewer. Consequently, in addition to information about the local flora contemporary with the fort, it also provided evidence for the diet of the soldiery. The presence of wheat fragments comparable with those in modern wholemeal flour is no surprise, nor is the occurrence of native edible fruits such as raspberry, blackberry, strawberry and bilberry; less to be expected are remains of exotic plants—figs, celery and opium poppy.

3. *Internal features*

For comparable evidence for the diet of medieval castle-dwellers, as well as other biological evidence, we may turn to the internal features of castles: pits, especially garderobe pits, drains and miscellaneous layers of rubbish. An outstanding instance, in terms of the full publication of the plant and insect remains, though not, as yet, of the other contents, is Pit F1/27 at Hen Domen.[47] This pit, 3 m square and at least 6.6 m deep, may have been an unsuccessful attempt to dig a well: certainly there is no evidence that it was a latrine pit. It was filled with a small quantity of kitchen refuse, including fish bones, egg shells, mammalian bones, and even a goose's wing; but the principal infilling was of plant debris, partly derived from buildings in the form of thatch, wattle and other timber, but mostly having the character of stable bedding. The plant remains are essentially local material brought in from neighbouring cornfields, meadows, marshes and woodlands: a flora normal in central Wales today.

If Pit F1/27 tells us about the countryside around Hen Domen, a more intimate picture of human activity within a castle is provided by the contents of a blocked fifteenth-century drain from the kitchen at Barnard Castle.[48] The variety of food species present suggests that what we have here are traces of food prepared for the high table of the castle hall. The most conventional items comprised cuts of beef, mutton and pork, along with veal, lamb and sucking pig. Game animals are represented by red, fallow and roe deer, and hare. Goose and chicken

---

[44] Rees and Bartley (1983a); Smith *et al.* (1983a); Smith *et al.* (1983b).
[45] Evans (1972).
[46] Knights *et al.* (1983).
[47] Grieg *et al.* (1982).
[48] Donaldson *et al.* (1980).

(and also eggs) appear to have been regular items, supplemented by wild birds which ranged in size from grouse and partridge to small song-birds. Fish were also important: herring was the most abundant small fish, but cod and ling may have been more important, as well as haddock, pike, conger eel and, more rarely, common eels, trout, whiting, gurnard and flat fish. Rivers, inshore waters, and the sea to a depth of 100 m or more were all exploited. No surprise is caused by the occurrence of oysters, cockles and mussels. Finally, vegetable remains include oats, peas, sloe and elder. While it is not possible to quantify the relative importance of all these elements in the diet of the medieval aristocracy, their sheer range must evoke our interest and admiration.

The kitchen-drain deposit from Barnard Castle is altogether exceptional both qualitatively and in terms of its content. Animal bones and other food remains have been reported, however, from a wide variety of deposits—pits, gullies, occupation layers, refuse layers, ditch fills—from castles which range from simple ringworks like Llantrithyd, through baronial strongholds like Threave or Sandal, to a royal castle like Portchester.[49] The bones appear to be principally from food or kitchen refuse, and they often yield information about methods of butchery. The principal species represented are domestic, with cattle to the fore: the ratios of sheep (and/or goat) and pig are more variable, both from site to site and from period to period on any one site. Immature as well as adult animals are normally present, with sucking pig strongly represented: given the prolific breeding of pigs, this was probably as rare a delicacy as beefburgers today. Red, roe and fallow deer all occur, and at Portchester they became increasingly important through the middle ages. Domestic fowl and geese were kept for the table. Horse bones are rare, presumably because the horse was not eaten. Dogs are often present in numbers, and cats were needed to keep down the mice and black rats. Smaller game animals included the hare and a variety of birds, some of which had probably been taken by the goshawks recorded at Portchester and Llantrithyd. Fish bones are poorly represented, and the predominance of cod may be a function of the robustness of cod vertebrae.

In published reports on animal bones, it is customary to proceed from lists of individual bones to inferences about the relative proportions of the various species, especially of domestic animals; the minimum number of animals present; perhaps even the lean carcass weight available; and hence the contribution of particular animals to the diet.[50] It is also possible to estimate the stature of domestic animals, and the age at which they were killed. On this basis we may hope to build up a model of medieval animal husbandry, and its role in the economy. This ambitious programme is not without its snags. Some of these are well outlined in the Portchester report,[51] but others deserve discussion here. For a start, there is no complete agreement as to how the proportions of the different species should be calculated. It has been suggested that the number

[49] Llantrithyd: Noddle *et al.* (1977); Threave: Barnetson (1981); Sandal: Griffith *et al.* (1983); Portchester: Grant (1977); Eastham (1977).

[50] Chaplin (1971).

[51] Grant (1977).

of fragments, gross weight of bones, and estimated minimum number of individuals should all be used because 'none of them alone gives a true picture'.[52] Moreover, conventional methods of estimating the killing-age of animals sometimes imply an animal population that was slaughtered before it had time to reproduce itself.[53] This may be because one customary method of calculating age at death—that based on the fusion of the epiphyses of long bones—is said to 'contain a serious flaw in its logic'.[54] The relevance of tooth-wear to age—looking in the horse's mouth—has also been questioned.[55]

These technical problems are, however, relatively minor compared with the primary issue: how relevant and representative is our sample? Essentially the problem has two levels: how completely was the potential sample recovered for analysis; and how representative is the sample itself of human activity on the site? The limitations on completeness of recovery begin with the proven inability of excavators themselves—the actual wielders of trowels—to recognize and retrieve all the evidence, whether artefactual or environmental, which they turn over in the course of digging.[56] This is compounded in the case of botanical and zoological evidence. Leaving such microscopic material as pollen grains out of account, there is still a great variety of small items which cannot easily be retrieved by conventional excavation techniques. In relation to diet, these would include seeds and grains, and small bones, especially of birds and fish. In wider environmental terms, vegetable, entomological and molluscan specimens are all involved. It has been recognized for over a decade that the only way to improve retrieval rates is by techniques of flotation and wet-sieving: even these cannot guarantee total recovery.[57] Such techniques were indeed employed on material from the Barnard Castle drain and Pit F1/27 at Hen Domen; but at Portchester the 'possible sources of error and bias that may affect an unsieved site' are pointedly mentioned by Grant.

Assuming that refined techniques of sieving could raise the recovery rate to a high level, how valid would the material thus recovered be for inferences about the original animal population and hence about diet and husbandry?[58] For a start, we must recognize that not all the bones discarded from a kitchen or a hall had equal survival value. In particular, the bones of young animals and of certain species such as pig are especially likely to decay. More important, however, is the relationship between discard or deposit on the one hand, and sample on the other: between what was thrown away where on the original site, and which parts of the site happen to be excavated. Much thought has been devoted in recent years to formulating strategies for sampling on excavations, so that the excavation of a limited area might still yield evidence that

[52] Noddle *et al.* (1977), 63.
[53] Alcock (1975).
[54] Watson (1978).
[55] Grant (1978).
[56] Clarke (1978–79).
[57] Payne (1972a).
[58] Payne (1972b).

was representative enough for valid generalization about the site as a whole.[59] Some of these strategies have been based on mathematical concepts of probability: their validity depends on the occupants of the site having acted in a mathematically random manner in their activities of building houses, laying hearths, cooking and discarding food refuse, and so on.

Is such random behaviour likely? Common human experience suggests that it is not; but can this be tested? In relation to activities in the past, it can only validly be tested by the total excavation of an archaeological site: the one hundred per cent sample. Much attention has been paid recently to establishing an empirical basis for general laws by observing the discard patterns and other activities of modern peoples: but hunter-gatherer groups and the Tucson, Arizona, garbage survey are poles apart from castle-studies. Perhaps more relevant is South's generalization, on the basis of excavations at Fort Moultrie and other sites in South Carolina,

'On British-American sites of the
eighteenth century a concentrated
refuse deposit will be found at
the points of entrance and exit.'[60]

In other words, you went to the back step and chucked. This is not random activity, but highly structured; and it is so in relation to another kind of structure, namely, a building and its door; and this in turn is the physical manifestation or functional realization of a structured social organization.

Negatively, it follows from this that probabilistic sampling, on the basis of a random number table, is inappropriate for exploring the archaeology of a complex, structured society. But there is also a positive implication. Given some knowledge of the physical structures of a society—its buildings—we can begin to predict where the richest and most interesting samples might be found. The relevance of this to castle excavations is obvious, for there we normally have a good idea of the layout before excavation starts. True though this is, we still need a wide data base, empirically derived, before we can begin to predict where our best samples will be found. As it happens, the buildings which are most important in social terms are not likely to be rich in evidence. A primitive demonstration of this is provided by the distribution of pottery around, rather than within, the hall at Castle Tower, Penmaen. It is reinforced by the observation that the bones from the motte top of Baile Hill, York, were remarkably fragmented—and therefore difficult to identify—probably because 'the floor of the castle was regularly cleared and all the larger fragments removed'.[61] At present, our outstanding source of information about discard on a castle is the Sandal excavation report. Here the recording is sufficiently refined for us to

---

[59] Cherry *et al.* (1978) for a general overview; Hinton (1983), 6–7 for comments in a medieval context; Astill and Lobb (1982) for a view *contra* that expressed here.

[60] South (1977), 48. Much theory has been developed to account for the ways in which artefacts come to be discarded on archaeological sites. The weakness of a flow diagram like that of Schiffer (1972) is that it is two-dimensional and unilinear, whereas it should be four-dimensional and multilinear.

[61] Penmaen: Alcock (1966), fig. 7; Baile Hill: Rackham (1977), 146–47.

be able to compare the distribution of pottery—and by implication, other refuse—at various periods in the castle's occupation, including the moment of time represented by the siege of 1645.[62] It is particularly salutary to learn that although the barbican ditch was the main rubbish dump, it was not the only one; a great deal of material was evidently disposed of elsewhere. This has implications for the overall validity of the sample of animal bones from the barbican ditch.

In conclusion, it is clear that the study of zoological material from castles has a great deal to tell us about the diet of the inhabitants—and about other conditions of life as well, when we include rats, stable flies and intestinal parasites. Vegetable samples contribute less simply because of their sheer scarcity. Much of this information we could not derive from documentary sources. Given improved techniques of recovery, and more thought about where to sample, the yield of information will be even greater. At the same time, we must recognize that the problems of establishing minimum numbers of animals, yield of animal protein, or age of killing will not easily be solved. This imposes limits on our inferences about animal husbandry and its role in the economy. At present we can learn more from economic documents, and especially from medieval manuals of husbandry, than we can from the specialist bone analyses appended to excavation reports. There is a lesson here for the archaeozoologists as well; for it would surely be useful for them to compare the excavated material with the expectations of Walter of Henley.[63]

C. EXPERIMENTAL ARCHAEOLOGY

Experimental archaeology has two principal strands which may be distinguished analytically, but which in practice are often intertwined.[64] By replicating ancient structures and other artefacts, it is possible first to test hypotheses about site formation in both the constructional and decay phases; and secondly, to examine the effectiveness of artefacts, and the reasonableness of our functional interpretations. In relation to castle-studies, the first strand is represented especially by the construction and weathering of earthworks; but the erection of timber buildings and their destruction, especially by fire, is also relevant. The second strand finds expression especially in the fabrication and testing of weapons.

General Lane Fox Pitt–Rivers appears to have been the first archaeologist to dig a ditch with the express purpose of observing the processes of silting, so that he might use his observations to check the interpretation of the silted ditches found on archaeological sites. More recently, carefully designed ditch and bank earthworks have been built on both chalk and sand subsoils.[65] Primitive tools such as antler picks and rakes and ox scapula shovels were used in an attempt to assess the effort involved in digging the ditch and casting up the bank. Thereafter, the silting of the ditch, the collapse of the rampart, and the

---

[62] Moorhouse (1983), 169–73; Brears (1983), 219–23.

[63] Alcock (1975); contrast Barker (1978), and note especially his account of the diet at the garrison post at Monte Ingenio. For the use of medieval manuals of husbandry, Lauwerier (1983).

[64] Coles (1973); Coles (1979).

[65] Jewell and Dimbleby (1966); Evans and Limbrey (1974).

shifting and decay of deliberately placed artefacts and organic materials were carefully monitored.

Given that many castles have an earthwork element—the circuit of a ringwork, the mound of a motte, the bank of a bailey or burgus—it is evident that there is much here of relevance to castle-studies. In particular, observation of the weathering of ditch sides, and of rampart collapse and weathering, are helpful in controlling our interpretation of the original form of a ditch-and-bank rampart. Again, the rate and character of ditch silting, the movement of artefacts, and their incorporation in the silts, must control hypotheses about the post-constructional history of an earthwork, and about the chronological significance of stratified finds. Given the differences between neolithic and medieval tools, or between student labourers and gangs of *fossatores*, there is less value in current inferences about the man-hours required to build an earthwork.

It should also be emphasized that much of our present information comes from only two earthworks; and that in neither case has the experiment been carried through as systematically as had been intended. There is clearly great scope for medievalists to build, for instance, a *Holzerdemauer* on a clay site; or, even more ambitious, a motte complete with timber tower. In this respect, the present experiments provide no guidance on the stability, or rates of subsidence and consolidation, of a high-piled mound. Despite such limitations, it is clear that all excavators of medieval earthworks should be fully aware of the existing experimental evidence.

Turning now to weapons: here we are interested in them solely in relation to castle-warfare, not on the wider field of battle. Nor are we concerned with gunpowder: the idea of experimenting with replicas of early cannon seems hazardous for the experimenters, and insufficiently rigorous, because we do not know the strength of either late medieval iron or early gunpowder.[66] Here, at least, we must be content with our historical records.

So far as the effectiveness of artillery using natural torsion or tension is concerned, there is a large body of experimental evidence from the Greek and Roman world: notably the reconstruction of both full-scale and small-scale models by Payne-Gallwey (whose work goes far beyond the medieval concept of the crossbow), Schramm, and, recently, Marsden.[67] The continued use of tension- and torsion-powered artillery makes all this relevant to the middle ages as well. But the great invention of the castle-period was the trebuchet, which depended for its power not on torsion or tension, but on a counterpoised weight. Here, of course, we come into Cathcart King's home territory. Combining schoolmastering and castle-studies, he had some seventy trebuchets built, to a one-sixteenth scale, by his young charges.[68]

The first significance of this work is the level of replication involved. Far too much so-called experimental archaeology is still at the anecdotal level of the single experiment. With the model trebuchets, it was possible to vary the

[66] Kenyon (1981), 231.
[67] Payne-Gallwey (1903); Schramm (1980); Marsden (1969–71).
[68] King (1982).

weight of the counterpoise, the weight ratio of counterpoise to shot, and the ratio between the two lengths of the counterpoised arm. Overall, the experiments demonstrated in miniature the elegant simplicity and effectiveness of the trebuchet: above all its ease of maintenance, its smoothness of action and its freedom from shock loading. Useful information was also obtained about the ballistic characteristics of the machine, including its ability to clear high walls. If one has a reservation about the conclusions—and King will surely forgive this—it is about the mathematics involved in multiplying the height and range achieved by the models sixteen times in order to calculate the range and trajectory of the medieval weapon.

Another well-conceived series of experiments, by Jones and Renn, has examined the military effectiveness of arrowloops.[69] It has long been obvious that the visual field scanned by a human eye pressed to the outer limits of an arrowslit is greater than that actually commanded by weapons. A major reason for this is the difficulty of handling both the long bow and crossbow within the narrowing confines of a turret embrasure. The Jones–Renn experiments used original slits at White Castle. It was shown that neither weapon could be deployed satisfactorily within an embrasure; the long bow at least had to be fired by an archer standing behind the wall. Despite this, it was found with both weapons that an archer could hit almost everything that he could see. Moreover, extrapolating from the evidence of the two slits used for the experiments, it appeared that White Castle was well covered by arrow-fire. More surprising was the possibility that an attacker could place an arrow through a slit: a probable score of 30 per cent at a range of twenty-five yards.

One further area of experimental archaeology of potential value to castle-studies is that of the full-scale reconstruction of timber buildings from the evidence of excavators' plans. Hitherto this has been largely—but not exclusively—confined to Iron Age and Roman structures. For medieval buildings, such as those of earth-and-timber castles, we have only the scale models of museum exhibits, which raise none of the stress problems of a full-scale structure;[70] or paper reconstructions, ranging from Sorrell's would-be realistic scenes[71] to more schematic drawings, often by excavators with no architectural knowledge. Recently there has been vigorous, and not always charitable, discussion of the principles and practice of such paper reconstructions.[72] At the conclusion of one of these debates, and after summarizing the conflict of interpretation between an excavator and an architectural historian, Barker concluded 'someone ought to construct a full-scale model!'[73] With such a view I would strongly concur; and I would add, in view of a reservation expressed earlier, that I should also like to see a full-scale replica of a trebuchet. It would be fitting, and in a good medieval tradition, to call such a machine the Great King: *ultima ratio regis*.

[69] Jones and Renn (1982).

[70] For hardware and other models, Clarke (1972), 13–14.

[71] Sorrell (1981).

[72] Drury (1982a), especially Part IV; Rahtz *et al.* (1982).

[73] Rahtz *et al.* (1982), 47.

Acknowledgements: I am deeply grateful to friends and colleagues who have answered queries, corrected errors, and helped to improve both the content and presentation of this paper: in particular M. J. Aitken, E. A. Alcock, P. A. Alcock-Parkes, I. Bailiff, M. G. L. Baillie, A. J. Clark, J. W. Hancock and E. A. Slater. In more general terms, my understanding of both possibilities and problems in the field owes much to stimulating discussions with fellow-members of the Science-based Archaeology Committee of the Science and Engineering Research Council.

Mottes and castle-ringworks in Wales

C. J. SPURGEON

CASTLE-RINGWORKS, hereafter termed ringworks, were the subject of a masterly and detailed discussion by David King and Leslie Alcock in 1969.[1] Subsequently David King added a perceptive general paper on mottes.[2] These papers remain central to any study of the earthwork castles of Wales, supplemented in princely fashion by David King's many and varied published contributions to the history and archaeology of castles in Wales, and crowned by his monumental *Castellarium Anglicanum*. Having first met 'King of the Castles' twenty-four years ago at the appropriate border setting of Castell Bryn Amlwg, where Shropshire meets Radnorshire and Montgomeryshire, his subsequent company in the field in Montgomeryshire, and further afield in Britain and abroad, has been a joy and an education. Wales, in particular, is greatly in his debt in the matter of castle-studies, and the following contribution is a quite inadequate tribute to the inspiration of his energetic fieldwork and published works.

King and Alcock identified 723 mottes and 204 ringworks in England and Wales, the latter figure excluding fifty possible sites.[3] They suggested that the true proportion of mottes to ringworks might prove to be about three to one, after due allowance for the likely potential of future excavation and fieldwork; more ringworks are likely to be discovered than mottes, which have been more easily identified, or on occasion mis-identified.[4] Recent fieldwork in Glamorgan by the Royal Commission supports this suggestion: four unrecorded ringworks have been identified, but no additional mottes, while excavations have added two further ringworks beneath stone castles.[5]

The suggested proportion of three to one is supported by figures for Wales. A count of sites, based on fieldwork in Cardiganshire, Glamorgan and Montgomeryshire, the Commission's archive, and the published literature, including, above all, David King's *Castellarium Anglicanum*, produces totals of 242 mottes and seventy-seven ringworks. In addition there are eleven stone castles with

---

[1] King and Alcock (1969).

[2] King (1972).

[3] King and Alcock (1969).

[4] For example, Deepweir Tump (Mon.), which proved to be a mound of builders' rubbish (Probert 1967), and Bettws Newydd (Mon.), which was found to be a cairn (Knight 1964).

[5] At Loughor and Rumney. See Lewis (1975) for the former; for Rumney, see Lightfoot, *Medieval Archaeol.*, forthcoming, and Lightfoot (1979), (1981), (1982) and (1983).

plans which suggest primary ringworks, of which only three or four would give
us a 3:1 ratio.

For present purposes no account is taken of the various types of ringwork
defined by King and Alcock, or of the presence or absence of baileys. It is
also assumed that each motte was the primary castle on the site, an assumption
requiring some explanation in the light of recent evidence that some were formed
by filling in ringworks,[6] or were added to earlier ringworks.[7] Excavations in
Glamorgan at Loughor and Rumney have revealed infilled ringworks crowned
with later masonry.[8] In retrospect, however, neither was a typical motte, given
their exceptionally low and broad profiles; had they retained their curtain walls
they would surely have been classed with similarly levelled ringworks at Ogmore
(Pl. I) and Coity. The secondary addition of a motte to the perimeter of an
earlier ringwork is less easily detected, and has only been suggested at Gypsies
Tump (Mon.).[9] Wales has no certain example of a motte heaped up against
an initially free-standing tower of masonry, as at Lydford (Devon),[10] though
an early record of a foundation in the motte at Caerleon (Mon.) has been suggested as an indication of something similar.[11] The ruinous keep fragment at
Kenfig (Glam.) has an inserted vault masking a blocked ground floor loop,
but externally the accumulation of blown sand hides the possible addition of
a mound when the vault was inserted.[12]

Welsh evidence for the primary nature of mottes is stronger. At Hen Domen
(Monts.) the motte was primary.[13] Tre Oda motte (Glam.) was again the primary
castle, utilising as its core a Bronze Age cairn.[14] Rûg motte (Mer.) showed
an identical sequence,[15] while Twyn y Gregen (Mon.) proved to be a motte
scarped from a moraine.[16] In 1982 a section of the motte at Llansantfraidd
Cwmdeuddwr (Rads.) was exposed, revealing a low marginal 'marker bank'
of turves, soil and gravel representing no more than the initial phase of construction.[17] Adding to these excavated examples the many mottes which are self-
evidently scarped moraines or natural eminences, and noting the generally small
size of most of those in Wales, it seems reasonable to suppose that few might
prove to be infilled ringworks.

With these reservations, the earthwork castles of Wales may be broken down
into the following groupings in the historic shires, divisions which approximate
far more closely to medieval boundaries than those of recent creation.

---

[6] For example, Aldingham in Lancashire (Davison 1969–70).

[7] For example, Castle Neroche, Somerset (Davison 1971–72; King 1972, 105–06).

[8] See note 5.

[9] Alcock (1963), 215; King and Alcock (1969), 101.

[10] Saunders (1980).

[11] Knight (1963).

[12] Richard (1927).

[13] Barker and Higham (1982), 72.

[14] Knight and Talbot (1968–70).

[15] Gardner (1961).

[16] O'Neil and Foster-Smith (1936).

[17] Clwyd–Powys (1982), 11.

Table 1. The distribution of earthwork castles in the old Welsh counties (see map, Fig. 1).

County	Mottes	Ringworks	*(possible sites)*	Totals	*(possible totals)*
Anglesey	1	1		2	
Brecknockshire	23	6		29	
Caernarfonshire	7	1		8	
Cardiganshire	20	7		27	
Carmarthenshire	30	7		37	
Denbighshire	10	0		10	
Flintshire	13	0		13	
Glamorgan	16	27	(7)	43	(50)
Merionethshire	11	2		13	
Monmouthshire	29	5	(1)	34	(35)
Montgomeryshire	33	3		36	
Pembrokeshire	18	16	(3)	34	(37)
Radnorshire	31	2		33	
Totals	242	77	(11)	319	(330)

The counties with most earthwork castles are Glamorgan, with forty-three or more, and Carmarthenshire, Montgomeryshire, Pembrokeshire, Monmouthshire and Radnorshire, which all have over thirty sites. In contrast, Anglesey has only two, and Caernarfonshire eight. Earthwork castles are most numerous in the counties of the border and south coast, a distribution matching those of manorial centres in general,[18] and of moated sites.[19] Our sites may also be tabulated in relation to the main divisions of medieval Wales (see Tab. 2, p. 26).

The sparsity of earthwork castles in Gwynedd is clear, with fewer found only in the much smaller adjacent territory of Perfeddwlad, an area claimed by Gwynedd and hotly disputed with the Normans. Powys has the largest total (58), followed by Dyfed (49) and Glamorgan/Gwynllwg (38). The latter grouping is appropriate, these territories falling to Robert fitz Hamon in the late eleventh century, though maintaining separate administrative identities thereafter. The Glamorgan sites lie mainly on the lowlands of the south, the Vale of Glamorgan, and constitute the most closely grouped series. Other thick concentrations may be noted in the eastern parts of southern Powys (Powys Wenwynwyn), Rhwng Gwy a Hafren and Brycheiniog. Sites thin out westwards, excepting only thickly-clustered Dyfed and the adjacent group in the Teifi Valley. Broadly, the distribution reflects topography, with few sites in the mountainous interior, and most in the more fertile areas of Norman settlement to the east, south and south-west. Recorded Welsh castles are few. In Ceredigion, held only spasmodically by the Normans (1093–94; 1110–36; 1158–?64), most castles were Norman foundations, as were at least four in sparsely-castled Gwynedd.

[18] Rees (1951), Pl. 47.
[19] Spurgeon (1981), 21, Fig. 2.1; RCAM (1982), 72, Fig. 33.

Table 2. The distribution of earthwork castles in the main territorial divisions of medieval Wales (see map, Fig. 2).

Gwlad	*Mottes*	*Ringworks*	*(possible sites)*	*Totals*	*(possible totals)*
1. Gwynedd	12	3		15	
2. Perfeddwlad	9	0		9	
3. Powys	54	4		58	
4. Ceredigion	20	7		27	
5. Rhwng Gwy a Hafren	34	4		38	
6. Brycheiniog	20	4		24	
7. Dyfed	29	20	(3)	49	(52)
8. Ystrad Tywi (inc. Gower)	21	11		32	
9. Glamorgan/Gwynllwg	19	19	(7)	38	(45)
10. Gwent	24	5	(1)	29	(30)
Totals	242	77	(11)	319	(330)

Notes: i. Numbers given to each territory correspond to those on maps, Figs. 2 and 3.

ii. For the *cantrefi* and *cymydau* making up each territory see Lloyd and Rees.[20]

EARLY MASONRY CASTLES

Mottes and ringworks with Norman or later masonry upon them have been included in our figures, since most, if not all, began as earth and timber castles. Very few employed masonry at their foundation, and of these the earliest was that of William fitz Osbern (1067–71) at Chepstow in Gwent, and where later Norman keeps were built at Monmouth, Usk and White Castle. Glamorgan also had twelfth-century stone keeps without identifiable earthwork defences at Kenfig and Penllyn, while others may be represented by collapsed heaps of masonry at Dinas Powys, Llanblethian and Sully. Further west, in Pembrokeshire, there is a square twelfth-century tower at Manorbier, and a square foundation at Haverfordwest has been interpreted as a Norman keep, while a re-used Norman capital at Kidwelly (Carms.) is thought to represent another. At Dinas (Brecs.) there is a large rectangular foundation, and Hay (Brecs.) has an early rectangular tower. No early masonry is recorded in Rhwng Gwy a Hafren, Powys or Perfeddwlad, though it has been suggested that Robert of Rhuddlan's castle of *c.* 1088 at Degannwy was a stone keep and bailey.[21]

Early Welsh masonry castles are even rarer, and seemingly all of the later twelfth century. Rhys ap Gruffudd, the Lord Rhys, rebuilt Cardigan in stone and mortar in 1171,[22] but no trace of this work survives. Rhys may also have been responsible for the vestiges of a keep at Ystrad Meurig (Cards.) and the twelfth-century masonry defining two wards at Dinefwr (Carms.). Beyond his

[20] Lloyd (1939), map at end of Vol. 2; Rees (1933); Rees (1951), Pl. 22.
[21] Alcock (1967), 198, 200.
[22] *Brut (Hergest)*, 155.

dominion, Rhys captured Castell Nanhyfer (Pembs.) in 1191, where the clay-bedded keep and bailey of the 'Inner Castle' are probably his,[23] and in 1177 he founded a castle at Rhaeadr (Rads.), now almost vanished, though possibly of stone.

In Gwynedd the well-preserved keep at Dolwyddelan (Caerns.), reputedly Llywelyn Fawr's birthplace, but of early thirteenth-century date, has a predecessor in the masonry footing excavated on the nearby outcrop of Tomen Castell.[24] The unique stone-revetted 'motte' at Cwm Prysor (Mer.), though of uncertain date, should also be noted.[25] The scant vestiges of Carn Fadryn (Caerns.) and Penrhyndeudraeth (Mer.) terminate the roll of early Welsh stone castles.

MOTTES AND CASTLE-RINGWORKS (GENERAL)

Problems are posed by two distinct types of earthwork castle. Mottes occur in all counties, their totals ranging from one in Anglesey to thirty-three in Montgomeryshire. Ringworks, absent from Denbighshire and Flintshire, range elsewhere from one in Anglesey and one in Caernarfonshire, to twenty-seven in Glamorgan. Table 2 shows a great preponderance of mottes over ringworks in medieval Powys. Mottes are least common in Gwynedd (12) and Perfeddwlad (9), but so also are ringworks, with three and none respectively. The greatest concentrations of ringworks are in Dyfed (20) and Glamorgan/Gwynllwg (19).

Ringworks are rare in north Wales, with only seven in the six counties which together correspond with ancient Gwynedd, Powys and Perfeddwlad; the same area has seventy-five mottes. The remaining seventy ringworks lie in south Wales, where their distribution is inconsistent with, for example, five ringworks and twenty-nine mottes in Monmouthshire, but twenty-seven ringworks and sixteen mottes in adjacent Glamorgan.

Discussion of these uneven patterns of distribution cannot ignore the admirable and detailed paper by King and Alcock.[26] Three of their broad conclusions will be considered in turn, though here only in relation to sites in Wales.

1. *The chronology of mottes and ringworks*

> Mottes and ringworks were seemingly '... straightforward alternatives from the beginning of the Norman period.'

> 'There is no reason to look for the difference in date as a determining factor ... in view of the rapid spread of Norman power over England and much of Wales.'[27]

This rejection of any chronological significance with regard to mottes and ringworks was mildly tempered by the further observation that where the two

[23] King and Perks (1950–51).
[24] Wilson and Hurst (1965), 193; Jones (1964); RCAM (1956), 83.
[25] Gresham and Hemp (1949).
[26] King and Alcock (1969).
[27] Ibid., 99, 103.

types lie closely adjacent, and where one seems to have replaced the other, '... the ringwork seems more commonly to be the older of the two.'[28] Six such pairs were described: in four cases the ringworks appeared to be the older castles, in two the mottes. This slight indication of a greater antiquity for ringworks might be negated if we added the mottes at Ystradowen (Glam.) and Nevern (Pembs.), both seemingly replaced by suspected ringworks at Talyfan and Newport respectively.[29] A greater sample of earthwork castles might be gauged if we scrutinize those for which there are foundation dates or a reasonable indication of their most likely period of first use.

1(a). Castles of the period 1066–1100

Ringworks certainly appeared very early in England, but in Wales not one is known to have existed before 1100. In contrast, twenty mottes may be reasonably attributed to the reign of the first two Williams (map, Fig. 3). Roger of Montgomery built his motte at Hen Domen (Monts.) between 1071 and 1073, and at about this date Robert of Rhuddlan was given Rhuddlan motte (Flints.), raised at the Conqueror's command.[30] The Conqueror may also have built the fine motte at Cardiff in 1081 (Pl. II), conventionally ascribed to Robert fitz Hamon as *c.* 1093, a possibility with wide implications which are discussed in the appendix. Domesday Book gives good reason for suspecting a further eight mottes by 1086. In the north Earl Hugh of Chester held Iâl, where Tomen y Faerdre (Denbs.) was his probable *caput*. Hugh also held Hawarden (Flints.), where there is another fine motte. Roger of Montgomery's sheriff, Rainald, held the commotes of Cynllaith and Edeyrnion, where the respective mottes of Sycharth (Denbs.) and Rûg (Mer.) may be his, the latter probably the 'Ruc' where Gruffudd ap Cynan was captured in 1081.[31]

Domesday Book also identifies Roger of Montgomery as the lord of Arwstli in the upper Severn Valley, where the fine motte at Moat Lane (Monts.) is surely his. By implication, others of the five mottes along the line of the Roman road between Hen Domen and Moat Lane might also be his, and particularly the impressive site of Gro Tump.

In Gwent, Caerleon motte was appurtenant to Chepstow and held by Turstin fitz Rolf. Though no castles are mentioned, both Caerwent and Caldicot, each with a motte, were possessed by Durand, the sheriff of Hereford.

Under William Rufus a further eight mottes are indicated by the records. Four were in Gwynedd, where Aberlleiniog (Ang.), and Caernarfon and Aber (Caerns.) were established by Hugh d'Avranches *c.* 1093,[32] and Tomen y Mur (Mer.) by Hugh, or by William Rufus, who encamped there in 1095. In the middle march Bernard de Neufmarché's motte at Brecon was in being by 1093, and William de Braose (d. 1095), or his son Philip, had probably built Builth

---

[28] Ibid., 100.

[29] King (1983), **1**, 170–71; King (1983), **2**, 395.

[30] *Orderic Vitalis*, 138–39.

[31] This was first suggested by Jones (1910, 172, fn. 2); see also Lloyd (1939), **2**, 385 and fn. 89.

[32] Following the death of Robert of Rhuddlan in 1093, rather than the usually cited 1088. See *Orderic Vitalis*, xxxiv–xxxviii.

before 1100. In Gwent the motte at Abergavenny must surely have preceded the foundation of the priory there by Hamelin de Ballon, before his death *c.* 1090. Finally, in the south-west, William fitz Baldwin, by command of the king, founded a castle and mint at Rhyd y Gors in 1094, which castle was probably the motte at Carmarthen.[33]

Besides these twenty mottes, at least six other castles were built before 1100 (map, Fig. 3). Of these, only the masonry hall and ward of William fitz Osbern at Chepstow may be securely classified. Later masonry has made it impossible to identify the form of Arnulf of Montgomery's Pembroke (1093), or William fitz Osbern's Monmouth (by 1071). The excavator of Degannwy suspected a stone keep and bailey constituted Robert of Rhuddlan's castle of *c.* 1088.[34] The site of Roger of Montgomery's Cardigan (1093) is uncertain; either it was on the site of Cardigan Castle and now completely masked by later masonry, or it is represented by the scarped and embanked riverside knoll a mile down the Teifi from Cardigan, which is not typical as motte or ringwork. Finally, a castle might be suspected at Radnor before 1100. Held by the king in Domesday, it was granted to William de Braose by 1095. William's son, who succeeded him in 1095, had a borough at Radnor,[35] and surely a castle. The site of the original Radnor poses problems, with three or four claimants.[36] Of these, New Radnor is by far the most likely site, its massive earthworks and the scarping of a strong natural eminence recalling the Braose castle of Bramber (Sussex). Alone of the alternatives, New Radnor has an appendant town, its earthwork defences substantially intact. Though *New* Radnor does not figure in the records until 1252–53, this may signify no more than an expansion, rather than a change of site. The curving line of the west defences and the irregular street pattern at that end of New Radnor, which contains the church, contrasts with the rectilinear form and gridded streets of the east end, and may represent the Braose borough.

By 1100, then, we have some evidence for at least twenty mottes, one stone castle (Chepstow), three castles of uncertain type on particularly strong natural sites (Pembroke, Degannwy and, probably, New Radnor), and two others of uncertain type at Monmouth and Cardigan.

The mottes include seven of the eleven listed as the finest in Wales.[37] Of these Rhuddlan and Cardiff were seemingly raised on the orders of the Conqueror, and Carmarthen and possibly Tomen y Mur for William Rufus. Cardiff, Abergavenny, Caerleon, Caerwent, Caernarfon, Carmarthen, Tomen Y Mur, and, possibly, Builth, were mottes sited within or near Roman forts, while Hen Domen, Gro Tump and Moat Lane lie along the line of a Roman road. Roman forts are also suspected near Chepstow and Monmouth. The earliest Norman

---

[33] *Brut (Hergest)*, *Brut (Peniarth)* and *Brenhinedd*, *s.a.* 1094 and 1096. Alternative sites are discussed by James (1980, 34–35, 44 and Fig. 4.8) who now favours Banc y Castell, a vanished site south-west of the town.

[34] See note 21.

[35] Lloyd (1939), **2,** 403 and fn. 11.

[36] King (1983), **2,** 410, 564–65.

[37] King (1972), 104, fn. 12.

invaders obviously sought prime sites on existing lines of communication, and most of them developed into lasting administrative centres.[38]

While there is good evidence for Norman mottes before 1100, if none for ringworks, the Welsh cannot be shown to have erected any castles as early as this. Surviving documentation suggests that mottes were overwhelmingly preferred by the Normans in Wales in the late eleventh century, unless this was the castle-form favoured for more significant castles which would more readily attract chroniclers' attentions. The latter possibility, though pure speculation, might dimly reflect Professor de Boüard's observations on earthwork castles in Normandy, where mottes occupy sites in the villages and often beside the parish church, while the ringworks are in more isolated positions.[39]

1(b). Castles of the period 1100–36

Robert de Bellême's Carreghofa (Monts.), built in 1100, is seemingly the earliest recorded ringwork in Wales, soon followed by others at Kidwelly (Carms.) *c.* 1106, Old Aberystwyth (Cards.) in 1110 and Sentence Castle (Pembs.) in 1116. In the lordship of Glamorgan excavations indicate this period for the ringworks at Llantrithyd and Dinas Powys,[40] while those at Newcastle and Ogmore are first mentioned in 1106 and 1116, and the recorded presence in the lordship of the Turbervilles, Umfravilles and de Wintons suggests this period for others at Coity, Penmark, Llandow and Llanquian. In contrast, no motte is known to have been founded in the lordship in this period. In the neighbouring lordship of Gower, invaded in 1106, both mottes and ringworks were raised, with excavation evidence available for ringworks at Penmaen and Loughor,[41] and documentary references to mottes at Swansea and Llandeilo Talybont.

In Ceredigion seven mottes were raised soon after Gilbert fitz Richard was granted the territory by Henry I in 1110. These were his own castle at Blaenporth, and those of his followers at Caerwedros, Castell Gwallter (Walter de Bec's castle), Dinerth, Humphrey's Castle, Lampeter and Ystrad Peithyll. If Tomen Llanio is accepted as the lost site of Richard de la Mare's castle, we have eight mottes, all probably raised between 1110 and the uprising of Gruffudd in 1116. By 1116 Gilbert had also built his ringwork at Old Aberystwyth and the castle at Ystrad Meurig, where the eroded remains are not easily classified. At Cardigan, though its precise location is disputed, Gilbert rebuilt Roger of Montgomery's castle of 1093. It has been shown that these eleven castles have a

---

[38] In contrast, only six twelfth-century or undated earthwork castles lie on or near Roman forts: the mottes at Treflis (Brec.), Myddfai (Carms.), Colwyn (Rads.), and Tre Oda and Gelligaer (Glam.); and the ringwork at Loughor (Glam.). It might be added that Roman forts are also suspected at or near Bronllys, Tretower and Trecastle (Brec.), Ruthin (Denb.) and Painscastle (Rads.). The eleventh-century motte at Rhuddlan (Flints.) was placed within the Saxon burgh of Cledemutha, and the motte of 1212 at Mathrafal (Monts.) is also within a very probable Dark Age enclosure.

[39] Boüard (1964), discussed in King and Alcock (1969), 102.

[40] Alcock (1963), 73-93, though the paucity of pottery, and tradition, might link Dinas Powys with the last native prince of Glamorgan who was dispossessed conventionally by Robert fitz Hamon; but see appendix. For Llantrithyd see Charlton (1977).

[41] Alcock (1966); Lewis (1975).

close correlation with the ten commotes of Ceredigion, which seemingly served as 'units of penetration'.[42]

Elsewhere mottes at Tretower and Crickhowell (Brecs.), Welshpool (Monts.), Llandovery (Carms.), Cymmer (Mer.) and Painscastle (Rads.) were built by 1135, and those at Cwmaron and Colwyn (Rads.) were first mentioned when rebuilt in 1144. All but two of these were Norman castles. At Welshpool, Cadwgan ap Bleddyn was building a castle, almost certainly Domen Castell, when he was slain in 1111,[43] and Uchdryd ab Edwin built Cymmer in 1116. These two mottes are the earliest Welsh castles that can be identified.

Overall there is some evidence for the foundation of eighteen mottes and fourteen ringworks in Wales in the reign of Henry I, a surprising change from the earlier period, but not an illuminating one, in view of the concentration of ten of the ringworks in the county of Glamorgan, where historians and archaeologists have been most active, and where, uniquely, ringworks outnumber mottes.

1(c). Castles of the period 1136–1200

Most castles recorded before 1136 continue to appear in the records for the remainder of the twelfth century. Between 1136 and 1200 additional castles are first mentioned in all counties except Anglesey and Caernarfonshire, with some twenty-one mottes and eight ringworks. For reasons given above, Colwyn and Cwmaron mottes have not been included. Most of the additions are again Anglo-Norman foundations, though more Welsh examples are now emerging.[44] Of the twenty-one mottes, four are Welsh: Tomen y Rhodwydd (Denbs.), built by Owain Gwynedd in 1149; Ysgubor y Coed (or 'Aberdyfi', Cards.), built by Rhys ap Gruffudd in 1156; Castle Caereinion (Monts.), built by Madog ap Maredudd in 1156; and Tafolwern (Monts.), possession of which was contested by Owain Gwynedd and Hywel ap Ieuaf in 1162. There is also one account of the building of a castle by Owain Gwynedd in 1165 at Corwen (Mer.),[45] where there are three mottes, including the eleventh-century Rûg.

Of the eight ringworks added for this period, two were Welsh: Castell Cynfal (Mer.), 1147,[46] and Llanrhystyd (Cards.), 1149, both the work of Cadwaladr ap Gruffudd, brother of Owain Gwynedd, and the only ringworks known to have been founded by the Welsh.

1(d). Late use of earthwork castles, 1200–1403

Thirty-four mottes and three ringworks, all without trace of masonry additions, are recorded in Wales in this period, the last being Owain Glyndŵr's Sycharth, destroyed in 1403. Four of the mottes were first built in the thirteenth century, two Welsh and two English. First, in 1210–12, the earl of Chester built Holywell (Flints.), and in 1212 Robert Vipont raised the motte at Mathrafal (Monts.)

---

[42] Edwards (1956).

[43] *Brut* (*Peniarth*), 36; *Brenhinedd*, 119.

[44] For a recent illustrated account of the native castles of north Wales, see Avent (1983a), with earthwork castles discussed on pp. 2–6.

[45] *Brenhinedd*, 167.

[46] Classed as a motte by King (1983), **1**, 278, but it has a distinct bank around its summit.

for the king (Pl. III). In Ceredigion, Trefilan was built by Maelgwn ap Rhys in 1233, and Garth Grugyn by Rhys Fychan in 1242.

The three late recorded ringworks are Carreghofa (Monts.), where royal expenditure is recorded in 1212-13;[47] Old Aberystwyth (Cards.), taken by Llywelyn Fawr in 1221; Sentence (Pembs.), destroyed by Rhys Fychan in 1257.

Late sites show a higher proportion of recorded sites in Welsh hands than earlier, including former Norman sites like Old Aberystwyth (1221) and Dinerth (1208), though it was King John who restored Owain Gwynedd's Tomen y Rhodwydd in 1212. In 1244 John l'Estrange fortified one of the mottes at Flint in timber,[48] while service is recorded at the motte at Welshpool in 1299.[49] At Hen Domen excavations show continued activity until *c.* 1300.[50] Only Anglesey and Caernarfonshire have no late earthwork sites, and most of those that are known are to be found in areas with few masonry castles. Montgomery has five mottes, Mathrafal, 1212, Tafolwern, 1244, Llanfyllin, 1257, Welshpool, 1299, and Hen Domen, *c.* 1300. Ceredigion has six, the ringwork at Old Aberystwyth, 1221, and the mottes of Ysgubor y Coed, 1206, Dinerth, 1210, Nant yr Arian, 1216, Trefilan, 1233, and Garth Grugyn, 1242.

After 1300 only four mottes are recorded: in Pembrokeshire, Wolf's Castle and Castle Morris, both in 1326; in Glamorgan, Llandeilo Talybont, 1353, and in Denbighshire, Sycharth, 1403.

Some tentative conclusions may be drawn from this survey of the chronology of earthwork castles in Wales. Before 1100 there is an apparent preference for mottes of a generally impressive nature; thereafter ringworks were certainly in use as an alternative castle-type. Both types were built by the Welsh, though in general they made far less use of castles, as their rarity in Gwynedd demonstrates. Only the brothers, Owain Gwynedd and Cadwaldr of Gwynedd, and Rhys ap Gruffudd of Deheubarth are to be seen raising new castles in any consistent fashion to strengthen the borders of their territories, the brothers at Tomen y Rhodwydd, Corwen, Cynfal and Llanrhystyd; Rhys at Rhaeadr, Ysgubor y Coed (=Aberdyfi) and the 'Inner Castle' at Nanhyfer. We have also noted the possibility that Rhys was the pioneer of Welsh masonry fortification, though only Dinefwr, Nanhyfer and Ystrad Meurig retain any visible vestiges.

2. *Geology and the problems of ringwork distribution*

In considering the illogical localized grouping of ringworks,

> '... The character of the subsoil would seem likely to supply an explanation, but this too has only to be considered to be rejected: few, if any, of our groups of ringworks correspond to any sort of uniform area on a geological map, while if we take the two principal counties where ringworks predominate, there is

[47] Colvin (1963), **2,** 602–03.
[48] King (1983), **1,** 153.
[49] Ibid., 300, fn. 28, citing *Cal. Inq. P.M.,* **3,** 432, and King (1983), **2,** 567; Spurgeon (1965–66), 54.
[50] Barker and Higham (1982), 19–20, 48, 93–94.

little in common between the soft chalk and later deposits of Hampshire and the hard and ancient rocks of Cornwall.'[51]

A certain degree of surprise seems to be implied in this rejection of a geological explanation for the uneven patern of motte and ringwork distributions. It would certainly seem that the motte would normally require a reasonably tractable subsoil, or a natural or artificial eminence amenable to scarping and reforming. Such conditions would be equally suitable for the construction of ringworks, which could therefore be expected in areas where mottes were common. Where ringworks form localized groups to the exclusion, or near exclusion, of mottes, they might represent the only feasible alternative in areas with an intractable subsoil. Such ideas were inspired during a survey of the castles of Glamorgan, where ringworks form an exclusive group in the Vale of Glamorgan, with mottes occupying an area further north. It was soon apparent that many mottes were formed of glacial material, and it is illuminating to consider a brief study of the mottes of north Wales by a geologist, the late E. Neaverson.[52]

Neaverson considered the geology of mottes in the counties of Anglesey, Caernarfon, Denbigh, Flint and Merioneth, with comments on twenty-three of the forty-two mottes now known in those counties. These, he found, were built on glacial drift deposits. Robert of Rhuddlan's castle on the volcanic rock of Degannwy was '... exceptional, for the Normans seem to have avoided building on solid rock wherever possible ...' He offered two general conclusions of relevance to our discussion:

> 'The Drift deposits (including the alluvium) are important ... because they comprise the only non-consolidated rock-material in North Wales, and they obviously determine the distribution of the artificial mounds·on which the early Norman castles were built.'

> 'The construction of these strongholds requires the presence of a suitable substratum which could be rapidly fashioned into conical mounds. Hence the distribution of Norman castles is limited in general by the presence of Drift deposits, the only non-consolidated rocks in North Wales.'[53]

Neaverson comments on the particular drift deposits of twenty-three mottes: in Flintshire: Hawarden, Holywell, Mold, Prestatyn, Tyddyn Mount, Leeswood, Rofft Mount and Rhuddlan; in Caernarfonshire: Aber and Caernarfon; in Anglesey: Aberlleiniog; in Merionethshire: Tomen y Mur, Castell Prysor, Castell Gronw, Crogen, Llanfor, Owain Glyndŵr's mound and Rûg; and in Denbighshire: Pentrefoelas, Erddig, Tomen y Faerdre, Tomen y Rhodwydd and Llys Gwenllian.

Neaverson mentions no ringworks, but we might suggest that the presence of abundant glacial land-forms along the routes of early Norman expansion in north Wales may well have contributed to their rarity in these five counties. Montgomeryshire, not covered by Neaverson, is an adjacent area equally blessed

[51] King and Alcock (1969), 103.
[52] Neaverson (1947).
[53] Ibid., 6, 17.

with an abundance of glacial features which have often been mistaken for mottes,[54] and there also mottes greatly outnumber ringworks.

We need not doubt the Normans' frequent choice of sites which enabled them to erect castles speedily and with the minimum of effort, not merely from easily reformed drumlins or moraines, but also over pre-existing cairns or defensive enclosures. Wales may have two mottes over remains of Roman gateways, at Tomen y Mur and Colwyn, if nothing quite as striking as the motte of 1203 at Meelick (Co. Galway), which was heaped over a church. In areas of 'ready-made' mottes in the form of prominent glacial features, we need not be surprised if mottes greatly outnumber ringworks, though these may also occur.

Neaverson's study is the only geological appraisal of the mottes in Wales to have been published, but current work in Glamorgan has already shown that only two sites there appear to lack the required 'suitable substratum'. Uneven observation, and isolated reports on other mottes in Wales,[55] seem to confirm the frequent, if not universal, validity of his theory. A few exceptions, with rock-cut ditches, might even prove the rule: at Castell Gwallter and Ystrad Peithyll (Cards.), and at Nantcribba and the hybrid 'ring-motte' of Cefn Bryntalch (Monts.), the builders seized upon conveniently prominent outcrops requiring limited effort in creating mottes.

For ringworks, Neaverson's theory can only offer the negative speculation that they might cluster in those areas where 'suitable substratum' was rare or lacking. Unfortunately, however, glacial drifts in their various forms blanket much of Wales, and are particularly thick in those valleys and lowlands where we find the densest manorial settlement. At its greatest extent, however, the Welsh ice-sheet did not extend to four coastal areas: southern Pembrokeshire and the adjacent western extremity of Carmarthenshire, the southern part of the peninsular of Gower, the greater part of the Vale of Glamorgan, and most of Gwent. These four limited areas on the south coast are precisely those designated by King and Alcock as the centres of the only concentrations of ringworks they identify in Wales.[56] Our map (Fig. 4, A) plots sites in these areas in relation to the southern limit of the Welsh glaciation. South of the limit are thirty-eight or thirty-nine ringworks, about half the total for the whole of Wales. Even more striking is the complete absence of mottes from two of these areas, namely, southern Gower and the Vale of Glamorgan, which have five and fifteen ringworks respectively. The Dyfed ice-free zone has thirteen or fourteen ringworks to seventeen or eighteen mottes, and Gwent has five closely concentrated ringworks to eighteen mottes.

The Dyfed sites are so inter-mixed that a geological explanation is not immediately apparent, and must await correlation with drift features derived from the Irish Sea ice which passed over south Pembrokeshire, south Gower and the Vale of Glamorgan, though in the latter areas very little drift survived erosion and fluvio-glacial scouring from the more massive Welsh ice-sheet.

[54] Spurgeon (1965–66), 1, 56–57.
[55] For example, Twyn y Gregen (Mon.; see note 16), Tre Oda (Glam.; see note 14) and Hen Domen (Monts.), all of which were raised on glacial material.
[56] King and Alcock (1969), 104, map.

In the lordship of Gower the *caput* at Swansea was a motte, now vanished. The only other motte in the lordship was Llandeilo Talybont. Both of these were built on glacial drift. South-west of these, on the Gower peninsular, are eight ringworks. Why only ringworks were built here is not immediately apparent, drift maps presenting a varied and complex picture. Penmaen and North Hill Tor are certainly built on sites where rock is near the surface, but glacial deposits are widely if irregularly present.

In Gwent we have five ringworks, excluding the possible example of Grosmont. The five form a concentrated group in the vicinity of Usk, in which lordship they outnumber mottes. In the surrounding lordships there are many mottes, with as many as five in Monmouth and eight in Abergavenny. This singular group of ringworks has yet to be tested for any possible geological anomaly.

The lordship of Glamorgan furnishes strong evidence that the character of the subsoil was the major factor responsible for the generally segregated distribution patterns of its mottes and ringworks. The historic *county* of Glamorgan has sixteen mottes and twenty-seven ringworks. Of these, two mottes and eight ringworks are in the lordship of Gower, and two ringworks are in the south-western extremity of the lordship of Gwynllwg,[57] leaving the medieval *lordship* of Glamorgan with fourteen mottes and seventeen ringworks.

A map of the Vale of Glamorgan (Fig. 4, B), prepared with the generous guidance of Dr R. A. Waters of the British Geological Survey, shows the earth-work castles in relation to the surface geology. Thick drift deposits define the southern limit of glaciation, following a rough arc from the vicinity of Llanilid to Welsh St Donats, and on to Bonvilston, beyond which it approximates to the line of the A48, the ancient 'Portway' and the Roman road, which it follows as far as Ely. South of this arc the predominant outcrop is Lias Limestone, with lesser localized outcrops of Carboniferous Limestone. The Lias gives the Vale its characteristic features: a relatively level surface, with an abundance of shallow bedded limestone and a thin, stony, but very productive soil.

The map covers the area where most of the lordship's castles lie. Ten of the fourteen mottes are plotted, and sixteen of the seventeen ringworks, as well as the two in Gwynllwg, to the east of Cardiff.

The mottes are seen to lie, with one exception, on glacial drift or alluvium. The exception, Castell Coch, which lies on Carboniferous Limestone, is the motte suspected, but difficult to prove, beneath the restored thirteenth-century masonry castle. Of the four mottes in the lordship which are beyond the bounds of the map, only that at Ruperra would seemingly join Castell Coch as a motte built on intractable rock, in this case nodular limestone. Very largely, then, including the two mottes on drift in the lordship of Gower, those in both the county and lordship of Glamorgan support Neaverson's observations. Not one motte is to be found among the many ringworks on the shallower soils over the limestone to the south.

Sixteen of the seventeen ringworks in the lordship are shown on the map,

[57] Rumney and St Mellons, both included under Monmouthshire in King (1983), **1**, 287–88, but respectively brought within the old county of Glamorgan by boundary changes in 1938 and 1951.

as well as the two in Gwynllwg. Of the sixteen, fourteen lie south of the drift: seven on Lias Limestone,[58] four on Carboniferous Limestone,[59] and three on Triassic rock.[60] This broad expanse of shallow soils also has four of the seven stone castles with plans suggesting possible primary ringworks.[61] The only certain ringworks on the drift are Llanilid, and, beyond the area of the map, Gwern y Domen, near Caerphilly. It is interesting to note that these ringworks in the zone where mottes predominate are both hybrid sites at which elevated glacial mounds are crowned with ring-banks, presenting difficulties of classification noticed by Alcock.[62]

The emphatic and exclusive use of ringworks in the southern Vale demands explanation. The area is the most fertile part of the lordship, and among its lords it counted some whose wealth and standing were equal to the later conversion of their ringworks into strong stone castles,[63] or, in one case, to the erection of a stone castle on a new site.[64] Such men included the two de Cardiff lords of Llantrithyd ringwork who were sheriffs of Glamorgan, William in 1102 and 1118, Ralf in 1126. It seems very probable that only the nature of the subsoil could have prevented at least some of these important lords erecting mottes, particularly in view of their regular attendance at the *Comitatus* at Cardiff, in the shadow of their chief lord's great motte.

One further observation may be made, though one not immediately capable of explanation. Excepting only the chief lord's castle at Cardiff, and the vestiges of the early abandoned castle of the de Sturmis at Stormy, the mottes of Glamorgan lordship lack any firm documentary record or hint of their manorial context. In complete contrast, the ringworks of the Vale are almost all linked, with a reasonable degree of certainty, to families and their manors. Such speculation is the province of the medieval historian, but the archaeologist is bound to wonder whether the mottes of the lordship of Glamorgan might for the most part represent an initial Norman settlement associated with Cardiff, possibly under the Conqueror. They certainly form an effective screen to the north of the *caput*, reminiscent of the mottes in the Vale of Montgomery.[65] This interesting possibility is further discussed in the appendix. It is most unlikely that the mottes clustered to the east and north of Cardiff are Welsh foundations: mottes, excepting the fragment at Ynyscrug in the Rhondda and the tiny Twyn Castell at Gelligaer, are absent from the Welsh upland commotes.

---

[58] Beganston, Bonvilston, Gelli Garn, Howe Mill, Llandow, Pancross and Walterston.

[59] Dinas Powys, Llanquian, Llantrithyd and Ogmore.

[60] Caerau, Coed y Cwm and Coity.

[61] The four are Newcastle, St Donats, Penmark and Barry. Two others, Talyfan and Llantrisant, are also shown, the seventh, Neath, being beyond the area of the map.

[62] Alcock (1963), 214.

[63] De Londres at Ogmore, Turberville at Coity, the chief lord at Newcastle; at the suspected ringwork sites: de Hawey or Butler (St Donats) and Umfraville (Penmark).

[64] De Someri at Dinas Powys, where the multivallate ringwork was dismantled, possibly uncompleted, and surely replaced by the nearby stone castle.

[65] King and Spurgeon (1965).

3. Personal preference in castle-building as a factor in motte and ringwork distribution

King and Alcock could find no better explanation for the uneven distributions of mottes and ringworks than the accident of personal preference of certain lords for one of these castle types:

> 'It seems that the human variable is the only explanation. The pattern of lordship gives us some slight assistance; in three cases, concentrations of ringworks correspond with compact baronial holdings: Cornwall, Glamorgan and Gower.'

> 'We are left, indeed, with little more than the accident of personal preference to account for any choice of ringwork as against motte, or *vice versa*. The evidently irrational grouping of our earthwork castles can hardly be explained on any other basis. Our compact groups of ringworks may be explained either by the local castle-builders having imitated some conspicuously successful earthwork in the neighbourhood, or by the personal preference of the local overlord or his military advisers—who may well have aided and counselled his tenants in the building of their castles.'[66]

They noted, we should add, that the ringwork concentrations in Cornwall, Gower and Glamorgan did not occupy the full area of their respective fees, and that each of them had its mottes, though these were away from the ringworks.

Personal preference, like the factor of geological necessity, cannot be dismissed, particularly in Wales, where, in all but the confined southern coastal area described, the widespread glacial drift offered suitable subsoil, for either type of earthwork. Personal preference was first suggested in regard to the overwhelming predominance of mottes in Montgomeryshire.[67] The early erection of mottes by Roger of Montgomery at Hen Domen and westwards along the Severn Valley to Moat Lane by 1086 could well furnish the model for the many undoubtedly Welsh mottes to the north of the Severn. Roger had a motte in Normandy, and had also raised one of the finest examples in England, at Arundel, and held a further fine one at Shrewsbury. He has also been seen as the probable instigator of the resettlement of 'waste' in the Vale of Montgomery, the Rea-Camlad gap east of Hen Domen on the main route to Shrewsbury, where a remarkably uniform and close-set group of small mottes is to be found.[68] Roger's preference for mottes may be further strengthened in considering the ringworks of Shropshire. Twelve of these were listed by Barker in 1964,[69] and increased to fifteen in *Castellarium Anglicanum*. It appears from Domesday Book that five ringworks were on land held by Roger Corbet, while the lands of Roger de Lacy and Picot de Say each have two, and those of Siward, Elmund and Alward, and Roger of Montgomery himself, only one each.[70] The Montgomery invasion

---

[66] King and Alcock (1969), 103, 106.

[67] Spurgeon (1965–66), 5–6.

[68] King and Spurgeon (1965), 80–86.

[69] Barker (1964), 222.

[70] Corbet: Ritton, Hawcocks Mount, Westbury, Wollaston and Pontesbury; de Lacy: Diddlebury and Rushbury; de Say: Castell Bryn Amlwg and Hopton; Siward: Wistanstow; Elmund and Alward: Amaston; Earl Roger: Wilcott. Oldbury is a siege-castle, and two cannot be placed with confidence in any holding (Selattyn and More).

of Ceredigion and Dyfed in 1093 offers no further help; the nature of the only recorded castles of this campaign, at Cardigan and Pembroke, is not known.

The Ceredigion earthwork castles are not easily explained in terms of personal preference. Mottes predominate again, with twenty against seven ringworks. The only recorded eleventh-century castle is the unknown Cardigan of Roger of Montgomery, though Roger seemingly built others which may well have been mottes.[71] We have seen that with the return of the Normans in 1110, under Gilbert fitz Richard de Clare, eleven castles are known to have been built, or rebuilt, by 1116. Cardigan is certainly stated to have been over Roger's earlier castle, but this, like Ystrad Meurig, another built by Gilbert, is of unknown type. Some preference for mottes is certainly shown by the followers of Gilbert, who raised seven recorded mottes, including Tomen Llanio, which has been identified as the castle of Richard de la Mare. Unfortunately, however, the remaining two of the eleven are the well-known motte at Blaenporth and the ringwork at Old Aberystwyth, an awkward mix in this context for their builder, Gilbert fitz Richard, the lord of Clare and Tonbridge, two of the largest mottes in England.[72]

The absence of ringworks in the earl of Chester's lands of Cheshire and much of Staffordshire has been interpreted as a dislike for them which might explain their absence in Flintshire and Denbighshire.[73] While this may be so, we have also offered a geological reason for the preference shown for mottes in north Wales.

The cluster of five ringworks around Usk, in Gwent, might merit an investigation of their manorial devolution, as would the more complex pattern of ringworks in Dyfed.

Regarding the less numerous Welsh earthwork castles, it may only be said that the princes of Powys seem to have displayed a preference for mottes, as did Owain Gwynedd. Owain's brother, however, built the ringworks at Llanrhystyd (Cards.) and Cynfal (Mer.).

APPENDIX

Cardiff and the coin evidence for Norman activity in south Wales under the Conqueror

In considering castles recorded in Wales before 1100, we noted the possibility that the fine motte at Cardiff was erected in 1081 for William I. Three Welsh chronicles [74] record the founding of Cardiff by that king, at the time of his expedition to St Davids directly after Rhys ap Tewdwr had attained pre-eminence in south Wales by his victory at Mynydd Carn. William's pilgrimage (so termed by the Welsh chroniclers, but in reality a diplomatic expedition in strength) achieved a binding feudal compact with Rhys, effectively curbing further hostile Norman encroachments in south Wales until

---

[71] The chronicles record that the Welsh in 1094 destroyed all the *castles* of Ceredigion and Dyfed except Pembroke and Rhyd y Gors (*Brut (Hergest)*, 35; *Brut (Peniarth)*, 19; *Brenhinedd*, 87).

[72] King (1972), 103.

[73] King and Alcock (1969), 106.

[74] *Ann. Marg.*, *Breviate of Domesday* and *Brenhinedd*. See *GCH* (1971), 9, and fns. 51 and 52; Nelson (1966), 103–05.

shortly before Rhys's death near Brecon in 1093. Rhys, as 'Riset' in Domesday Book, rendered £40 annually to the king, the same amount as that rendered by Gruffudd ap Cynan, Rhys's ally at Mynydd Carn, for his fee-farm of Gwynedd, though this obligation had soon fallen to his gaoler, Robert of Rhuddlan, who seized the northern prince soon after the battle. Territorially, Domesday Book records the effectiveness of the pact with Rhys, unlike that with Gruffudd, with the limited Norman advance into south Wales halted at Caerleon and Radnor, in contrast to the deep inroads made into mid- and north Wales by 1086. This simplified outline of events in south Wales under William I has long been accepted.[75] Its implications, however, seem to have been best appreciated by numismatists. Historians and archaeologists, constrained by the limitations of Domesday evidence, have not adequately contemplated the possiblity of peaceful if limited Norman settlement beyond the Usk under the Conqueror. Growing numismatic evidence, together with a diversity of minor documentary references, suggests that a reappraisal of this early period is long overdue.[76]

In any reconsideration, the recorded founding of Cardiff in 1081 is central. Understandably, the rejection of this early foundation by Sir John Lloyd, the father of Welsh history, has been hard to counter.[77] The great motte at Cardiff, however, is by far the largest in Glamorgan, and one of the best in Wales. Though no castle is mentioned in 1081, we must remember the Conqueror's personal direction of castle-building at Exeter, Warwick, Nottingham, York, Lincoln, Huntingdon and Cambridge, as described by Orderic Vitalis, and also the persistent, if disputed, claims of a pre-Norman Norse settlement at Cardiff.[78] We might also note that the last pre-Norman bishop of Llandaff (1056–1104) was Herewald. His name, like that of his son Lifris (=Leofric), was clearly English, and the small apsidal church at Llandaff, replaced by his successor, Bishop Urban, might indicate Norman influence in Glamorgan at an early date.[79]

Even before 1081, the battle fought on the banks of the Rhymni in 1072, just east of Cardiff, signals Norman involvement in Welsh dynastic conflicts. At that battle Caradog ap Gruffudd of Gwynllwg, with Norman help, defeated and slew Maredudd ab Owain of Deheubarth, thereby averting the absorption of Glamorgan in a greater Deheubarth where he himself had claims.[80] The Norman help was no doubt provided by Roger fitz William fitz Osbern, a debt not forgotten three years later, to judge by the account of a posthumous miracle of St Gwynllyw, written in the 1130s.[81] This recounts the flight of three Norman knights to Caradog's court following their part in an abortive conspiracy against William I, no doubt that which caused the downfall of the house of fitz Osbern in 1075. Caradog promised to protect these knights '... *though he should lose everything he held from the king*'. William's response, we are told, was to dispatch an army under William Rufus which ravaged Glamorgan and subsequently suffered the saint's miracle near Newport in Gwynllwg, the culmination and whole purpose of this addition to the life of Gwynllyw.

In deciding what credence might be given to the Life of St Gwynllyw, the tale of the three knights should be considered in its widest context. There exists yet another

[75] Lloyd (1939), **2**, 393–94; Lloyd (1899–1900), 162–64; Edwards (1956), 161–62; Nelson (1966), 35–41; *GCH* (1971), 8–9.

[76] An opinion shared by my friend Jeremy Knight, who inspired the present review of the evidence and drew my attention to many of the documentary references.

[77] Lloyd (1899–1900), 162; Lloyd (1939), **2**, 396, fn. 132.

[78] Charles (1934), 151–59; Paterson (1920); Paterson (1921).

[79] *GCH* (1971), 91; Fenn (1962), 25–28; Brooke (1963), 320–22; North (1957), 54–55.

[80] *Brut* (Hergest), 27; *Brut* (Peniarth), 16; *Brenhinedd*, 77.

[81] *Vitae Sanctorum*, 191-92; Knight (1970–71), 33–35.

indication of Roger fitz William's close associations with the Welsh in the charter of another Caradog (ap Rhiwallon), of *c.* 1075, in which lands at Llangwm, near Usk, were granted with the guarantee of Roger as lord of Gwent.[82] Few would dispute the strong probability that Roger assisted Caradog ap Gruffudd at the battle of Rhymni in 1072, or doubt that Roger's rebellion of 1075 provides a remarkably good historical context for the flight of the knights. The acceptance of these bare details would go far to explain the formative events of 1081. Caradog had seemingly acknowledged some undefined feudal obligations to the Crown, and knowingly risked the consequence of defying such obligations in sheltering the rebel knights. His ascendancy over Glamorgan, achieved with Roger's help in 1072, may perhaps have been won at the price of some formal acknowledgement of the Crown. If such was the case, Caradog's fall at the battle of Mynydd Carn might have been seen as just retribution for his disloyalty in 1075, and help to explain the Conqueror's immediate urge to meet the victorious Rhys ap Tewdwr, who could now exercise authority over Glamorgan as well as Deheubarth. In this light, following the compact with Rhys at St Davids, William's foundation of Cardiff would seem a logical step to take, buttressing the eastern flank of his new Welsh ally. The exceptional motte at Cardiff might well have been raised for the king, particularly as the Anglo-Saxon Chronicle hints at the possibility of isolated Norman garrisons already in place beyond the border, in its reference to William freeing hundreds of men on his expedition.[83]

One further reference supportive of William's foundation of Cardiff raises serious problems. The Cartulary of Gloucester Abbey contains a confirmation of 1086 by William of Robert fitz Hamon's grants to the abbey of Welsh lands, including Llancarfan.[84] At this date the extensive estates centred on Gloucester, and held until her death in 1083 by Queen Matilda, were still in the king's hands. They were not granted to fitz Hamon until the early years of William Rufus's reign, after which, it is held, he conquered Glamorgan, and surely obtained this misdated confirmation from that king.

Finally, and above all, it is the coin evidence which compels serious consideration of the shadowy documentary evidence for greater Norman activity in south Wales under William I. The expertise and generous guidance of George Boon makes possible a brief discussion of this specialist aspect, and one he has covered in more detail in his publication of the recent Wenallt (Glam.) hoard.[85]

Four coins may be attributed to a mint of William I at Cardiff. The earliest, a Type VI penny of *c.* 1077–80/1080–83 in the National Museum of Wales, is a fragmentary stray find of 1930 from Cardiff Castle, for which Boon reads the moneyer's name as possibly HEREVI (Hervé) at CA[I]ER (Cardiff). With this he places an unpublished fragment of a Type VII penny in Stockholm, noticed by the late Professor Michael Dolley in 1976, and conceivably of Cardiff, CII[.]D[..] = ?CARDII. Finally, there are two certain William I Type VIII pennies, which were assigned to Cardiff by Brooke as long ago as 1916; the moneyers are Aelfsige and Swein, and the name of the town reads CAIRDII, and CIVRDI, with A upside-down.[86]

Besides these four Cardiff coins of William I, we must also take account of the contemporary coins attributed long ago to a mint at St Davids by Carlyon-Britton and Brooke.[87]

[82] *Liber Landavensis*, 274; Davies (1979), 129–30.

[83] Lloyd (1939), **2,** 393–94; Williams (1948), 15.

[84] *Hist. Cart. Glouc.*, 334; Nelson (1966), 104; *GCH* (1971), 584, fn. 53.

[85] Boon (1986), 37–82.

[86] Brooke (1916), **2,** 109–10, Nos. 582–83. He also identified a further specimen, not accepted by George Boon.

[87] Carlyon-Britton (1905), 49; Brooke (1916), **2,** 166.

The attribution of these coins depends on the interpretation of 'Devitun' as Dewi's Town. More recently this interpretation has been rejected, but without seriously attempting to identify the proposed alternative site for 'Devitun' in the Welsh Marches.[88] The rejection, however, despite '. . . marked affinities between the alleged Cardiff coins of William I and those of the mint of "Devitun"', was strongly influenced by '. . . grave doubts among historians as to the possibility of there being William I mints at Cardiff and St David'.[89] These doubts, indeed, have discouraged a full consideration of all the evidence, which, in the context of the 1081 treaty between Rhys and William I, would make mints at Cardiff and St Davids far more plausible.

The recent Glamorgan hoards from Llantrithyd and the Wenallt have immeasurably advanced our knowledge of early coinage, and demonstrated the importance of numismatics to a fuller understanding of the history and archaeology of the early Norman period. William I mints may now be restored to Rhuddlan, Cardiff and St Davids, and suspected at Abergavenny. To these, the reign of William II adds a mint at Rhyd y Gors (RVDCO, *Rytcors*, or Carmarthen), appropriately datable to William fitz Baldwin's foundation there for the king.[90] Under Henry I a mint was founded at Pembroke,[91] and also at Swansea for King Stephen.

Acceptance of mints of William I at Cardiff and St Davids would go far to explain puzzling aspects of the currently favoured accounts of the Norman conquests of Glamorgan and Pembroke. For Glamorgan there is an exceptional lack of any contemporary documentary evidence for its conquest, a deficiency contrasting with the recorded incursions of William fitz Osbern, Hugh d'Avranches, Roger of Montgomery, Robert of Rhuddlan and Bernard de Neufmarché. If William I established a Norman presence at Cardiff in 1081, as some records and the coins would suggest, it might reasonably be seen as a military and economic aspect of the pact with Rhys. The mint at Cardiff, as indeed that at St Davids, could not have functioned safely without a strong Norman military presence. Furthermore, both mints would provide the means of exchange by which the garrisons could be paid, and by which Rhys could acquire his annual fee-farm rent of £40. Such a negotiated Norman presence in and around Cardiff would perhaps explain the silence of the records, for fitz Hamon might then have easily assumed control at any time during Rhys's pre-occupation with his final campaigns leading to his death at Brecon in 1093.

The mint at St Davids, and its presumed garrison, would make more credible the campaign of Arnulf of Montgomery in 1093–94. From their base in the upper Severn Valley, the men of Roger of Montgomery over-ran Ceredigion and Dyfed, and Arnulf established a castle at Pembroke. Despite the severance of his lines of communication in 1094, when Cadwgan ap Bleddyn of Powys recovered Ceredigion, he held on to Pembroke.

Acknowledgements. Sincere thanks are due to my colleagues of the Royal Commission on Ancient Monuments in Wales: Mr H. J. Thomas has shared with me the current work on the castles of Glamorgan; Mr W. G. Thomas read and much improved an initial draft of this article; and Mr Peter Smith, Secretary

---

[88] Jones (1955–57), who also points out that one comes from an altered Bristol reverse die; Dolley (1962) and Dolley and Knight (1970), 79–80.

[89] Dolley (1962), 76.

[90] Carlyon-Britton (1911) attributed it quite impossibly to a Llywelyn ap Cadwgan 'Rex'.

[91] Cf. Carlyon-Britton (1905), 54–56. The known coins of Pembroke are conveniently listed under lot 1175 in the F. E. Jones sale catalogue (Glendining's) of 13 April 1983.

of the Commission, has permitted the incorporation of material gathered for the forthcoming inventory dealing with the Glamorgan castles. In dealing with geological matters, Dr R. A. Waters of the British Geological Survey has given much appreciated advice, and Professor D. Q. Bowen has allowed me to incorporate his published southern limit of the last glaciation on Fig. 4, A. The initial inspiration for the appendix came from Mr Jeremy Knight, together with some valuable suggestions regarding the sources, and the vital numismatic evidence is owed entirely to the interest and kindness of Mr George Boon.

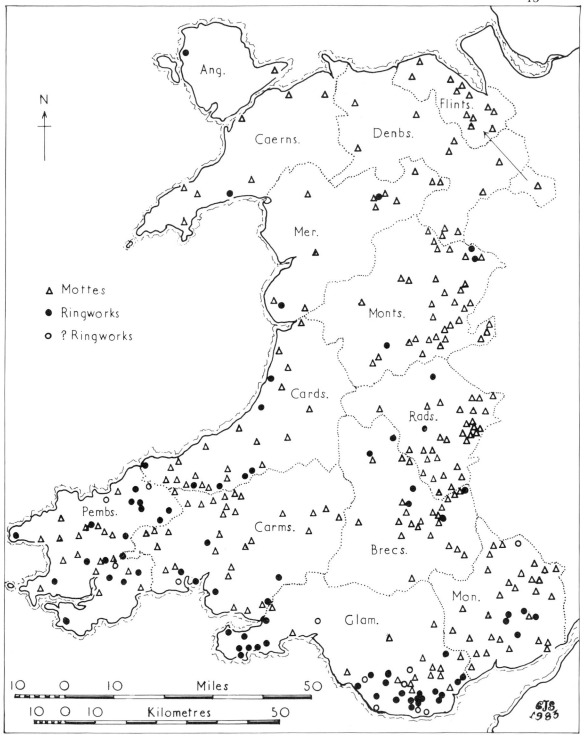

N

△ Mottes
● Ringworks
○ ? Ringworks

Ang.

Caerns.

Denbs.

Flints.

Mer.

Monts.

Cards.

Rads.

Pembs.

Carms.

Brecs.

Mon.

Glam.

ETS
1983

10 O 10   Miles   50

10 O 10   Kilometres   50

Fig. 1   Distribution of earthwork castles in the old Welsh counties.

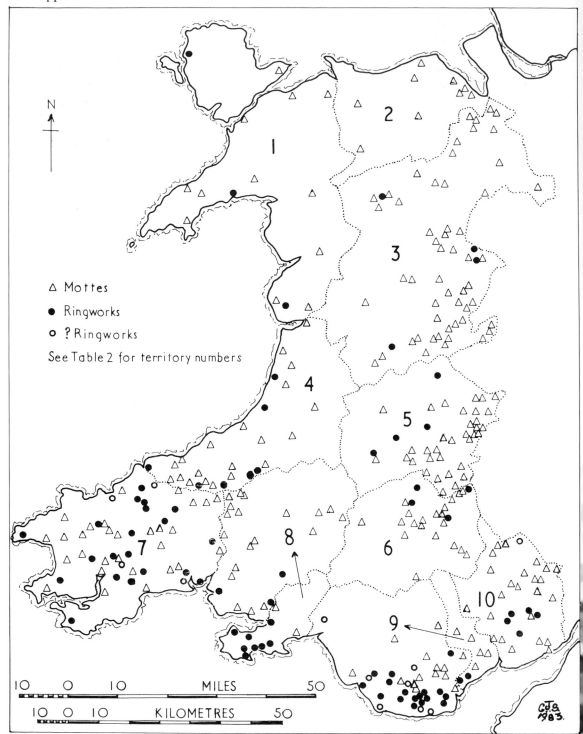

Fig. 2   Distribution of earthwork castles in the main territorial divisions of medieval Wales.

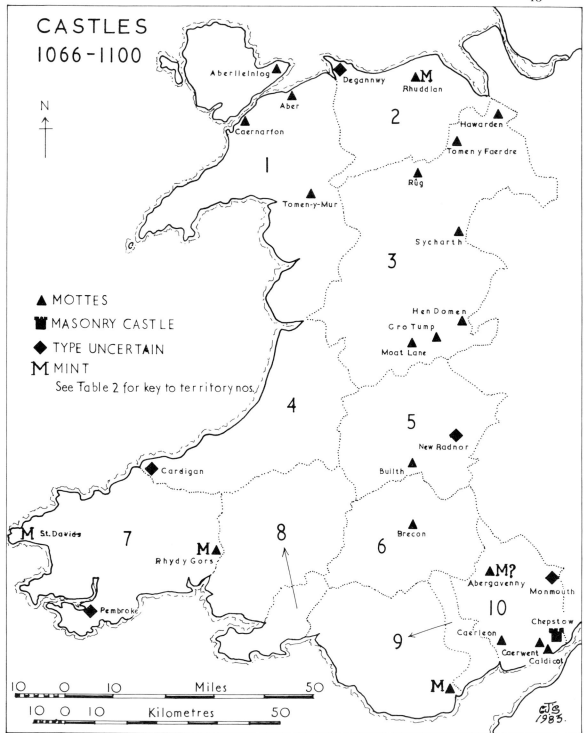

CASTLES
1066–1100

N

▲ MOTTES
♜ MASONRY CASTLE
◆ TYPE UNCERTAIN
M MINT
    See Table 2 for key to territory nos.

Aberlleiniog
Aber
Caernarfon
Degannwy
Rhuddlan M
Hawarden
Tomen y Faerdre
Rûg
Tomen-y-Mur
Sycharth
Hen Domen
Gro Tump
Moat Lane
New Radnor
Builth
Brecon
St.Davids M
Rhyd y Gors M
Pembroke
Cardigan
Abergavenny ▲M?
Monmouth
Chepstow
Caerleon
Caerwent
Caldicot
M

1   2   3   4   5   6   7   8   9   10

10   0   10   Miles   50
10   0   10   Kilometres   50

cJg
1983.

Fig. 3   Castles recorded, or strongly suspected as being founded, before AD 1100.

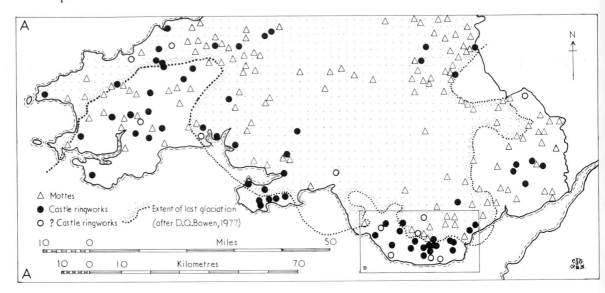

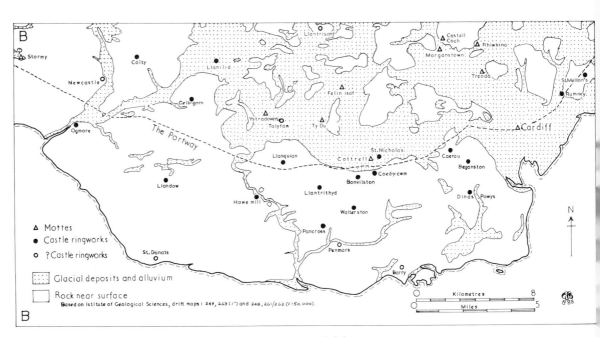

Fig. 4   Earthwork castles and glacial deposits in south Wales.

I   Ogmore Castle, Glamorgan.
(*Crown copyright reserved*).

II   Cardiff Castle, Glamorgan.
(*Crown copyright reserved*).

III   Mathrafal motte and bailey castle, Montgomeryshire.
(*Crown copyright reserved*).

Hen Domen revisited

PHILIP BARKER

THE excavation of Hen Domen, Montgomery, and particularly the interpretation of the excavated evidence,[1] has been profoundly influenced by presuppositions based on all that we know, or think we know, about the period following the Norman Conquest, and in particular its defensive structures. The site was chosen for excavation because of its fine earthworks of 'motte and bailey' type, on the assumption that they were those of an early timber castle, and, further, that they were those of the castle built by Roger of Montgomery between *c.* 1070 and 1086, and which is mentioned by name among the Domesday entries for Shropshire.

Roger of Montgomery was one of William the Conqueror's greatest magnates and the castle was sufficiently important to him to be named after his birthplace in the Calvados region of Normandy. On the fall of Robert de Bellême and the demise of the Earldom of Shrewsbury in 1102, the castle passed to a lesser family, that of the de Boulers. The lordship attached to the castle was, nevertheless, quite extensive, comprising the lands in the immediate vicinity of the castle, the adjacent hundred of Chirbury, and outlying manors in Shropshire, and there were family possessions in other counties as far away as Suffolk and Wiltshire, acquired through marriage during the course of the twelfth century.[2] Moreover, the first head of the de Boulers family, Baldwin, was married to a woman, Sybil de Falaise, who was perhaps one of the bastard daughters of Henry I. Montgomery Castle (that is, Hen Domen, as it later came to be known) was the *caput* of the new marcher lordship, and remained until the early thirteenth century the military, social and judicial centre of the estates held by the de Boulers.[3]

Since the beginning of the excavation, therefore, our understanding of everything found, from the plans of buildings to pottery, arrowheads to horseshoe nails, has been coloured by the knowledge that this was an aristocratic site of crucial strategic importance in this part of the Welsh border, since it is situated close to a major ford over the river Severn.

But there have been, even after twenty-five seasons of intensive excavation, no finds which could dispassionately be called 'aristrocratic', nothing, apart from the defences themselves, to suggest that the site was occupied by a succession of wealthy and powerful families.

---

[1] I am most grateful to my colleague, Dr Robert Higham, for discussion, both on and off the site, of the problems of interpretation touched on here.

[2] Barker and Higham (1982), 17.

[3] Ibid.

It therefore occurred to the writer, during the 1983 season, to wonder how, if we could clear our minds of all preconceptions, we would interpret Hen Domen? What conclusions would we draw about the people who lived here if we knew nothing of medieval life? What, in fact, distinguishes it from a small prehistoric defended site?

The presence of the motte precludes the earthworks from looking prehistoric, but there are a number of ringworks in the region which cannot, on inspection, be dated more closely than within a bracket which includes the later Bronze Age at one end and the later thirteenth century at the other, and, if one stands with one's back to the motte, the bailey at Hen Domen could well be one of these.

The structural evidence revealed by the excavation is very varied,[4] but none of it is different in kind from the methods of timber-building used in the previous thousand or more years. The most sophisticated structures implied by the Hen Domen evidence are timber-framed, with their sills lying on the ground or in sleeper-beam trenches. Such buildings require accurate joints, and two water-logged timbers found in the outer ditch demonstrate this,[5] though the preserved sill-beam of the earliest bridge (presumably built on the orders of Roger of Montgomery himself) has crude joints with unnecessarily large and therefore less efficient mortices.[6] There is nothing here which could not have been fashioned at least from Roman times onwards—there are no suggestions of the highly elaborate joints of only slightly later date found in barns and church roofs.[7]

Other forms of buildings, with post-holes and wattle walls, or clay walls streng-thened with small irregularly-spaced posts are undatable in style, as were perhaps the buildings they represent. The writer always intended, when reconstructing the Hen Domen buildings, to have them bristling with dragons at the corners, like the motte towers on the Bayeux Tapestry, or the stave churches of Norway, or the church at Kilpeck, only fifty miles away. But though a good deal of waterlogged worked timber has been found, none of it has any decorative carving, even of the simplest kind—all is utilitarian. Nor have any of the pieces of leather found been tooled or punched decoratively.

In fact, the earliest levels on the site, those datable before *c.* 1125, yield almost no finds at all. There are tiny scraps of pottery derived from pots thought to have been imported from elsewhere, probably the Midlands.[8] The only finds of metal are nails, knives, arrowheads and other less identifiable objects. The finds are, in fact, little different in quality or quantity from those found at a small defended Cornovian site at Sharpstones Hill, Shrewsbury, dug by the writer and others in 1965 (forthcoming), and the Cornovii have been described by Graham Webster as 'a poor, backward rural community.'[9] We seem to be getting close to Wheeler's description of William the Conqueror as a 'scratch-markware chieftain'.

---

[4] Ibid., 89ff.
[5] Ibid., 41, Fig. 40.
[6] Ibid., Fig. 68
[7] Cf. the work of Cecil Hewett, exemplified in Hewett (1969) and Hewett (1972).
[8] Barker and Higham (1982), 74
[9] Webster (1975), 14.

Is this fair? Did Roger's men and Baldwin's family live like Cornovian peasants? (Or was the Iron Age site itself the home of a Cornovian aristocratic family? Their round houses were certainly bigger than any building yet found at Hen Domen, even if not so substantially founded . . . .)

It may be argued that a closer prehistoric parallel to Hen Domen is the hill-fort on Ffridd Faldwyn, only a few hundred yards away, excavated by B. H. St J. O'Neil.[10] Here the defences were built on an increasingly formidable scale, and the structural timbers, attested by the size of the post-pits, were massive. Although only a comparatively small proportion of the site was excavated, the area was as great as that at Hen Domen, yet only one sherd of Iron Age pottery was found, together with a very small number of other finds[11] from a community which must, on any reckoning, have been large and flourishing.

The contrast with the Roman sites of the area, such as Forden Gaer and Wroxeter, sandwiched in time between Fridd Faldwyn and Hen Domen, is startling. At Wroxeter the quantities of pottery and small finds of all kinds are enormous—86,000 sherds of pottery have been recovered, from the upper layers only, of an area approximately 140 m × 30 m; the annual yield of coins is about 250 and there are hundreds of brooches, hairpins and beads, together with all kinds of decorative metalwork, carved objects of bone, shale and jet. There is also much evidence of trade with the Continent and as far away as the eastern Mediterranean. The object traded furthest to Hen Domen seems to be a jug from the Stamford area of Lincolnshire. Nothing even from Normandy can be identified.

Yet both Wroxeter and Hen Domen lack one vital strand which we know was of the greatest significance in the lives of their inhabitants—at neither site is there any evidence of Christianity. If we knew nothing of Romano-British or Anglo-Norman culture we should have no inkling from these sites of that all-pervading influence. Yet there is every reason to believe that there was a bishop of Wroxeter from the fourth century onwards, that is, the period under excavation there, and the Normans were devout fighters who did penance for the souls of those they killed.

It should be noted that the building at Hen Domen identified, with some reservation, as a chapel[12] is only considered to be so because of its tri- or quadripartite apsidal shape and because, by analogy with so many surviving stone castles, one expects a chapel in a castle. A building of similar plan on a Romano-British site would be differently interpreted since many apsidal Romano-British buildings seem to be purely domestic. As an extension of this somewhat tendentious way of thinking, the vessel identified as a stoup for holy water[13] was only thought to be so because it came from the 'chapel' area and because similar mortar-like vessels have elsewhere apparently been used in this way, for example, mortared into the porches of existing churches. In another context, this interpretation would probably not have occurred to us.

[10] O'Neil (1942–43).
[11] Ibid., 54.
[12] Barker and Higham (1982), 44.
[13] Ibid., 45.

If so powerful a force as Christianity cannot easily be detected, other aspects of the spiritual and intellectual life of the site will be equally elusive. We may guess from the deer and wild boar bones on the site that Baldwin and his entourage enjoyed hunting, but we do not know their taste in poetry and music—if any. And though we can assume from what we know of castle life in general that Baldwin's wife and children lived with him, there is little, if anything, among the finds to suggest the presence of women and nothing, such as toys or feeding bottles (known elsewhere in pottery), to suggest children. It is probable that Roger's first castle was a garrison entirely manned by soldiers and that from 1102 onward the castle became residential,[14] but there is at present no *archaeological* evidence to support this assumption.

This is rapidly becoming an essay on the limitations of archaeological evidence, which was not the original intention. What, therefore, can we say positively about the site in its earlier years and about the people who lived there?

Everything points to a life of great simplicity, shorn of extraneous trappings and ornament. The bailey is at all times crowded with buildings, but only two have any sign of heating (though the use of braziers, perhaps even in upper rooms, and therefore not archaeologically discernible, cannot be discounted). The impression one gets is of a life of great hardiness, lived mainly out of doors, except in the worst weather and at night—not unlike all-year-round camping. There is nothing to suggest literacy among any of the castle's inhabitants; they clearly used very little coin (one coin only has been found in twenty-five years of excavation); they ate, as one would expect, beef, mutton and pork and some deer (though there is less antler, worked or unworked, than one would expect); there is very little bread wheat and no sign of any cultivated fruits, such as plum or apple (though there are some wild blackberries) and no imported delicacies such as figs or grapes.[15] The picture is, in fact, very close to that of the hard simple life, spent chiefly in the open, and with few social graces, that one would deduce from the excavation of prehistoric sites here or elsewhere on the border.

By the early thirteenth century all had changed. The new stone castle at Montgomery was decorated with stiff-leaf capitals as fine as those at Westminster, Wells or Lincoln, and with elegant mouldings for the glazed windows, and it is reasonable to assume that the rest of the castle was in keeping. Even allowing for the fact that New Montgomery Castle was a royal foundation, and that the de Boulers were, by comparison, poor, nevertheless, Hen Domen is the site of their only castle and one might expect what movable wealth they had to be concentrated there. It has been suggested that the de Boulers and similar families might have had their wealth tied up in livestock rather than in finery—if so, the comparison with prehistoric peoples is even closer. At Hen Domen, and particularly in the earlier decades, we seem to be in a quite different world from that of the courtly aristocratic life commonly envisaged in the medieval castle.

[14] Ibid., 93–94.
[15] Ibid., 61ff.

'Chastel de Dynan': the first phases of Ludlow

DEREK RENN

A straight line drawn across a map between Bristol and Chester passes through Ludlow exactly halfway along its length. Ludlow is thus in the very centre of the Welsh March, on the line of the medieval road Chester–Shrewsbury–Leominster–Hereford–Gloucester. The town and castle are sited on a ridge protected on three sides by the rivers Corve and Teme: only eastward is the ground both level and dry. The plan of the town and the visual delights of its ecclesiastical and domestic buildings have been frequently described. There is so much to see that the remarkable state of preservation and interest of Ludlow Castle can be easily overlooked. Its preservation is due first to its continued use as the headquarters of the Council in the Marches of Wales until 1689 and latterly to the earls of Powis who first leased (1772) and then bought the castle from the Crown in 1811.

The archaeology of Ludlow is dominated by the very detailed description of the castle by William St John Hope, followed by his short but very percipient paper on the town plan.[1] Since then the town plan and the domestic planning of the castle have been re-examined by other writers,[2] and I should like to offer a review of the evidence for the origin and early defences of Ludlow Castle.[3] The first certain reference to the castle is during the siege in 1139, when King Stephen rescued his hostage, Prince Henry of Scotland, from a grapnel thrown down its walls,[4] but the architectural evidence suggests a rather earlier date for the walls and towers of the inner bailey.

LUDLOW IN DOMESDAY BOOK

John Horace Round declared that the *Lude . . . terra R. de Laci* which Eyton had identified as Ludlow was Lyde in central Herefordshire, and concurred with Hope that the site of Ludlow was included with Stanton Lacy and that the place had no existence before the castle was begun.[5] Let us take each of these statements in turn.

[1] Hope (1908); Hope (1909).

[2] Conzen (1968), 113–20; Faulkner (1958), 177–82.

[3] Figs. 8–11 are based upon Harold Brakspear's survey (SA Ludlow) with the permission of the Society of Antiquaries of London.

[4] *Henrici Hunt.*, 265; *Chron. John Worc.*, 54.

[5] Eyton (1857), 280; Hope (1908), 324.

First, there is some duplication of places and entries in the relevant folios of Domesday Book, not to be wondered at in a border area. There are two consecutive *Lude* entries on folio 184, and two folios later the same Osbert fitz Richard is recorded as holding successively *Stantone, Lude, Ludeford* and *castellum Aureton*. This last is reasonably identifed as Richard's Castle,[6] and this is the folio Eyton was referring to.[7] Assuming that the enquiry proceeds southward along the medieval road, *Lude* is surely Ludlow.[8]

Second, although a late nineteenth-century plan shows the 'great tower' of Ludlow Castle as being in the parish of Stanton Lacy,[9] the castle had remained extra-parochial (as former Crown property) until the conclusion of a dispute between the Poor Law commissioners and the Powis estate which had lasted from at least 1824 until 1862, including the legal fiction of a 'Ludlow Castle Parish' at one stage.[10]

Last, the apparent silence of Domesday Book is not positive evidence that Ludlow Castle had not been begun by 1086;[11] this would be particularly true if the castle had been built on a virgin site as Hope and Round claimed. Personally, I find it difficult to believe that so fine a position was not inhabited before the reign of William II; the area adjoining the castle to the south is called Dinham, a name with a fine Saxon ring to it, whatever its exact meaning.

LUDLOW IN LEGEND

The thirteenth-century romance *Fouke le Fitz Waryn*[12] gives a spirited account of the early history of Ludlow Castle. Roger de Bellême (that is, Roger of Montgomery, *vicomte* of the Hiémois) is said to have begun castles at *Brugge* (Bridgnorth) and *Dynan* (Ludlow). After his son's rebellion and disinheritance in 1102, 'Dynan' was given to Joce de Dynan who finished the castle and built a stone bridge across the Teme. The author clearly knew his Ludlow, mentioning the three baileys and two ditches, and the highest tower within the third bailey. In the course of the fighting between Joce de Dynan and the Lacy claimants (c. 1145–53?), the gate of Dynan towards the river is opened, a tower over a gate is burnt and the high tower largely overthrown.[13]

Doubts have been cast on this account on the grounds that Roger of Montgomery was never lord of Ludlow.[14] But are we certain of this? Roger arrived in England in December 1067 and was given the county of Shropshire in 1071.[15] Even if we could be sure which Domesday entry covered the site of Ludlow

---

[6] Curnow and Thompson (1969), 106.

[7] Eyton (1857), 235–36.

[8] *Stanton* is an even more common entry: two separate ones on f. 254, two consecutive ones on f. 256[b], one referring to Helgot's *castellum*, and another on f. 260.[b]

[9] *Ex. inf.* Dr Trevor Rowley.

[10] SRO Walcot.

[11] Wightman (1966), 135, fn. 1.

[12] BL Royal MS 12C XII.

[13] Hathaway *et al.* (1975), 3, line 31; 4, lines 8, 12, 14; 13, line 28; ix; 17, line 29; 18, line 36.

[14] Eyton (1857), 233–35; *VCH* (1908), 288–90.

[15] Mason (1963).

Castle, identification of its holders *T.R.E.*, 1066 and 1085, does not rule out an unrecorded intermediate owner who had time enough to begin a castle. If Roger's son Robert was the castle founder (and to my inexpert eye the text is not clear on this point), this is supported as regards Bridgnorth by Orderic Vitalis,[16] and Ludlow might be part of the same secondary southward expansion of the earls of Shrewsbury in 1098 × 1102, a not impossibly short length of time for the first building phase, and only a few years after the dates of Roger de Lacy I (1085 × 1095) whom Eyton and Hope believed to have been the founder.[17]

We must, however, remember that *Fouke le Fitz Waryn* was composed to belittle the Lacys, so we should examine their claim as founders in terms of historical probability.

THE SOUTHERN WELSH MARCH 1055–75

Hereford was burnt by Gruffudd ap Llywelyn in 1055, and Edric the Wild's later rising was only crushed when William fitz Osbern was given palatine authority in 1067. Walter de Lacy I first appears in the region in 1067, apparently with separate grants of land and authority from the Crown. Later he acquired some Shropshire manors from Roger of Montgomery about 1074, and also profited from the disgrace of Roger fitz Osbern in 1075.[18]

Principally on the evidence of Domesday Book, William fitz Osbern is believed to have created a system of castles protecting the western frontier of his earldom of Hereford before his death in February 1071, refortifying Ewyas Harold and building Clifford and Wigmore castles on waste land further north, and Chepstow and Monmouth castles further south (Fig. 5).[19] The first three castles named have mottes with traces of stone shell keeps on top, and the latter two have stone halls on river cliffs, although only at Chepstow is there enough architectural detail to attribute some of the masonry to the period 1067 × 1071. The fitz Osberns, father and son, might have fortified Ludlow as a site on the northern border of the earldom, at the confluence of the two rivers, just like Chepstow, Hereford and Monmouth castles, about 25 kilometres apart along the medieval road already mentioned. The other castles are also about 25 kilometres apart, except for Wigmore, whose site was probably selected to control the Roman road to Hereford where it entered fitz Osbern's territory.

The earldom of Shrewsbury was created in 1074; before then, Roger of Montgomery may only have been a tenant-in-chief of fitz Osbern, the paramount earl of the whole March. Walter de Lacy I died in 1085 as the result of a fall from scaffolding while superintending the building of St Guthlac's church in Hereford, which suggests a fatally close interest in building (Hugh de Lacy met a violent end at the building of Durrow Castle a century later).[20] There

[16] Mason and Barker (1961), 41; Mason (1963), 12, 26.
[17] Eyton (1857), 274; Hope (1908), 323–24.
[18] Lewis (1985), 203–05; Wightman (1966), 117, 120, 168.
[19] Renn (1964), 129–30.
[20] Wightman (1966), 168, fn. 1, 191.

had to be a reorganization of marcher defences first in 1075, and again in 1094–1102.[21] I would vote—narrowly—for Ludlow's foundation *c.* 1075.

'DINHAM' AND LUDLOW

It has previously been believed that the town began as a market street running eastward from the outer gate of the castle to the parish church, followed by a re-orientation of a chequer of north-south streets (Broad Street, Mill Street, Raven Lane) intersected by Bell Lane and Brand Lane, ligatured by the erection of a town wall and the creation of a new Old Street on the east side of the town.[22] All this seems to have taken place very quickly: the earliest surviving part of the parish church, and the outer gate of the castle, date from the late twelfth century, Ludford bridge and the whole length of Broad Street were there by the 1220s, and the town walls may have been begun in 1233.[23] A tallage indicates that the town existed by 1189, and *temp.* John it was rebuilt when *Ludelowe* replaced *Dynan*.[24]

What previous writers have overlooked is that the castle itself was re-orientated when the outer bailey was added (Fig. 6). The inner gate looks southward, not east along the ridge, and the substantial postern towers of both baileys lie on the west side.[25] Public rights of way here are tenacious: when the posterns were closed up (and one converted into a residence) the wall of the castle nearby was pierced in two places to keep the paths of Dinham open. The Dinham area still has the air of a separate village, with a late twelfth-century chapel on the over-built village green, facing the entrance to the first castle. Extension of the castle has blocked and diverted the northern end of Dinham's main strect and back lane.[26] Dinham bridge was rebuilt in 1772, but the piers of an earlier bridge running rather north of east are said to be visible at low water.[27] This, or its predecessor, would be that built by Joce de Dynan (who probably took his name from here, rather than from Dinan in Brittany), and he was attacked upon it by the Lacys and rescued by the young Fulk le fitz Warin. Dinham bridge has easier approaches than Ludford bridge, and is better controlled by the castle. It serves little traffic today, although minor roads can still be followed from it to Knighton and Wigmore.

NORMAN FEATURES OF LUDLOW CASTLE

Although it has lost its roofs and floors, the castle is otherwise almost intact, occupying the north-west corner of the bluff on which the town stands. The river cliffs have been graded to form public walks round the castle which continue

---

[21] Mason (1963); Wightman (1966).
[22] Conzen (1968); Hope (1909).
[23] Lloyd (1979); 5, 10; *Cal. Pat. R. 1232–47*, 35.
[24] Hunter (1844), 94; Hathaway *et al.* (1975), 22, line 18.
[25] Curnow (1981), 12.
[26] Morley (1964); Rowley (1972), 98.
[27] SRO Walcot; Hope (1909), 387, pl. XLIX.

along the line of the filled-in outer ditch towards the town (Fig. 6). The plan is roughly square, the north-west quadrant of the site being cut off by a steep-sided rock-cut dry ditch to enclose the early castle. A late twelfth-century addition formed an outer bailey, quadrupling the area enclosed. The later curtain wall of this bailey butted against the north-east and south towers of the inner bailey; it was very poorly provided with towers, none of them covering the three exposed angles. The oblong tower projecting from the northern part of the east curtain has offsets on the east side only, and has been converted into a house. It once had a fellow at the east end of the south wall, possibly the 'Norman tower in a garden beyond the outer bailey' mentioned early this century. A sketch plan of 1765 shows a sub-circular projection near the south end of the east wall as well.[28] The present entrance, in the middle of the east side, is through a gateway vaulted in two bays, the shallower projecting forward of the curtain wall; both vaults and much of the interior walls have gone. A later entrance was through a D-shaped tower in the opposite wall whose passage is now blocked but can be clearly seen, including a portcullis slot. Just north of this tower the parapet of the curtain wall is raised to the same height and width as this tower, as if to give the impression of a twin-towered gatehouse to a distant or casual observer.

I now turn to the inner bailey. Generally, the early walling is of local shale rubble, with ashlar dressings and quoins of red sandstone. Doorways are square-edged and round-headed. Significant differences from these norms will be mentioned.

THE INNER BAILEY AND ITS TOWERS (Fig. 7)

The quadrant plan of the curtain wall is composed of a number of almost straight lengths of rubble wall forming an overall convex trace, more pronounced to the south and the east than elsewhere; perhaps the best description is of a stout irregular vesica. Rectangular towers, originally open-backed, project from the north-east, north-west and south-west sides of the curtain; on one side of the south-west tower is a smaller (backed) square tower, and on the other side is the 'great tower', these latter three forming the corners of the innermost bailey. That both the curtain wall and the towers have been raised in height, some more than once, is most obvious just to the west of the north-east tower and of the 'great tower', where quoins begin at a level below the first floor of each tower. The two northerly towers have their external angles splayed back above ground level. Since their internal angles are rectilinear, this suggests that alterations have been undertaken.[29]

The north-east tower (Fig. 8) had wall-passages, now blocked, onto the flanking wall-walks, entered through first floor doorways, the western passage having small lighting slits in its north wall. Part at least of the later wall closing the gorge of the tower appears to be Norman. The north-west tower (Fig. 8) has

[28] SRO Walcot; Weyman (1914–17), 130.
[29] An idea suggested to me (for the similar plan of Christchurch keep) by the late Stuart Rigold.

more complicated passages. Doorways at ground level lead to passages rising in the thickness of the curtain; that running north-east is half-filled up and ends in the floor of a later window embrasure, while the opposite passage steps up (with three arch frames at intervals) to a recent blocking; it continued formerly to the battlements as a spiral stair.[30] At first floor level another passage, glimpsed from below, ran round three sides of the tower, blocked at each end by later alterations. A remarkable squinch arch, with a latrine vent, carried it across one return angle of the tower.

The next tower southward (Fig. 9) is smaller and the gorge is closed, but pierced by the inner of two doorways, one in the north and the other in the east walls of the tower, both being barred from within the castle. The interior seems to be perfectly plain; for the last hundred years it has been tightly closed. This form of 'bent entrance' has been studied in detail by David Cathcart King.[31]

The south-west angle tower (Fig. 9) has doorways at first floor level, one leading onto the wall-walk towards the 'great tower' and the other into a passage running south to a loop-lit latrine and north to a blocking. All the towers are blind at ground level and only have small lighting slits to their wall-passages over. They were designed, like the curtain wall, to be defended from the wall-walk. Their upper floors formed part of the continuous circuit, reached by the rising wall-stairs adjoining the north-west tower and in the 'great tower' described below, possibly supplemented by a ladder or other temporary staircase.

THE 'GREAT TOWER' I: GROUND FLOOR (SEMI-BASEMENT)

Hope saw that the present north wall of the 'great tower' was considerably later in date than the others, and excavated outside the tower, finding the bases of stairs rising against extensions of the west wall and within extensions of the east wall, with a blocked archway between them. All this had been cased in further masonry surrounded by a battering plinth, over which had been built two north-south walls of the innermost curtain (Fig. 10). Hope concluded that the 'great tower' had been originally a T-shaped gateway block contemporary with the inner curtain wall, with an outer lobby in front of its door.[32] This is so unusual a plan[33] that the evidence needs to be re-assessed. Hope's note-books[34] contain only two sentences about the excavation, and the two published photographs seem to be the only ones which survive.

In cutting the inner ditch, the rock was quarried back to leave rough abutments for a bridge, levelled up with mortared slabs of shale, on the front of the 'great tower'. So the original entrance was here, but blocked by about 1180 when the Transitional arch was inserted into the curtain a little to the east.[35] Other

---

[30] Hope (1908), 284.

[31] King (1977), 165; King (1978), 106–07.

[32] Hope (1908), 305–10.

[33] The late Romanesque church at the Templar commandery of Ydes (Cantal) has a vaulted porch with wall arcades in front of its double west doors.

[34] SA MS 785.

[35] Hope (1908), 316.

early Norman gate-passages which have been blocked and replaced by an adjoining opening in the curtain can be seen at Bramber and Exeter,[36] and the plan *ab initio* occurs at Bridgend, Chepstow and Lydney during the mid- to late twelfth century. Richmond will be referred to below.

The facing of the 'great tower' is partly of squared rubble and partly in ashlar, varying from a hard grey stone to a soft red sandstone. These changes in colour and texture suggest that the tower is not such a simple structure as had been thought. For example, the outer doorway has been torn out so completely that no dressings are left, except for a short length of chamfered impost in the wreckage within (A on Fig. 10), but the filling in a different coloured stone gives the impression of a pointed Gothic arch rather than a semi-circular one. At the level of the slabs capping the bridge abutment is a chamfered quirked offset course, not returned along the east and west faces. On the south face this course is partly underpinned with squared rubble, and the south-east corner spreads out as a bold sloping batter, returned unevenly northward to where the upper ashlar facing stands on shaly rubble, perhaps a plinth to the curtain wall at this point.

This ground-level offset and batter resembles that fossilized by the building of the innermost curtain wall over the masonry platform excavated by Hope. Could it be that an ordinary oblong gate-passage was entirely cased around? This would explain the lack of any ashlar in the south part of the interior of the semi-basement, and the awkward design of the present vault. Such encasing has been demonstrated at the keeps of Pevensey and Portchester, and perhaps at the Tower of London, but not at Colchester; at Castle Acre the manor house was lined rather than cased for its conversion into a keep.[37] I have shown the possible outline in pecked lines on Fig. 10. The main objection to the idea is the narrow wall-passage in the east wall of the semi-basement. It is clearly a primary feature, lined with hard grey ashlar similar to that of the fragments of wall arcade whose capitals are very crude indeed (compare Robin Hood's Tower at Richmond Castle) and suit an eleventh-century date. Hope took it to be a wicket, by-passing the main door, but:

(a) The north doorway has a lintel which is lopsided and supported on a re-used stone; scars above suggest that an arch or tympanum has been torn out.

(b) Shallow recesses in the jambs of this doorway would be for a door closed against the interior of the tower.

(c) The roof of the passage is partly slabbed and partly covered in mortared rubble.

(d) The southern end of the passage ends in a built-up face supporting one end of an original lintel, as well as a timber bressumer (there are many examples of old timber in the castle still bearing masonry).

(e) The jamb below the lintel has a wedge-shaped recess chopped into

---

[36] Barton and Holden (1977), 137.

[37] Coad and Streeten (1982), 149; Drury (1982b), 393; Munby and Renn (1985), 75–76; Renn (1971), 61–62; Sturdy (1979).

it; if this was a wicket to the main door, I should expect to find a better bar socket than this.

(f)   In the re-entrant (B on Fig. 10) there is a column with a well-finished scalloped capital in red sandstone, rather better in quality than those of the arcade further north. Hope interpreted this as evidence for a two-bay arcade, but it could have been part of the main archway.

I would suggest that the passage might either have

  (i)   given access to a latrine in the thickness of the wall, or

  (ii)   opened into the side of the main archway, as in contemporary work at Bamburgh, Chepstow and Colchester, or

  (iii)   turned south again to open to one side of the main arch as at Lincoln (West Gate), Loches (Indre-et-Loire) or, later, at Richard's Castle.[38]

It is perhaps more than a coincidence that the only other early curtain wall with open-backed towers at the corners is at Carisbrooke; it also had an original gateway beside one corner,[39] like untowered Lincoln and Newark. Carisbrooke was founded by William fitz Osbern, although I cannot prove the stonework to have been his.

THE 'GREAT TOWER' II: UPPER FLOORS AND ADDITIONS

The straight wall-stair rises to the level of the curtain wall (Fig. 11). Its original purpose was probably simply this, but when the gate-passage was cased in, the extra width provided room for vaulted lobbies on each side and a more sophisticated facade. The stair doorway is set in a tall recess with cut-back jambs. The door to the western wall-walk has one impost as if for a lintel, and the adjoining slit (with a slight external splay) has been widened and lengthened so that it cuts the external half-hexagonal string-course on this face. Although there are offsets at different levels on the flanks, this non-return of offsets reminds one of the north-east tower on the outer curtain wall. The wider window further west has an outer order supported on jambshafts; two similar windows can be traced in part around the inserted opening between them.

There is a distinct possibility that only the front of this floor was built at first (compare the West Gate at Lincoln). The best evidence for this is the vertical quoins (X on Fig. 11) and the change from grey to red sandstone (at Y) on the opposite wall. The external face of the east wall is largely of rubble, and changes to ashlar on the lobby faces only. Further north there appears to be a vertical break in the coursing, beyond which again there is a jambshaft with a re-used lintel, either taken from one of the windows just described or lighting some feature now gone.

The tower was carried at least one floor higher (Fig. 11), but on flanking offsets, not a vault. The two tiny rectangular loops (A, B) seem too small to light the sizeable room within suggested by Hope, although his photograph[40]

[38]   Curnow and Thompson (1969), 115; Héliot (1972), 46.

[39]   The gap at the north-west corner could be due to a demolished angle-tower, *pace* Rigold (1969), 137, fn. 20.

[40]   Hope (1908), 267.

indicates that one at least was larger (and unblocked) in his day. There are much taller slits lighting Hope's spiral stair in the other corner, reached by a very narrow wall-passage with two right-angle turns in it, and presumably once giving access to the wall-walk above the roof of the 'great tower'. I could see no evidence of any Norman work in the present top floor.

How these passages were originally reached from below is not clear; perhaps there were stairs and passages in the north wall of the 'great tower', so riddled that it collapsed before the twelfth century was out. Wall-passages are uncommon in Norman castles, except in lighting clerestoreys, but wall-stairs occur at Bamburgh, Beaugency (Loiret), Loches and Richmond.

The barrel-vaulted lodge is not bonded into the east wall of the 'great tower' and is probably contemporary with the present entrance. I have been unable to confirm the existence of the loops mentioned by Clark and Hope; neither is in the position of the jambshaft mentioned above.[41]

A block added to the west side of the 'great tower' seems to have been intended for latrines from the first. The ground floor 'pit' is spanned by an arch on imposts; the floor above has three (formerly four?) slits, with the south part walled off with a latrine shaft in the narrow slot against the curtain (Z on Fig. 11) covered by a two-bay vault like the north part. One slit on this floor is obstructed by the shafts from the floor above, suggesting that it is an addition; certainly the external masonry and quoins change at this level. Hope argued that his western stair ran up to this block before turning east into the 'great tower', but, since he only found its very lowest steps, it might equally have turned eastward before reaching the latrine block.

LUDLOW AND RICHMOND

A few words must now be said about Richmond Castle, with which Ludlow is sometimes compared. It too has an early curtain wall with a convex trace, pierced with several wall-passages, and has a tower with wall arcades resembling those in the 'great tower' at Ludlow, beside a tunnel-vaulted gateway with a lobby and latrine-block in the return angle. However, here all the towers are closed at the gorge, not open-backed, and the 'great tower' at Richmond began and developed rather differently from that at Ludlow. Its ground floor was built against the outer face of the curtain wall with straight joints, blocking the early arch through the curtain. There is no clear evidence for an early gate-passage or tower.[42] The upper floors of the 'great tower', added later, are reached from the wall-walk of the curtain by straight wall-stairs.

Internally Richmond's 'great tower' is Stygian dark, except on the first floor, which has three large roll-moulded openings cut through the outward-facing wall (the central one has a lintel). They might be for artillery use *à la mode greq*, but they might also form a ceremonial facade like the two tiers of windows

---

[41] Clark (1884), **2**, 277; Hope (1908), 268.
[42] *Ex inf.* Mr O. J. Weaver.

at Newark.[43] Both are dated to *c.* 1170,[44] and since Hope dated the casing at Ludlow to around 1180, this is a reasonable scenario. By the time that the innermost bailey walls were built, the northern casing can only have been less than a metre higher than now. Perhaps it was never completed, and the north wall shored up in some other way until it finally collapsed. The innermost bailey had little space to do no more than protect the entrance to the 'great tower', and reminds me of those baileys at Corfe and Kenilworth, probably both built soon after 1200.[45]

THE ROUND CHAPEL

The only Norman building remaining within the inner bailey at Ludlow, apart possibly from the east wall of the great hall, is the round nave of the chapel. Hope pointed out that the west doorway had been partly rebuilt, and I would add that the eastern arch may be secondary; its setting is odd, and the carving is more developed than the wall arcade within the nave, which in its turn is later than the arcade within the 'great tower'.[46] The nave was originally lit by three large double-splayed windows standing on the billet-moulded string-course externally. They have continuous roll-mouldings internally and at their narrowest part. Externally they are plain except for the western one which has a roll-moulding and carved voussoirs. At some stage a gallery on two levels was inserted, perhaps replacing some earlier covered approach (see the vertical break in the wallplaster). Hope excavated the foundation of the chancel,[47] but he gives no evidence for it being contemporary with the nave.

Round churches are usually associated with the Hospitallers or Templars, for example those at Garway and Hereford nearby. Gilbert de Lacy gave land to the Templars, and a Templar is mentioned in Ludlow,[48] but it seems most likely that the chapel began as a private one, like that at Woodstock.[49] Rhenish influence can be detected in the cathedral and bishop's palace at Hereford.[50] Is it too fanciful to attribute the inspiration of the Ludlow chapel to Charlemagne's rotunda at Aachen, the source of round chapels at Abingdon and Bury St Edmunds?[51] By itself, yes, but there are echoes of the palace gateway at Aachen in Ludlow's 'great tower' (Fig. 12), perhaps by way of Hersfeld and Jumièges abbeys,[52] with their arcaded *Westwerken* and upper rooms. However, I hope that I have demonstrated that the 'great tower' of Ludlow is not as simple as that.

[43] Braun (1935).
[44] Renn (1973a), 253, 295.
[45] Colvin (1963), **2**, 617, 683.
[46] Hope (1908), 272, 276; Renn (1973a), pls. XXIV–XXVI.
[47] Hope (1908), 274–75.
[48] Eyton (1857), 252, 280.
[49] Colvin (1963), **2**, 1012.
[50] Clapham (1934), 109–12; RCHM (1934), liv–lvi; Pevsner (1963), 26, 135, 185.
[51] Gem (1975), 36–37; Hugol (1966); Kreusch (1966).
[52] Conant (1959), Figs. 21, 72.

Gate-passages not projecting in front of the line of the curtain wall to each side were built at Bramber and Eynsford in the late eleventh century. At Saltwood Castle, the wall towers only project internally, and the original gate-passage also seems to have been inside the line of the curtain wall, although subsequently extended both forward and upward. The date of the early work at Saltwood is uncertain, although the pilaster buttresses to the wall towers suggest a Norman origin. The open-backed rectangular towers on one side of each of the western gateways at Gisors (Eure) only project slightly in front of the curtains, and have wall-passages reminiscent of those at Ludlow, but the arrowloop embrasures are similar to those at Dover and Framlingham castles, indicating a date in the last quarter of the twelfth century.

Many Roman town defences exhibit the 'envelope effect', with their gates on or behind the line of the walls. A particularly good example is Lincoln, where the earliest medieval West Gate to the castle seems to have copied its Roman town wall predecessor of a few yards away. Unfortunately, the gates of Wroxeter, the nearest Roman town to Ludlow, have not been excavated yet. The first phase of the stone castle at Ludlow is clearly Roman-esque (the hyphen is deliberate). The three open-backed towers are ingeniously sited to flank almost the entire 'envelope'; the omission is a small area to the south-east, exactly where the ditch is blocked by a drystone wall now carrying an iron railing, but which might have been deliberately built to bottle up any attack in the 'dead ground'. The one seemingly superfluity of the design is the backed postern tower, but this perhaps was to form part of the symbolic continuity of purpose for the first *caput* of the Shropshire branch of the Lacys.

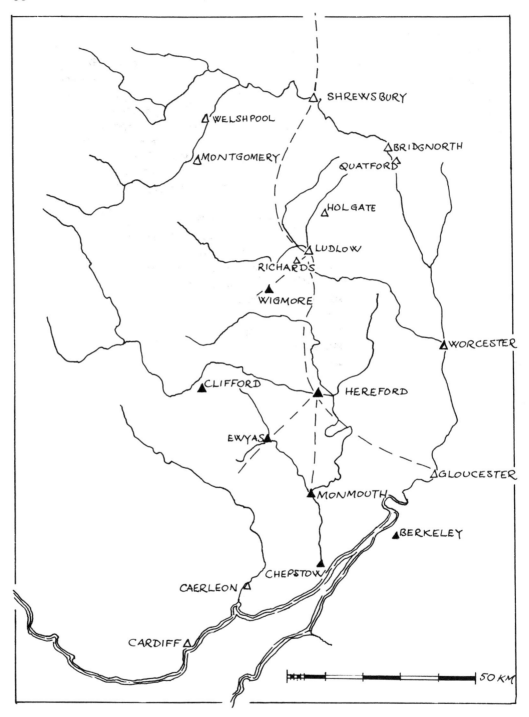

Fig. 5 Eleventh-century castles of the southern part of the Welsh March. Those begun by William fitz Osbern are shown in solid black: dotted lines indicate medieval roads.

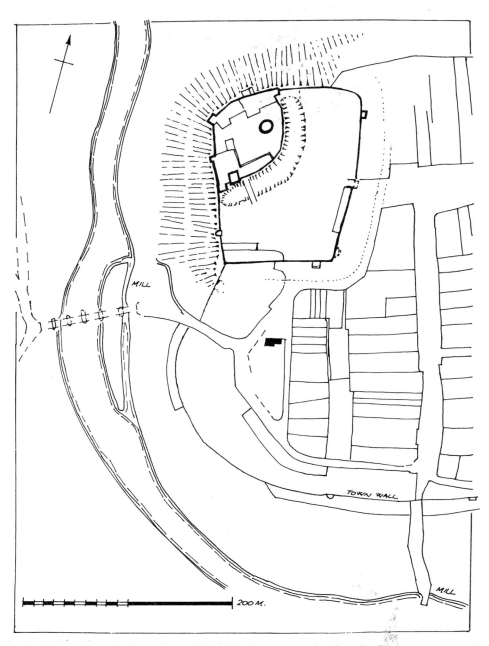

Fig. 6 Sketch plan of the western part of Ludlow town, showing the Dinham area south of the castle. Continuous property boundaries and site of the early bridge from air photographs.

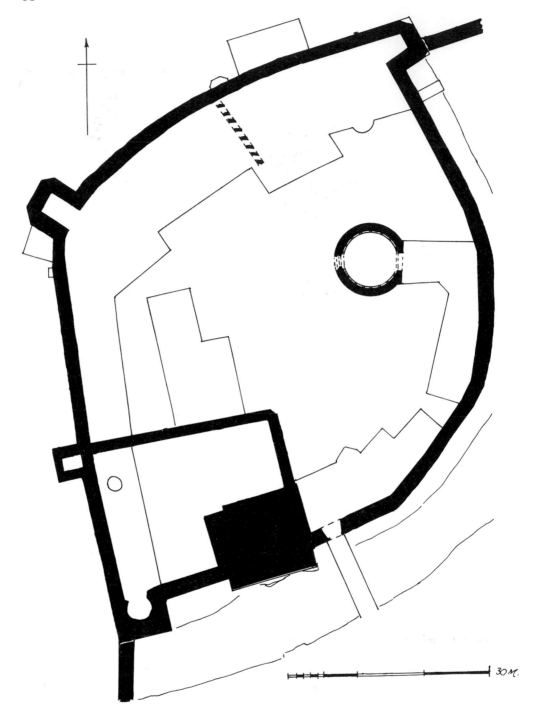

Fig. 7   Block plan of the inner bailey of Ludlow castle. Norman walling in solid black.

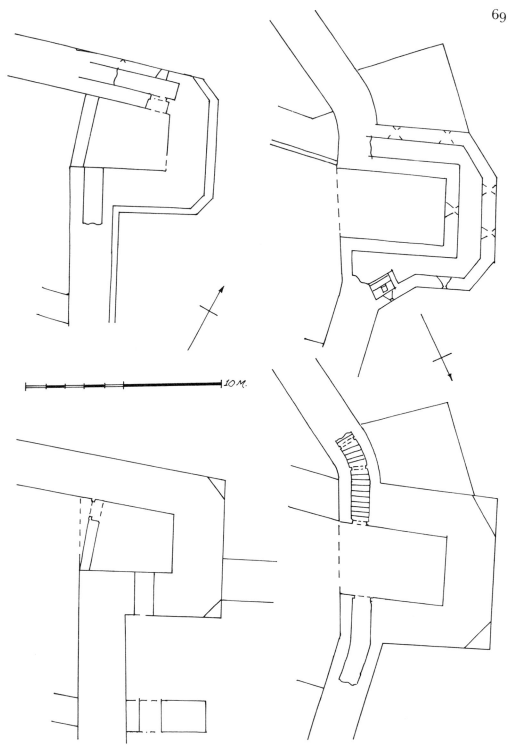

Fig. 8 Plans of the north-east (left) and north-west (right) angle towers of Ludlow Castle at ground (below) and first floor (above) levels. Post-Norman alterations omitted.

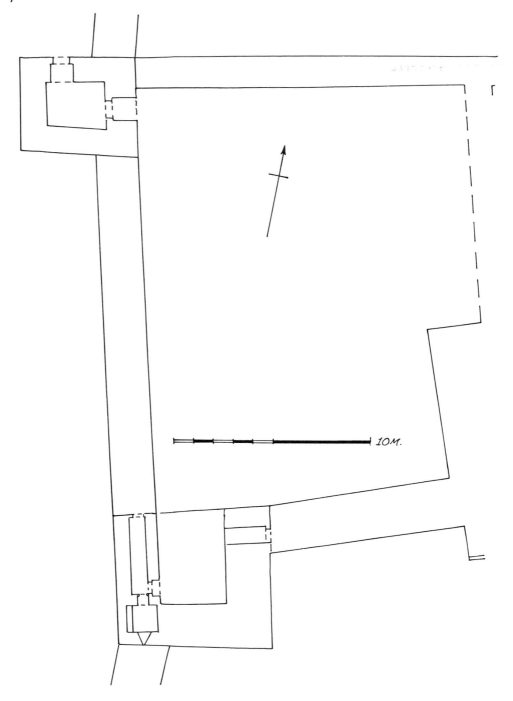

Fig. 9   Plan of south-west part of inner bailey of Ludlow Castle at ground level apart from south-west angle tower (shown at first floor level since ground floor filled by oven).

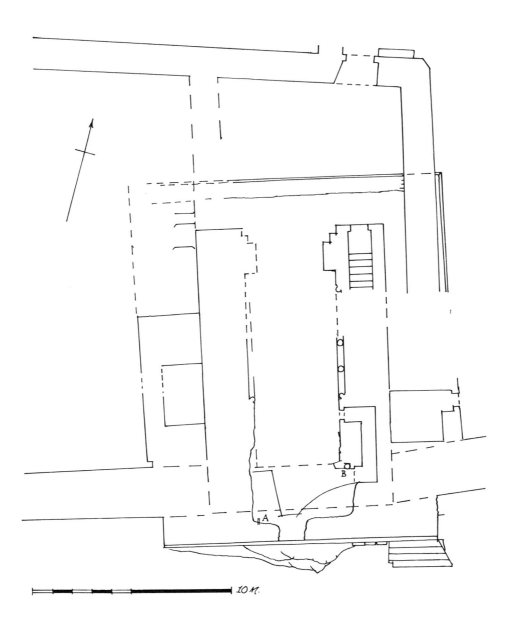

Fig. 10   Plan of Ludlow Castle's 'great tower' (immediately adjoining previous figure to the east) at ground level. Post-Norman alterations omitted.

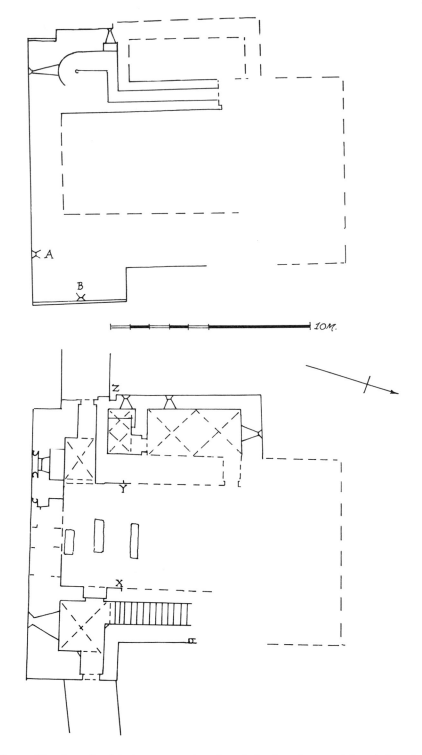

Fig. 11 Plans of Ludlow Castle's 'great tower' at first (below) and upper (above) floor levels. Post-Norman alterations omitted.

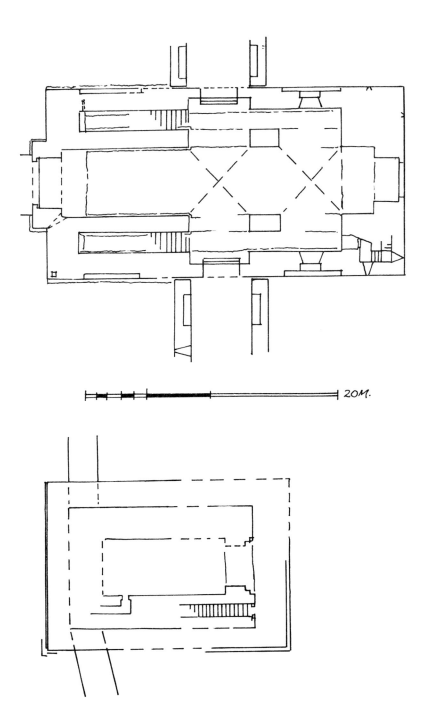

20M.

Fig. 12 Comparative ground plans of the gateways at Aachen Palace (above)—after Kreusch 1966, Abb. 14—and Ludlow Castle (below).

The road to Harlech: aspects of some early thirteenth-century Welsh castles

JEREMY K. KNIGHT

ANYONE concerned with the castles of Wales will need as a basic tool of his trade the lists published in *Archaeologia Cambrensis* for 1963, 1967 and 1970 by David Cathcart King and A. H. A. Hogg, as well as the definitive studies of individual castles published over the years by David King, culminating of course in *Castellarium Anglicanum*. The dating evidence for individual castles set out in the lists can range from an almost chance entry such as 'Aber . . . a(ttacked) 1222', with little relevance to the overall history of the castle, to the magisterial finality of 'Harlech. b. 1285–90'. The present essay is concerned with the chronology and planning of a group of well-known castles of the southern March, all described in detail elsewhere, which have as a common factor their association with William Marshall the elder, earl of Pembroke, with his sons, or with Hubert de Burgh, earl of Kent, ally and neighbour of the Marshalls and aligned with them not only against the power of Llywelyn the Great, but at times against a far from uniformly grateful king of England.

Innovation in castle-building in a particular area often came about when a magnate whose military career had been passed in one area of the western world found himself transferred by the wheel of fortune, with the resources and motive to build, to another area. William Marshall and Hubert de Burgh, though both English-born, had spent most of their distinguished military careers in France, and after they had obtained their marcher lordships—William by marriage in 1189, Hubert by royal grant in 1201—it would be surprising if their castles did not show a familiarity with up-to-date French practice. The role of castles such as Chepstow in the introduction of the fluent new defensive modes of the thirteenth century is well-known, though direct documentary evidence for the dates of the castles we shall be discussing is almost totally absent and has to be surmised from the castles themselves, combined with what we know of the careers of their builders. The cross-channel influence in military architecture was not a one-way traffic, as Villandraut (Gironde), a Gascon Harlech built by a royal clerk of Edward I, Bertrand de Got, who became Pope Clement V in 1305, can serve to remind us.[1]

---

[1] Gardelles (1972), 234–35, Figs. 154–57.

PEMBROKE CASTLE: WILLIAM MARSHALL THE ELDER

William Marshall's marriage in 1189 forms the *terminus post quem* for his work at Pembroke, Chepstow and Usk, though the danger of circular argument is obvious. Pembroke was one of the strategic key points of the Marshall domains, the link between their lands on the Welsh March and their vast inheritance in southern Leinster. Detailed description of Pembroke is unnecessary,[2] and comment here is confined to aspects of the circular keep, probably the earliest of the Welsh round keeps.[3] Comparison with a French keep such as Laval (Mayenne), which is probably a shade earlier,[4] is instructive. They are of similar size, though Laval would be the taller even without its spectacular wooden hourd and conical roof. Both contain three storeys over an unlit basement, with first floor entry and with floor levels marked externally by chamfered ashlar offsets, a feature found at Chepstow, on the Garrison Tower at Usk, and on several of Philip Augustus's round keeps, for example, Lillebonne (Seine-Maritime) and Chinon (Indre-et-Loire). Both towers are lit by long arrowloops supplemented on the upper floors by very similar two-light windows, those at Laval being of rather earlier type, 'Romanesque' rather than 'Transitional'. Both were roofed with elaborate hourds. That at Pembroke has to be reconstructed from its beam holes, but at Laval hourd and roof survive, with a spacious circular fighting gallery around the perimeter of the wall top, its close set arrowloops giving all-round field of fire (Fig. 13). Hourd and roof are supported by giant cart wheels of radiating timbers joined to a mast-like central post. At Pembroke, the hourd and central space were roofed separately, though the hemispherical domed 'sentry box' over the vault may have been finished with a small conical timber roof like the upper part of the Laval roof.

One difference between Pembroke and French round keeps is of course that the latter were almost invariably vaulted throughout in stone, whereas the single stone vault at Pembroke is unique among the Welsh round keeps.[5] Further discussion might bring other round keeps such as Lillebonne into the picture, for this shows a number of the features discussed, but such discussion would only emphasize points already made, namely, the strong French influence on Pembroke, its primary position among Welsh round keeps,[6] and the contrast between the French keeps, vaulted in stone, and the Welsh round towers, floored and roofed in timber.

CHEPSTOW II: WILLIAM MARSHALL THE ELDER

When William Marshall inherited William fitz Osbern's castle at Chepstow (Chepstow I) it was about 120 years old. We do not know how its vulnerable

---

[2] See King (1978).

[3] King (1977); King (1978), 98–105, 117–18; Renn (1967–68).

[4] Pré (1961).

[5] King (1977) discusses its affinities.

[6] On the latter see Renn (1961), though one should note that the Romanesque voussoirs at Longtown are now known to be reused pieces.

eastern face was then defended, but the Marshall replaced whatever existed with a stone curtain wall with two projecting round towers. This is in the Carboniferous Limestone rubble on which the castle stands, with dressings of 'Dundry stone' from the Bristol area. 'Dundry stone' is a convenient and familiar term, sometimes backed up by specific reference to the quarries on Dundry Hill, south of Bristol, as in the Newport Castle (Gwent) building accounts of 1448.[7] Geologists, however, emphasize that it is not possible specifically to attribute stone to these quarries on geological grounds alone. A detailed catalogue of the use of this stone in medieval Welsh buildings, similar to Dudley Waterman's study of Dundry stone in Ireland,[8] would be most valuable. It is a cream-coloured granular Jurassic limestone, easily distinguished from the white 'Sutton' limestone from near Bridgend which is the other main medieval freestone of the region. A more oolitic version can occur, as on the chapter house capitals at Llanthony, but it is doubtful whether this is geologically distinct.

The entry through William Marshall's curtain is a simple archway of two orders tucked in between the river cliff on the north and one of the half-round towers covering it at close range on the south. The pointed front arch has stop-chamfered jambs with simple carved capitals on the inner order. The second circular tower, at the south end of the curtain, links the new work with fitz Osbern's curtain. Long arrowslits in tower and curtain cover the approach over the now filled-in ditch. The northern tower has a chamfered offset at the top of its external plinth and another at first floor level. The southern tower has a similar offset surviving at an upper level and it is possible, though not very likely, that others lower down have been lost in later refacing; but there is a curious lack of homogenuity in the work as a whole, which extends, as we shall see, to the detailing of the arrowslits. The original entry to each tower was through a door with ashlar jambs in the centre of its flat rear face at ground floor level. Both are now blocked and only visible internally, that on the south also being blocked by the springing of an inserted vault. Two chamfered ashlar jambs on the interior face of the curtain between the gate and the river cliff might suggest a single guardroom to the rear of the gate, with stairs to the wall-walk, but they may not be original.

The curtain wall has a pair of arrowslits, one covering the inner face of each tower (Fig. 14, 2–3). Both are long and tapering, with circular basal oillets, of Sailhan type IIb.[9] Both narrow as they taper downwards, the southern one slightly so, from 70 mm width at the top to 50 mm at the bottom, the northern one markedly. It has a shouldered head and is no less than 200 mm wide at the shoulder (Fig. 14, 3). It is now blocked and part of its ashlar rear arch is visible on the internal face of the curtain. The embrasure of the second loop survives in a much ruined form as an untidy and partially blocked hole recently exposed by the removal of modern refacing during conservation. It is possible that these unusual loops date from a time when the art of standing back and

---

[7] Pugh (1963), 227–28.
[8] Waterman (1970).
[9] Sailhan (1978)

aiming through a narrow loop was still something of a novelty, and its practitioners less than fully confident. The northern tower has a more conventional Sailhan type IIb slit at ground floor level (Fig. 14, 4) and plain rectangular slits (Sailhan Ia) above. The southern tower has a slit with neat pentagonal oillets top and bottom (Fig. 14, 1), a variant of Sailhan IIIa, at first floor level and plain slits above. At ground floor level an inserted door and later curtain butted against the tower have removed any evidence, though frustratingly the only unblocked embrasure of this period is inside this tower, its slit blocked by the later curtain. There is also a slit with 'inverted T' oillet (Fig. 14, 5) above the door of the northern tower, the type's good downward arc of visibility making it particularly suited for such a position. Altogether, the slits form an oddly diverse miscellany.

USK CASTLE: WILLIAM MARSHALL THE ELDER (Fig. 18)

In 1938, Bryan O'Neil contrasted the main period of work at Usk with the more advanced work of Hubert de Burgh *post* 1219 at Skenfrith and Grosmont, and attributed Usk to William Marshall the elder who died in that year.[10] Later writers have accepted this attribution. The square Norman keep may be de Clare work of pre-1174, but the following phase made Usk a major stone castle. The curtain encloses a trace which might equally be described as a shallow-angled octagon or as a rectangle with its sides angled out as shallow echelons. The corners, orientated to the cardinal points, each carried a tower; the Norman keep on the east, round towers on the others, though only a small part of the south tower now survives. Entry, as at Chepstow, was by a simple arch through the thickness of the curtain, and facing this entry across the ward is a large circular tower whose modern name is the Garrison Tower. Though integrated with the curtain, this shows affinities with the round keeps of the region. The Garrison Tower and adjacent curtain have a series of arrowloops with small square basal oillets (Fig. 15, 4), a type not in Sailhan. I have suggested elsewhere,[11] on circumstantial historical grounds, a possible date of 1212–19 for Usk, and there is a series of identical loops in the surviving tower of Caerleon Castle, seized by William Marshall from its Welsh lord in the autumn of 1217.

The plan of Usk invites comparison with several contemporary castles (Fig. 18). Le Coudray-Salbart (Deux-Sèvres) near Niort received English subsidies for fortification in 1202 and 1227, and was an important frontier castle in Angevin Poitou in the years after John's loss of Normandy and the Loire. Hubert de Burgh was incidentally 'mayor' or seneschal of Niort from before 1212 until 1215 and must have been familiar with Le Coudray-Salbart. Its plan[12] is reminiscent of Usk: a similarly proportioned rectangle with round or beaked corner towers, a gate in the centre of one long side, and a round tower of, as Curnow points out, keep-like size and affinity with first floor entry. The variation here is that this forms one of the corner towers, and the place of the Usk Garrison

[10] O'Neil (1938).
[11] Knight (1977).
[12] Eydoux (1967); Curnow (1980).

Tower, mid-way along the other long side, opposite the entrance, is occupied by a small round tower.

King John's Dublin (Fig. 18), the mandate for which was issued in 1204, is now a near-total rebuild, but its original plan is known from seventeenth-century maps.[13] It matches Le Coudray-Salbart closely, even to the small circular tower in the centre of its long rear face, though it lacked, so far as we know, a Great Tower. Its twin-towered gatehouse was probably later, but Le Coudray-Salbart's distinctive circular gate tower with 'straight-through' gate-passage recurs at Trim (Co. Meath), seized by King John in person in 1210 and allegedly complete by 1220. Curnow cites[14] other parallels in France and at Ludlow. We seem to be dealing with a small group of related castles linked to the concerns of King John and his immediate circle of magnates in Poitou, Ireland and Wales in the final decade of his reign, following the loss of Normandy. A few other castles might be regarded as belonging to the same generation of development, for example, Fère-en-Tardenoise (Aisne), built by Robert II, count of Dreux, soon after 1205 with six shallow-angled sides, angle towers and a highly experimental gatehouse; but such developed polygonal castles as Boulogne (Pas-de-Calais) of 1228–32[15] and Bolingbroke (Lincs.) of the 1220s[16] are later, though such a plan is basically a geometricized version of the looser polygonal traces of the twelfth century and perhaps needs no formal parallel.

CAERLEON CASTLE: WILLIAM MARSHALL FATHER AND ELDEST SON 1217+

In the autumn of 1217 William Marshall seized Caerleon from its Welsh lord, Morgan ap Hywel, and forced him to issue a charter, aptly described by one nineteenth-century historian as an 'incredible document', by which he granted his castle to the Marshall. The Welsh annals *sub anno* and the *Histoire de Guillaume le Maréchal*[17] agree that this followed the truce between Louis of France and the English in September 1217, a truce which the Welsh saw as a betrayal by Louis of his allies. Morgan continued the war since the Marshall held other territory of his in the Magor-Undy area. The long-drawn-out dispute continued until Morgan's death in 1248, but he never regained his castle. There was time for one building season before the Marshall's death at Easter 1219, and if work had begun on new defences at Caerleon they must have been completed by his son. The castle was a motte and bailey between the Roman fortress and the river, guarding bridge and river-crossing. An apparent shell keep on the motte's top survived into the eighteenth century, but that is almost all that we know of it.[18] The foundations of a twin-towered gatehouse remain at the foot of the motte, covering the stairs to its top, but the only standing masonry is a corner tower next to the Hanbury Arms Hotel. This is circular, with three

[13] Maguire (1974).
[14] Curnow (1980), 53.
[15] Héliot (1947).
[16] Thompson (1966).
[17] *Hist. Guill. Mar.*, **2**, 277–79.
[18] Knight (1970).

long arrowslits with small square basal oillets like those at Usk (Fig. 15, 1–3). The lower 600–800 mm of each loop is formed of neat ashlars of Dundry stone, but above this are larger and less well-shaped blocks of Bath stone, yellowish and friable, clearly reused Roman work. David Zienkiewicz's excavation of the fortress baths has shown that they survived as substantial and perhaps roofed ruins until the twelfth or thirteenth century, when they were demolished by stone robbers. Caerleon Castle could have been an obvious beneficiary, but other sources, for example the amphitheatre, are also possible. Evidently the builders were initially unfamiliar with local resources and used imported freestone, but soon found an alternative source of supply.

Cilgerran Castle: William Marshall the younger 1223+ (Fig. 16)

On Palm Sunday 1223, William Marshall the younger landed at St Davids from Ireland. His army took Carmarthen and Cardigan, then marched to Cilgerran 'and there began to build an ornate castle of mortar and stones'.[19] It is in a plain style, without ashlar, the arrowloops formed from the same shaly rubble as the rest of the walling. In consequence, they have no oillets, but are otherwise similar to those of William Marshall and his brothers at Chepstow III, dated 1225–45,[20] with horizontal sighting slits set fairly high up. The plan recalls Hubert de Burgh's Grosmont of 1219 onwards (Fig. 16), with a curtain enclosing a trapezoid ward, round angle towers and a rectangular gate at one of the more protected angles. The rear is protected by an earlier hall at Grosmont and at Cilgerran by the natural slopes of the promontory. There is a similar plan at Limerick, with the Shannon to the rear. All three were probably influenced by earlier ringworks.

The Marshalls in Ireland

The historical links between Anglo-Norman Wales and Ireland have left little trace in the military architecture. We have no equivalent to William Marshall's church at New Ross, the town and port which were a rival to King John's Waterford lower down the Barrow estuary, or to Marshall's foundation of Tintern Minor in Co. Wexford. New Ross is architecturally reminiscent of Llanthony, whose building history was much influenced by the fate of its extensive de Lacy lands in Ireland. The chief Marshall castle, Kilkenny, is a massive seventeenth- and nineteenth-century rebuild, though the trapezoid plan with corner towers is probably original. Trim, Carrickfergus II and what we know of Dublin suggest an interesting phase of castle-building under John, but there is disappointingly little subsequent development. McNeill, however, has noted several parallels between the castles attributed to Hugh de Lacy as earl of Ulster (for the second time) in 1227–43 and those of the Marshalls and de Burgh in south Wales.[21]

[19] *Brut (Peniarth)*, 100.
[20] Perks (1967).
[21] McNeill (1980), 22–27.

He compares the outer gates of Chepstow and Carrickfergus with their circular towers and draws attention to Greencastle in Co. Down (not to be confused with its Donegal namesake), which is another variation on the Skenfrith-Grosmont-Cilgerran theme. It has a trapezoid ward with round corner towers and a rectangular first floor hall with clasping angle buttresses massive enough to be described as a keep. This hall recalls Grosmont, but is central, like the Skenfrith keep. These links between Ulster and the southern Welsh March might suggest that the Marshall castles of Leinster once contained similar work, though McNeill would prefer the direct influence of an Anglo-Welsh master-mason or engineer.

The odd Leinster group of rectangular hall-keeps with round corner turrets at Carlow, Ferns (Co. Wexford) and Lea (Co. Laois)—all Marshall castles at some stage—are sometimes ascribed to the younger Marshalls, but they are quite unlike any other Marshall work, and what detail survives suggests a mid-thirteenth-century date.[22] The continuing fondness for rectangular hall-keeps into the thirteenth century, as at Athenry (Co. Galway), and the sporadic use of round keeps recalls the castles of the princes of Gwynedd,[23] though both groups have their own special features. Like their owners, the Anglo-Norman castles of Ireland soon became distinctly Anglo-Irish (see Addendum).

THE CASTLE-BUILDING OF HUBERT DE BURGH IN WALES

Hubert de Burgh, of a modest Norfolk family, first comes into view in the household of Prince John in Normandy in 1198. In July 1201, John granted him the Three Castles (Grosmont, Skenfrith and White), but by the end of 1203 he was back in France as constable of Chinon, which he held against Philip Augustus in a year-long siege until its fall in June 1205. Hubert, who had shown notable personal gallantry, was a prisoner of war in France until perhaps 1207, and in the autumn following his capture John granted the Three Castles to William de Braose, the rival on the March of the Marshall-de Burgh alliance. By coincidence, de Braose also held the honour of Limerick, originally conquered by Hubert's brother, William 'The Conqueror' of Connaught. Hubert did not recover his lands on the March until January 1219, though in the meantime he had held various royal offices in France and England, including the custody of an impressive list of castles, and had added a second notable siege (Dover 1216) to his battle honours. His career[24] after this need not concern us, save that after his fall in 1232 he was probably never again sufficiently secure to risk the king's suspicions by fresh fortification. If this was so, his castle-building in Wales must fall into two phases, 1201–04/5 and 1219–32. His work at Skenfrith, Grosmont and, as adviser, at royal Montgomery, has been described elsewhere, but a few general comments on their planning and affinities may be useful.

---

[22] Leask (1936), 168–76.
[23] Avent (1983a).
[24] On which see Ellis (1952) and Walker (1972).

Skenfrith, Grosmont and Usk can be seen as variations on a theme. They have trapezoid or sub-rectangular wards with corner towers, often orientated to the cardinal points, a hall or round keep serving as a Great Tower, and a simple gateway. Kilkenny and Cilgerran are similar in plan, but lack the Great Tower. *Grosmont*[25] (Fig. 16) utilizes the line of an earlier ringwork, with the hall-keep of Hubert's first phase of 1201–05 serving as the Great Tower to his castle of 1219–32, whose gateway is contrived in one of the four corner towers. The castle is of the local red sandstone, without imported ashlar, and surviving arrowloops are simple slits. A couple of circular oillets are reused decoratively in a house at the foot of castle hill, looking incongrously like 'inverted keyhole' gunloops, but there is no indication of whether they belong to the de Burgh phase.

Skenfrith[26] lies on a flat site beside the Monnow and the pre-existing castle was levelled, making possible a castle planned *de novo*. A decorated Romanesque capital, found since Craster wrote, suggests that the earlier castle possessed a stone hall. The new castle is trapezoid in plan with a central round keep. The Buck print suggests that the now ruined entrance originally had an arch raised well above ground level and presumably reached by a timber forebuilding. The entries to the corner towers from the ward are similarly raised. Two arrow-slits, one with a serif basal oillet, Sailhan IIc, one a cross-oillet like Chepstow III (Fig. 14, 6), survive. The simple gateway forms a contrast with the twin-towered gatehouse at Montgomery, begun in the autumn of 1223.

Montgomery resulted from the crisis at the end of John's reign and after, which brought home the need to strengthen the keypoints of the March against Llywelyn, who had allied with the baronial opposition and the French. Matthew Paris described how 'the king's advisers pointed out to him a place where a most impregnable castle might be built' (*locum illum idoneum ad inexpugnabile castrum construendum*),[27] and behind the bland phrase 'the king's advisers' lurks the formidable justiciar, to whom the unfinished castle was granted in 1228.

The site chosen was a high north-south ridge, the result of volcanic activity. There is some evidence that a timber castle was quickly run up in the autumn months of 1223, following the king's visit in September during which the formal decisions had been taken. Work in stone would then have begun in the spring of 1224 and continued until 1232 or 1233. The castle[28] is in a different tradition of castle-planning, mainly due to its site. The wards in line along a ridge recur, for example, at Chinon, which Hubert defended in 1204–05, the two sites having a marked visual resemblence. Dyserth, Henry III's only other castle built *de novo*, and Chartley (Staffs.), with its round keep, are similar. This separate tradition emphasizes how our earlier group are variations on a theme, and we have seen how the earlier careers of its composers suggest that it could be a French theme.

[25] Knight (1980).
[26] Craster (1967); Craster (1970).
[27] *Matth. Paris*, **2**, 247, *s.a.* 1221.
[28] Lloyd and Knight (1981).

The changes in military architecture in the decades on each side of 1200, introducing the new defensive modes of the thirteenth century, are still in some respects mysterious. They included planned batteries of crossbow slits giving covering fire to the curtain, as at Framlingham and Dover in *c.* 1185–90;[29] the development of projecting circular mural towers covering a geometrically planned trace,[30] and an evolutionary sequence in gatehouse planning. One line in gatehouse planning (though there were of course others) leads from a simple arch through the curtain, protected by a single flanking tower at close range, which may be rectangular (e.g. Newcastle Bridgend *c.* 1175–80) or rounded (Chepstow II, Ste Suzanne in Mayenne), through an experimental stage (Le Coudray-Salbart, Fère-en-Tardenoise, Dover, Skenfrith or Skipton)[31] to the advent of the developed twin-towered gatehouse over a wide area in the 1220s (Angers (Maine-et-Loire), Boulogne, Bolingbroke, Montgomery). In these developments the Angevin area has a distinct internal cohesion, but they can hardly have evolved *in vacuo*. Older generations looked east to the Crusades or Byzantium —*ex oriente lux*—but there are other possible sources of influence nearer home.

The use of spaced circular or polygonal mural towers along a curtain or of twin-towered gatehouses was hardly a novelty in Europe at this date. Even today, a list of towns with standing late Roman defences in western Europe would be tediously long, and before medieval sieges and stone-robbing, Vauban and boulevards, it would have been much longer. Several of the more notable examples, Le Mans (Sarthe) and Pevensey for example, stood siege in the eleventh and twelfth centuries, and contemporary comment suggests that they were regarded as exceptionally strong and were accorded marked respect. Even round keeps could have found a model in some of the circular *cellae* of Roman temples. The 'Tour de Vesunna' at Périgueux (Dordogne), for example, is an imposing free-standing circular tower of Pembroke dimensions. Once the means of delivering an effective flanking fire had been evolved and once any problems of architectural engineering had been overcome, it would have been surprising if such defences and towers had not been studied and copied.

It is of course always a sound principle of military history to consider how a particular type of military 'hardware' has been influenced by developments in the comparable field 'over the hill'. The conquests of Philip Augustus, backed up by a solid programme of castle-building, broke English power in France north of the Loire. What follows makes no pretence of being an adequate discussion of the castles of Philip Augustus, but only seeks to say something of their general character in order to assess whether they might have influenced castle architecture in the areas we have been considering.

Philip Augustus's castle of the Louvre (Paris) existed by 1202, when instructions were given that the *turris Parisis* was to be used as a model for Dun-le-Roi, now Dun-sur-Auron (Cher). Neither now survives, but early plans and some inaccessible fragments in the basements of the museum of the Louvre show

---

[29] Renn (1969); Renn (1973b).
[30] Héliot (1947); Héliot (1965); Curnow (1980).
[31] For Skipton see Renn (1975).

that it had a square plan with three-quarter-round angle towers and half-round towers, single or paired for gates, mid-way on each face.[32] In the centre stood a large circular keep with an encircling ditch, a plan not unlike Skenfrith. Specifications for four round keeps were included in a register of 1204–12, but only one of these, Villeneuve-sur-Yonne (Yonne), survives.[33] It is a single tower, a strongpoint on the circuit of town walls like the Tour de Constance at Aigues-Mortes (Gard) or Philip's towers added to existing castles at Gisors (Eure) and Chinon. It thus tells us little of castle-planning, but with its battered base topped by a chamfered string-course and its first floor entry, it is not unlike such keeps at Skenfrith and Bronllys.

In 1222 Philip Augustus gave the care of the chapel in his 'new castle of Dourdan' to the church of St Germain. Dourdan (Essone)[34] is very similar in plan to the Louvre, save that the round keep is not central, but forms an enlarged corner tower, rather in the manner of Le Coudray-Salbart, isolated within a surrounding ditch. The curtain now linking the keep to the remainder of the castle is secondary. Philip used the same plan at Lillebonne and Arnold Taylor has shown how it was also used at Yverdon and Champvent in Savoy,[35] from whence it was to travel north again for Edward I's Flint in 1277 (Fig. 17). The precise square traces of the Louvre or Dourdan (Fig. 17) and their symmetrically placed towers and gates already foreshadow the planning of Harlech and Beaumaris, although they have of course only a single curtain, a stage on from the less formal trapezoid or multi-angular geometric planning, but one somehow has the impression that the influence of Philip's castles was specific rather than general, perhaps on Hubert de Burgh and, through Savoy, on the castles of Edward I.

ADDENDUM

Dunamase (Co. Laois)[36] is an imposingly sited castle which probably began as a Dark Age oppidum. It was in the hands of the Marshalls from soon after 1215. The outer ward is a barbican covering the only practicable approach. Its curtain has a series of long plain arrowslits such as are to be seen at Usk and Caerleon, but without ashlar. It is strikingly like the upper barbican at Chepstow, save for the latter's corner tower—which is an afterthought, as the partial straight joints on the exterior show. Unless the arrowslits are markedly old fashioned, it is unlikely to be after c. 1225. Dunamase is perhaps the one convincing piece of Marshall castle masonry in Ireland.

[32] Héliot (1965), 248.
[33] Vallery-Radot (1967).
[34] Humbert (1944).
[35] Taylor (1977).
[36] Leask (1936), 192–94.

Fig. 13   Laval (Mayenne): hourd on round keep (Pré 1961).

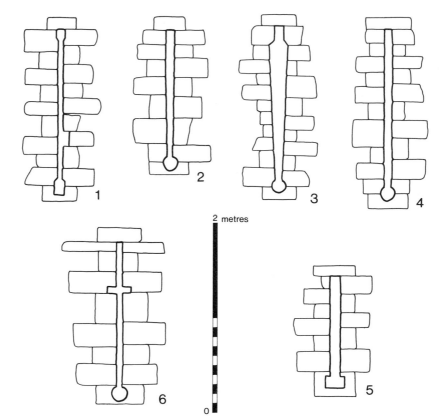

Fig. 14   Arrowloops: 1–5 Chepstow II (1189+), 6 Chepstow III (1225–45).

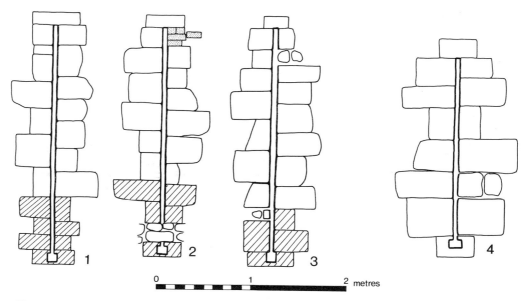

Fig. 15   Arrowloops: 1–3 Caerleon (1217+), 4 Usk, Garrison Tower (? 1212–19). Dundry stone hatched.

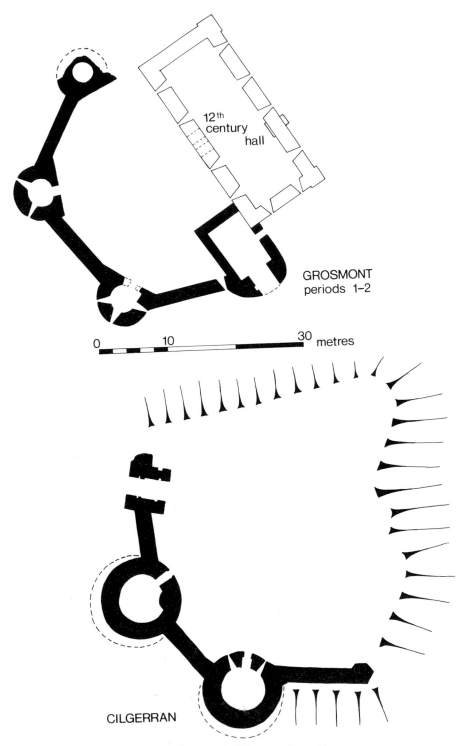

12th century hall

GROSMONT
periods 1–2

0   10   30 metres

CILGERRAN

Fig. 16   Castle-planning: Grosmont (1219–32), Cilgerran (1223+).

88

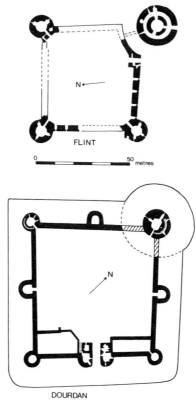

FLINT

0   50 metres

N ←

DOURDAN

N

Fig. 17   Castle-planning: Dourdan and Flint. Hatched masonry secondary.

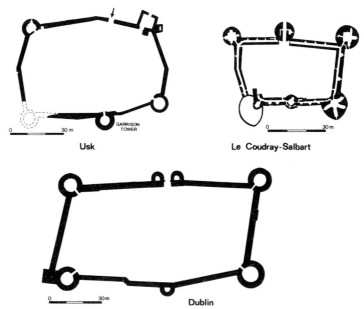

Usk

GARRISON TOWER

0   30 m

Le Coudray-Salbart

0   30 m

Dublin

0   30 m

Fig. 18   Castle-planning: Usk, Le Coudray-Salbart and Dublin.

Dryslwyn Castle

PETER WEBSTER

FOR well over a century the native Welsh castle at Dryslwyn, Dyfed, has been visible only as two massive sections of upstanding wall and sundry smaller wall sections and hillocks of collapsed masonry atop a rocky hill beside the river Tywi, five miles south-west of Llandeilo. The wealth of documentary evidence relating primarily to the later (English) occupation of the site was collected by E. A. Lewis in the early years of this century but regrettably has never been fully published.[1] The debt of anyone concerned with the history and archaeology of Dryslwyn to Lewis is enormous and his very detailed research into the site's history deserves to be better known than it is. Dryslwyn appears in the Royal Commission volume of 1917[2] but remained no more than a picturesque and gently decaying ruin until 1980, when it passed into the guardianship of the Welsh Office. Work was started immediately to consolidate upstanding walls and the author was invited to direct excavations in advance of further consolidation. Since 1980 a ground survey has been made and the general outlines of the inner ward determined by excavation and clearance. Some information on the associated town has also been forthcoming. This seems an opportune time, therefore, to summarise available information, both historical and archaeological.

The isolated hill on which Dryslwyn Castle stands is made up of mixed Ordovician shales, sandstone and limestone. It lies in the flood plain of the Tywi immediately adjacent to the present river course. In this area there are many meanders, and the river shows a tendency to form ox-bow lakes. It was probably as a result of river action that the hill became isolated and steepened by river erosion on its south side. From the hilltop the neighbouring castle of Dinefwr is easily visible, while Carreg Cennen Castle is visible in fine weather; both, like Dryslwyn, originally Welsh foundations. The highest part of the hill and the steepest slopes are to the south where the river is most easily commanded, and it is not surprising that it is this area which was chosen for the core of the castle.

The hilltop divides into three parts. To the south, as already indicated, is the core of the castle, the inner ward. Lying north-east of the inner ward, along the eastern side of the hill, is an outer ward joined to the inner ward only

[1] NLW Add. MS 455D. The Lewis collection was used extensively by Sir John Lloyd in *The history of Carmarthenshire*, 2v., (Cardiff, 1935–39). For a recent use of the collection together with other information on the area, see Solomon (1982). I am grateful to Mr I. Rees for drawing my attention to a number of the sources cited.

[2] RCAM (1917), 155–56.

by a narrow neck of rock outcrop (Fig. 19, no. 23). North and north-west of the castle wards lies a defended township.

Historically, Dryslwyn has a wealth of documentation mainly attached to the English siege (1287) and the subsequent period. Earlier references are sparse. The earliest located is for 1246, or possibly 1245, when, as recorded by the *Annales Cambriae*,[3] the seneschal of Carmarthen laid siege to the castle. At present we have no means of knowing how much earlier than this the first castle was actually constructed, but the small number of apparently twelfth-/early thirteenth-century sherds of pottery so far found on the excavations indicate that foundation at least a generation before 1246 is not impossible.

In 1271 Maredudd ap Rhys died at Dryslwyn[4] and was succeeded as lord of Dryslwyn by his son Rhys. In 1281 the latter was granted a charter by Edward I to hold a four-day fair at Dryslwyn,[5] 'one fair at his manor of Dryslwyn for four days duration, to wit on St Bartholomew's Day and the three days following unless the fair be to the damage of neighbouring fairs'. It would seem, therefore, that the township of Dryslwyn which is clearly closely tied to the castle grew up alongside it during the pre-siege thirteenth century.

In 1287 came the one event which drew Dryslwyn briefly into the full light of national events. Rhys ap Maredudd rose in revolt against Edward I and after initial success was besieged at Dryslwyn by a large English army under the earl of Cornwall. The events are detailed by Morris.[6] An army of over 11,000 was mustered for Dryslwyn between mid-June and mid-August 1287. It included sappers and other 'engineers', and it is clear that an engine was equipped using hide, timber, rope and lead, and quarrymen and carters employed to supply it with stone shot. At the same time, between 20 and 30 August, twenty-six sappers were employed to undermine the ramparts. The success of the latter operation came faster than the attackers would have wished for there was a collapse which resulted in loss of life, including some knights. The castle was taken or surrendered about 5 September 1287, and shortly afterwards Alan de Plucknet was made custodian.[7]

Considerable documentation attaches to the immediate aftermath of the capture of Dryslwyn, most particularly in the Pipe Rolls.[8] In 1287–88 we find Plucknet raising money by selling off animals and produce originally belonging to Rhys. One hundred and forty-seven animals are mentioned, but of greater interest are hay, apples, nuts and ox-hides which it is stated were found at Dryslwyn. Bacon is also mentioned as a product of the estate. The expenses show outgoings for a small garrison, and £129 4s. 10d. spent on masons, quarrymen and other petty workmen, £109 3s. 8d. spent on carpenters, smiths and charcoal burners engaged in the construction of a new mill, £36 5s. 1d. on the felling of wood

---

[3] *Ann. Camb.*, 86, fn. 1.

[4] *Brut (Peniarth)*, 116.

[5] *Cal. Chart. R. 1257–1300*, 253. Lewis mistakenly dated the charter to 1278. The editors are grateful to Mr D. Crook of the Public Record Office for clarifying this point.

[6] Morris (1901), 206–13. See also Taylor (1976), Smith (1965) and Griffiths (1966) with references.

[7] PRO Welsh R., 15 Edw. I, m. 8; PRO Orig. R., 15 Edw. I, m. 20.

[8] Cf. Rhys (1936), *passim*, but especially 38–63.

around the castle, on the renovation of the ditches *circa villam*, on cleaning the castle, and on breaking a rock at the entrance to the castle. Minor sums were expended on armour and equipment, crossbow equipment seemingly the most prominent, and a strangely small sum of 16s. 2d. on a bakehouse 'newly constructed' and another house at Dryslwyn. Could these be repairs to buildings constructed just before the seige? In 1288–89 we find Plucknet selling oats, lambs, pigs, wheat, mixed grain malt, apples and hay along with cattle 'from booty'. Work in the castle during this period seems to have been of a very minor nature as a total expenditure of only £13 10s. 10d. appears to have been spent on the fabric, and the wages of the workmen in 1288–89 only amounted to 10s. 6d., whilst in 1289–90 nothing at all appears to have been spent on the castle fabric.

The accounts of Alan de Plucknet for 1287 suggest, as one would expect, that a mixed agricultural economy existed on the castle lands. Building activity was restricted to a single year. The sums involved, if compared with the better documented activity in 1338 (see below), suggest that several buildings could have been constructed at this time. However, as no building is specified, apart from the new mill, it is probably better to see the expenditure as being connected with the repair of the very considerable damage which a siege, using sappers and a stone-throwing machine, is likely to have caused.

In 1294 a grant of burgages and land to the burgesses of Dryslwyn is recorded.[9] We learn more of the town in documents dating to 1300–01. The chamberlain's accounts for west Wales for that period were published by Lewis,[10] while his manuscript collection on Dryslwyn also includes a translation. From this we learn of an apparent thirty-seven burgages with rent of 12d. payable half-yearly at Easter and Michaelmas, and an apparent sixteen and a half messuages *in villa subtus castrum*, the town below the castle. There seems to be a slight discrepancy between this and the account of Walter de Pederton for 1298–1300, where it is stated that there were forty-three and a half burgages producing rent at Dryslwyn.[11] The latter account also records minor work and repairs at Dryslwyn at a cost of 49s. 10d.[12] In addition, £4 9s. 10d. was spent in 1300 'for the roofing of houses in Dryslwyn Castle, after the great wind ... in the month of January'. Throughout this period there is mention of the provisioning of the castle along with others in the area.

There is further mention of minor works in 1300–01,[13] and further accounts for 1303–04 and 1304–05,[14] both incidentally showing 37s. income which should betoken thirty-seven burgages. Lewis also notes court rolls for the period 1301–03[15] and a rental of 1302–03.[16] Of much greater interest to the archaeologist,

[9] PRO Orig. R., 22 Edw. I, m. 17.
[10] Lewis (1923).
[11] Rhys (1936), 70–71, 88–89; see also 194–95.
[12] Ibid., 120–21.
[13] Ibid., 218–19.
[14] Ibid., 304–05, 370–71.
[15] PRO Court R., 215, No. 17 and No. 20.
[16] PRO Rent. Surv., No. 773.

however, are some Exchequer documents of 1306.[17] These record in great detail the expenses relating to the construction of a new granary and bakehouse at the castle. Lewis gives a complete text and translation,[18] and the documents deserve fuller treatment than is possible here. It is worth, however, extracting some details.

For the new granary the following quantities of wood were obtained: 20 joists 26 ft long; 20 joists 16 ft long; 100 planks measuring 16 ft × 1 ft × 3 in; 40 turned 'laths' 8 ft × 1 ft; 72 chevrons 19 ft × 1 ft; 1,200 boards, and 1,200 laths for the roof. The roof laths came from the wood of 'Comcaulo', but all the rest of the timber was bought from three men, Ieuan Peen, Madog of Yskennen and William of Ybernia, who shaped it in the wood of Yskennen and Glyncothy. The total expended on these materials was £10 16s. 6d., with a further £12 13s. 4d. being paid to two carpenters for actual construction work, and 6s. paid to their six assistants.

Stone was employed for the foundations and roof of the granary. The foundations appear to have been laid with great care. A pit was dug 8 ft deep and 5 perches (82½ ft) around (*in circuito*), a phrase which does not imply a building of any particular shape. The pit seems to have been revetted with a wall and the interior filled in to provide a level platform for the wooden granary. It is interesting to see the breakdown of foundation costs. Materials (stone and lime) cost 6s. 7½d.; carriage of stone, lime and sand cost 12s. 4d., almost twice as much as the materials themselves. A sum of 16s. 8d. was paid to two masons for building the foundation wall, on a piece rate of 3s. 4d. per perch, and 16d. to two men for four days filling up the foundation within the wall to make it even. The roof was of stone slates, for a roofer was paid £1 6s. 8d. for obtaining and fixing stone slates, and a further 29s. was expended on carting the slate from a Carmarthen quarry to Dryslwyn, fifty-eight carts at 6d. per load. A further 3s. 2d. was spent on carrying the slates from the foot of the hill up to the castle, and 2s. 2d. upon lime for the roof. Two masons were also paid 8s. for work and materials connected with the construction of a 'step' up to the granary.

The catalogue of ironwork used in the granary is no less impressive. We read of 2 pairs of hinges with fastenings, 2 locks for the granary doors with nails, rings, plates and bolts for the same, 1,500 nails 'called spikenails' (spiknails), 800 smaller nails 'called boardnails', 200 'fixed' (*stagnatis*) nails 'called spikenails' for the door and windows, 4,000 nails 'called lathnails' for the roof, and 860 boardnails for the same. The total expended on ironwork actually used in the structure was 27s. 11d., but in addition, 8 iron 'buttresses' and a ladder of 32 feet were bought apparently for use during the construction process. The total cost of the granary was £25 16s. ½d.

The new bakehouse built at the same time was of stone construction. Unfortunately, as will be seen, it is not possible to be certain of its dimensions. Stone was quarried for this work at a cost of 18s., while its carriage cost 36s. Two

[17] PRO E 101/486/18.
[18] NLW Add. MS 455D, 103–12, 281–88.

hundred and fifty quarters of lime was used at a cost of £3 2s. 6d. It was burnt at the bottom of the hill and cost a further 10s. 5d. to get it to the top. The carriage of sand came to 16s. Masons were paid 3s. 4d. per perch for walling, as in the granary, and were paid a total of £4 for 24 perches (c. 396 ft). In addition, one of the two masons was paid 4s. for 'breaking the wall of the castle near the said bakehouse and making it even and level with the new wall of the said bakehouse in order to place wallplates thereon'. This could imply that the structure was in fact a lean-to against the castle wall.

Details of the expenditure on woodwork gives us further structural details relating to the stonework, for boards were bought for 'centres' (presumably formers) 'for the arch over the well' along with the two doorways and six windows at a total cost of 16d. Interestingly, this is the only mention of the castle's water supply, or of a well, noted in the records. Other woodwork obtained consisted of 100 chevrons 20 ft × 1 ft, 8 wallplates and 1,600 laths. The wood cost £1 7s. 4d. and the wages of the two carpenters a further £5, plus 6s. paid to six assistants for six days.

The wood for the roof was probably included in the general purchase of timber for the building. In addition, a roofer was paid 28s. 10d. for obtaining and fixing the roof slates, with a further 46s. being expended on carrying the slates from Carmarthen (92 cartloads), and 6s. 8d. on carrying them up the hill. 9s. 5d. was spent on lime and sand for the roof.

The ironwork purchased reflects the structural elements already mentioned. There were 300 'boardnails' for the 'centres', 4 hinges for the two doors, and 100 'fixed' nails for the same, ironwork for the six windows (*in ferramento sex fenestrae*) with fastenings, hinges and bolts (?). There were also 2 locks, 2 rings and 2 bolts for the doors, 6,000 'lathnails' and 1,100 'boardnails' for the roof. The total cost of the ironwork was £4 0s. 6d. An interesting additional expense was the sum of 5s. 4d. paid to two men over 16 days for 'breaking a certain rock in the said bakehouse'. The total expenditure on the whole bakehouse was £25 1s. 11d.

The detailed accounts concerning the construction work in 1306 are of considerable interest, and the archaeologist must hope that eventually the two buildings referred to will be located and identified, perhaps in the outer ward as there are no obvious candidates among the excavated buildings in the inner ward. There are, however, difficulties in translating the apparent exactness of some of the figures into actual structural evidence. It is noticeable, for instance, that the bakehouse required only about twice as much roofing material as the granary, yet it involved the building of 24 perches of walling as opposed to only 5 perches in the granary. In the granary the unit of payment for walls appears to be one perch by c. 8 ft in height. We are given no indication of the height of the bakehouse except that it was sufficiently high for wallplates for its roof to be placed on the 'castle wall', presumably an external ward wall. This ought to imply a structure of more than 8 ft in height, but even if one interpolates lengths of wall on top of one another and perhaps some internal walls also, it is difficult to get away from the concept of a very large building, as, indeed, is implied by the six windows and two doors mentioned in the accounts. Even if we suppose the granary was roughly square and gabled, thus maximising its roof area, while the bakehouse was oblong and lean-to, it is difficult to reconcile the figures. One must hope that excavation will eventually resolve these difficulties.

From 1287 there was a series of appointments to the post of constable of Dryslwyn.[19] In 1312 one of these, Sir Thomas le Blunt, had difficulty in obtaining possession due to hindrance by 'certain disturbers of the peace', and had to be assisted by the justiciar from Carmarthen.[20] In the same year the authorities at Carmarthen were ordered to repair and provision the castle.[21] This could well be the work recorded in an account probably of 1313,[22] an extract of which has been made or copied by Lewis.[23] This clearly referred to building repair and maintenance. It sounds as if the castle had been suffering from the weather for mention is made of a new gutter covering the 'office' of John de Havering, possibly the royal official of that name, although he had died in 1309,[24] and a new gutter for the stable. There is also payment for the making of a new aperture in the castle wall near the stable and for cleaning the court of the castle, and also mention of the repair of windows in 'the cellar under the hall where all the garnisture and victuals were stored'. Another entry shows that there were three of these windows and that the cellar was whitewashed. A repair of great interest to us is the four days of work by a carpenter repairing the planks of the middle storey of the high tower (*altae turris*), a structure which one assumes to be the round keep (Fig. 20, D). The same entry reveals that the hall contained planks, presumably as a floor. During the same operation a chest was bound in iron for 'keeping the chapel ornaments'.

In 1315 there was a further order for repairs,[25] and in the following year Thomas le Blunt sought extra men-at-arms to swell the garrison in response to the revolt of Llywelyn Bren.[26]

In the period 1317–21 the castle became a very minor element in the disputes between Edward II and Hugh le Despenser, on the one hand, and the anti-Despenser faction, on the other. The castle was granted to Despenser in 1317,[27] but the king had to issue an order the following year to his ministers instructing them to allow Despenser to enjoy his rights at Dryslwyn.[28] He resigned the grant in September 1318 only to obtain the castle again in November of that year.[29] A further series of what appear to be grants and counter-grants in 1321 is charted by Lewis,[30] but in May 1322 Dryslwyn was taken by the opponents

[19] For a complete list see Griffiths (1972), 255–66.
[20] Ibid., 257 with references.
[21] *Cal. Close R. 1307–13*, 477.
[22] PRO E 101/486/27.
[23] NLW Add. MS 455D, 126–28.
[24] Griffiths (1972), 94–95.
[25] *Cal. Close R. 1313–18*, 240.
[26] Ibid., 283.
[27] *Cal. Pat. R., 1317–21*, 56.
[28] *Cal. Close R. 1313–18*, 534–35.
[29] Cf. Griffiths (1972), 238 with references. Also PRO Orig. R., 12 Edw. II, m. 3, 14th September.
[30] NLW Add. MS 455D, 21.

of Hugh le Despenser. Despenser regained Dryslwyn soon afterwards and one might assume that some repairs were made, although no mention of them has so far been traced.

In 1324 there was a grant of a weekly market to the burgesses of Dryslwyn.[31] Routine maintenance of the castle may well have been neglected at this time for in 1338–39 there is a document detailing extensive work.[32] This is one of the yearly accounts submitted at Michaelmas by the constable. It records expenditure upon one wing (*uno pynguoun*), 'the upper half of which is entirely decayed through old age and fallen to the ground on the western side of the King's Hall'. There was also repair to the 'collateral' wall of the hall under the wallplates and work on 'other defects of the walls, towers and turrets'. It is of interest that the stone for this work came from a quarry near (*iuxta*) the castle. Transport from the quarry up to the castle took six men with horses (presumably packhorses) twenty days. Also of interest is the composition of the mortar used for 'covering and pointing' all turrets and walls. This included not only limestone burnt into lime but also sea coal. The latter was presumably used in lime burning but small fragments of coal can frequently be identified on site in the mortar itself. Carriage was again paid for the sand for mortar. At the same time a mason was paid for obtaining stone from the quarry *apud Iskennen* for making a doorway into the king's hall and a new window in the same building.

In the portion of the document relating to the work of the stonemasons we learn a little more about the decay of the hall and tower. The 'wing' on the western side of the hall is claimed to be 'entirely decayed from the middle to the top through old age and debility (*debilitate*) and fallen to the ground', and 'the top of the collateral wall of the same hall' was repaired beneath the wallplates so that a new roof could be laid. Apparently corbels were also fixed in the 'collateral' wall below the wallplates and gutters, presumably to give added support to the roof. It would be interesting to know if this is the origin of the corbels found among the debris of the large building in the south-west of the inner ward (see below, I-J-K-L).

The document makes clear that the hall was entirely re-roofed, but unfortunately the materials used are not listed separately. Joist posts and boards are mentioned but not specified, some anyway being used for a floor within the hall. Nine thousand laths were obtained for the hall roof 'and for the defects of other houses in the said castle', whilst 20,000 nails were used for unspecified purposes. Repairs to other buildings, not all being within the castle itself, were clearly going on at the same time. Along with work on the hall there was considerable repair to the large tower damaged and ruined in the inner ward of the castle (*in custod. interiori Castr.*), and also 'amending, repairing and partly restoring all other defects of the towers, turrets and walls both within and without the aforesaid castle'. Elsewhere, there is mention of repair to the 'houses and offices' of the castle and mention of pointing the bakehouse and the kitchen. Along with the masons and carpenters who have appeared frequently in other

---

[31] *Cal. Chart. R. 1300–26*, 461.
[32] PRO E 101/487/9.

accounts, this account includes a plumber engaged to repair defects in gutters and on certain unspecified house repairs using lead. The total expenditure on the 1338–39 repairs was £33 13s. 2d.

The charter of the town of Dryslwyn was confirmed in 1355 and again in 1391. On the latter occasion there were additional letters patent which gave the burgesses equal status with those of 'English' boroughs such as Carmarthen.[33] Further Ministers' Accounts exist for the period 1356–59[34] which show that at this time the town contained thirty-four burgages with a further fourteen outside on a street variously read as 'Budge Street' (Lewis) and 'Briggestrete'.[35] Mention of the town walls also occurs at this time. During 1356–57 £4 17s. ½d. was spent on carpenters, masons and tilers, some of it for the enclosure of a 'park', presumably outside the castle and town.

Throughout the fourteenth century there were regular appointments of constables and it is clear that the castle was being maintained periodically and kept supplied, and that it usually contained a small garrison.[36] The latter by the end of the century was probably smaller than it had been at the beginning, but there was still provision for at least a dozen men as the inventory for Michaelmas 1385 shows.[37] This lists the following items as in stock at the castle: 8 quarters of wheat, 4 quarters of beans, 2 pipes of honey, 2 quarters of salt, 4 crossbows, 12 helmets, 4 girdles, 12 adventals (a mail coif worn under a helmet), 12 pairs of gloves, 12 pairs of vambraces (armour for the arms), 12 habergeons (mail coats), 12 jacks (jerkins), 400 quarrels remaining from the previous year and 120 newly received.[38] This is hardly the equipment for a front-line garrison but it does at least show that the Crown was anxious to maintain a military presence at Dryslwyn despite what must have been its by now obsolete defences.

In 1402 Rhys ap Gruffudd ap Llywelyn Foethus was appointed constable of the castle for life, but in the following year Owain Glyndŵr entered the Tywi Valley and Rhys threw open the gates of Dryslwyn to him without resistance.[39] There is no mention of the fate of Dryslwyn in the extant documents, although some have supposed that it was destroyed.[40] Certainly the archaeological evidence suggests that the castle and town both ended in destruction by fire, but as yet the evidence can provide no more than a fifteenth-century terminus for this event, and, if anything, it points to a post-Glyndŵr demolition rather than destruction by Glyndŵr himself (see below). However, it is clear that interest in the military potential of Dryslwyn disappears from the early fifteenth century, and from 1407 the castle and town were granted mainly or wholly as a source of income, although one further constable was appointed in 1439.[41]

[33] *Cal. Chart. R. 1341–1417*, 328; *Cal. Pat. R. 1391–96*, 7–8.
[34] PRO Minist. Acc., 1158/7–10; 1221/11–12.
[35] Soulsby (1983), 133.
[36] Griffiths (1972), 255–66.
[37] PRO Minist. Acc., (1221), No. 16.
[38] I am indebted to John Kenyon for information concerning some of the terms used in this inventory.
[39] Griffiths (1972), 264 with references.
[40] E.g. Soulsby (1983), 134.
[41] Cf. Griffiths (1972), 264–66.

THE SITE

With excavation at Dryslwyn still in progress, any statement concerning the site must be of an interim nature. Regular summaries and interims have in fact already appeared,[42] and we will, therefore, restrict ourselves here to a general view of the remains visible at the end of 1985.

i) *The town*. In the area of the township both aerial and surface surveys have shown a number of house sites, although not nearly as many as are revealed in the documents. There appear to have been two entrances to the town. One was via a terrace (Fig. 19, no. 1) which runs up the north and south-east slopes of the hill. The other is more commonly used today and runs up the western side of the hill to a gap in the defences (Fig. 19, nos. 8 & 5). The ground rises from the latter entrance and a number of terraces are visible either side of a track (Fig. 19, no. 17). The terraces may mark house and garden locations. More clearly defined houses are to be seen on the higher parts of the hill where low mounds define wall lines, and a particularly well defined group are to be seen situated against the northern defences (Fig. 19, nos. 9–12). These and other likely house sites were plotted in the summer of 1980. During recent years summer vegetation has rendered most features all but invisible and further additions to the plan will need to be made in wintertime. The whole town is surrounded by a low bank which evidently masks the wall, and outside this is a substantial ditch. The latter follows the contours in the main, but on the southern limit of the town it rises noticeably to meet the inner ward defences just below their north–west corner. A section of the ditch showed it to be rock-cut with a flat base and a fill which seemed wholly medieval or later.

To test the nature of the observed features, a small excavation was undertaken in the town on a site overlapping an assumed building position (Fig. 19, no. 11) and the assumed town wall. The latter in fact proved to be a double wall whilst the house site clearly overlay a timber predecessor. The sequence of occupation on the site appears to be as follows. The earliest structure detected is apparently the outer portion of the town wall, and probably against the inner face of this a timber structure was erected with daub walls and a clay and stone floor. This building was demolished or possibly burnt down before the town wall was enlarged by building a new wall hard against the inner face of the existing wall. In the area investigated this inner wall was interrupted by a carefully constructed gap buttressed to either side. It is assumed that the second wall provided a rampart walk, while the gap marks the position of stairs giving access. Subsequently the access point seems to have gone out of use as a house on dwarf walls of drystone construction was built against the town wall completely closing the gap in the inner wall. This second house apparently reused the clay floor of its timber predecessor but was in use for so long that the interior surface was completely worn away right down to bedrock. The house later was destroyed by fire.

---

[42] Webster (1981); Webster (1983). Yearly summaries of the excavations appear in *Archaeology in Wales*, published annually by CBA Group 2.

The entire town sequence appears to fit within the period from the thirteenth to the fifteenth century. Obviously it will require much more extensive excavations to find out if the pattern is a general one, but we may note the dearth of either pre- or post-medieval finds and structures. There was a Roman coin and a few sherds of Roman pottery from the area but all the other finds and all structures were medieval. There were no signs of the often suggested Iron Age site and defences in the area investigated.

ii) *The outer ward.* This ward, which has yet to be excavated, lies along the south-east edge of the hill. The visible structures consist of a curtain wall still upstanding at one place on the north-west (Fig. 19, no. 22), with a lean-to structure adjoining. On the south-east, the curtain has fallen away and portions of it are visible on the hillside below (e.g. Fig. 19, no. 7). The remains of towers are visible on the north-east and south-west (Fig. 19, nos. 3 & 21). The north-east tower was apparently built to overlook the approach to the town and probably guarded the entrance to the outer ward itself. That on the south-west appears to be polygonal and guards the approach to the inner ward via a rock-cut ledge (Fig. 19, no. 23). The inner ward was additionally protected by a ditch on its north side. Near the entrance ramp a series of walls radiate from near the north-east corner of the ward, crossing the ditch and joining a wall running along the northern edge of the ditch. These are likely to have been an additional protection for the entrance. However, limited excavations in 1985 showed some buildings within these walls and so the area may, at some stage, have functioned as a small middle ward.

iii) *The inner ward* (Fig. 20). This ward has been the centre of excavation, clearance and consolidation over the last six years (1980–85), and as a result a clearer picture is now available of the general structure, although it will be some time before all the available archaeological details will be revealed. For ease of description, areas, buildings and rooms within buildings have been designated by letters on Fig. 20 and will be treated in alphabetical order.

The rock-cut ledge which provides the approach from the outer ward gives way to an area (A) which is clearly lower at its base than the ledge, although still filled with rubble. Access from A into the inner ward was probably via B, a room or tower on the north-east angle of the ward. B has been only partially cleared of rubble derived from its collapsed superstructure, and its floor level has yet to be revealed. Certainly a set of steps, eventually of stone but perhaps originally of wood, lead up and through a doorway into area C. Here further steps led up to a rock-cut ledge on the south side of C, which, in turn, gave access to steps leading up the east curtain wall, perhaps to an upper room in B but more certainly via an archway to a first floor entrance in the round keep D.

The round tower/keep D is one of the earliest features on the site as all adjacent upstanding walls abut it. Only the curving wall below E, shown in outline on Fig. 20, could possibly predate it. It is *c.* 12.25 m (*c.* 40 ft) in diameter externally where planned and the interior is *c.* 5.75 m (almost 19 ft) in diameter. The surviving portion forms part of the basal cone so that the upper tower may be assumed to be of slightly less girth. External clearance and excavation have been only partial and further work awaits progress in consolidation. Two internal openings are, however, apparent. One on the south-west does not penetrate the wall and may represent the position of a stairway leading to an upper floor. The other on the north clearly did run through the whole wall and still retains part of its vault. This belongs to a passageway of restricted height leading downwards and out of the building into the yard O. Internally the lowest floor was originally flagged over a mortar sub-floor with some features defined by post-holes in the sub-floor. It is clear that the floor was removed and that the whole keep perished in a fierce fire which has reddened the interior walls and left heavy deposits of burnt debris. What appears to be roof debris includes both clay and lead, but unlike most other buildings in the outer ward there is no sign of slate. The lead encountered was sufficient to glaze other debris extensively but it did not form pools, and it seems possible that the majority of the lead had already been removed from the roof before the conflagration.

Area E forms a passageway between keep D and the open area F. Beneath it lies the curving wall already described, and shown in outline on Fig. 20. In the developed castle it gave access to a double garderobe in the thickness of the south-east curtain and also to stairs, presumably leading to a wall-walk. Access was via a doorway between the north-east corner of G and keep D. This doorway appears to have been blocked at a late stage in the history of the castle.

Area F seems always to have been open. The earliest feature is part of the original curtain wall found only at the south end of F at the G-F-H junction. A wall running north-west/south-east at the north end of F may also be contemporary with the first curtain and is shown in outline on Fig. 20. Next to be constructed was building G which abuts the original curtain. Rubbish was then allowed to accumulate in F, and *c.* 2 m had built up before the south-east curtain was replaced. Immediately afterwards and perhaps as part of the same building operation, a thick layer of slate was dumped over F. This acted as a surface until the whole area was filled with destruction rubble. Building G abuts the first south-east curtain but appears to be subsequent to the I-J-K-L complex as its west wall has been formed by removing the facing from the walls of L and I and keying on the wall of G. The result is a wall which widens considerably as it moves southwards. At the north-west corner of G a doorway gives access onto the mortar-surfaced yard O.

Area H is subsequent to room G. There is slight evidence to suggest that the south-east curtain originally formed the south wall of G and that this was subsequently breached to accommodate the projecting area H. H has a lower room apparently without windows, and an upper storey with three lancet windows in the south wall and at least one in the east. This room has often been referred to as the chapel but there seems to be no hard evidence to support this supposition. The precise way in which G and H joined is at present unclear.

Rooms I, J, K and L formed a unit during the later years of the castle. The original building seems to have consisted of K and L with the area later occupied by J and I as an exterior courtyard; the splayed window between L and J belongs to this phase. Later J was incorporated into the building and its level built up to correspond to a first floor over K and L by the extensive dumping of clay and stone. It may have been incorporated in the building at the same time but the position here is anomalous and will be discussed later. At a still later date the south-west ward wall was replaced, probably because of a collapse, for the wall was widened and the buttress at the south-west corner added as an integral part of the new scheme. The new building had at least two floors with windows facing south-west.

Rooms K and L formed part of the original building scheme in this part of the ward. Between K and L lay a rounded pier of masonry apparently support-ing some feature in the room above. Later the feature was enlarged and walls added to separate K and L. In the final collapse of the building part of a chimney stack had fallen against the pier, and it may be assumed that the feature it supported was a fireplace, originally perhaps an open hearth and later a fireplace and chimney. Windows and a door let onto areas N and O to the north. Access to rooms above was provided by stairways in both K and L.

The I-J-K-L complex perished by fire. In K and L massive amounts of roof debris, including clay and slate, overlay burnt wood from floors and roof-struc-ture. Above lay the masonry debris of the building which appears to have col-lapsed upon itself. Amongst this debris were a number of red sandstone corbels, while fragments of window moulding and tracery found either side of the north-east wall of K and L will eventually give an indication of the upper floor windows overlooking the open areas N and O. Area I also contains destruction debris seemingly cut by drains on the south-east side of the room, but it seems likely that the debris here is from an earlier destruction than that in K/L.

Areas M, N and O occupy the triangular space to the north of K and L, and probably G. The small room M was created by adding a wall across the north-west corner of the ward. The level in M, N and O was raised by dumping rubble, whilst revetting walls were built to allow light to reach the windows in the lower rooms of K and L, and stairs constructed to link a doorway in L with the raised level of N and O. Area O, and probably N, was sealed with a stone and mortar floor subsequently renewed and patched several times. The creation of M, N and O is clearly later than the building of the ward wall and of the north wall of K-L, but it appears to have been part of the same constructional phase. No link has yet been established by excavation between O and D, but it seems likely that the passageway leading downwards on the north of D will link with the mortar surfaces in O. This would imply an open yard across the majority of the northern part of the ward and provide us with the essential means of access to all the buildings. It would also imply stairs in either B or A to link the level of the courtyard O with that of the rock-cut approach east of A.

CONCLUSION

As yet the excavations at Dryslwyn have not progressed far enough to enable us to link the documentary and archaeological evidence to any great extent. Nevertheless, for the inner ward at least we can propose an outline archaeological sequence and there are a few points at which this can be tentatively linked with the documentary evidence.

The first of the major inner ward buildings to have been built was the round keep. This was followed by the construction of much of the curtain wall and building K-L. Later K-L was enlarged to include J-I, and subsequently G was built. This provides us with all the major known buildings in the ward except H, and all seem most likely to pre-date the siege of 1287. This is partly because if it were otherwise the later parts of the sequence would have to be unreasonably compressed, and partly an argument from the silence of the admittedly incomplete documentation after 1287 on such major works. Apparently corroborative evidence is provided by a trebuchet ball of shaped stone found in the rubbish levels in F. This ball seems most likely to have been one of the many which the documents record as having been fashioned for the machine used in the 1287 siege. One cannot of course be sure that it was found where it originally fell, but this does at least seem possible. *If* the ball can be used to date part of the rubbish accumulation in F to pre-1287, then G, which it post-dates, and I-J-K-L, which G post-dates, are clearly also pre-siege. There seems no reason to doubt on grounds of style alone that the keep D is pre-1287.

Prior to the full excavation of H, it is not possible to be certain when it was constructed, although initial soundings show that it post-dates the first south-east curtain and probably is later than G as well. Its lancet windows would suggest a thirteenth-century or, at the very latest, an early fourteenth-century date, but construction either before or after the siege is, as yet, feasible.

Most of the subsequent work in the inner ward was in the form of repair and maintenance, although this could sometimes be on a fairly large scale. All the major developments so far detected could well belong to the major repairs of 1338. Crucial to this is the identification of building I-J-K-L. This is clearly the dominant residential structure in the inner ward; its debris has yielded the majority of the sandstone corbels found so far on the site, and we know that corbels were being used in reroofing the 'King's Hall' in 1338. The south-west corner of the structure has been rebuilt in a manner suggestive of partial collapse such as we know occurred to the 'West Wing' of the hall prior to 1338. It seems reasonable therefore to equate I-J-K-L with the so-called 'King's Hall'. The substantial layer of roof slate in area F was probably derived from a stripped roof. It immediately overlies the foundation offset of the curtain wall in F. If we could equate this slate level with the known period of roofing activity on the hall, then we can link this to the rebuilding of the F curtain, which must immediately precede the dumping of roof slate. The case is not proven but it is at least possible that all this activity took place in 1338.

The problems concerning the final destruction of the castle have already been mentioned. To date, both the historical and archaeological evidence is inconclusive. A coin from beneath the destruction debris in room K has a general fifteenth-century date and is, so far, the latest datable object from a significant context. Evidence is accumulating for the removal of both the contents of the castle and some of the building materials prior to the final destruction. The dearth of lead from the keep's roof debris and the removal of the lowest stone floor have already been mentioned. The steps to the east of area C appear also to have been robbed of their treads, while the drain capping at the foot of the steps from L to O, possibly an iron grille, is also missing. In addition, the destruction debris in both K-L and D has yielded fittings, but little suggestion of contents within the buildings concerned. The whole is suggestive of an empty and partially stripped structure prior to its final destruction by fire. None of these elements is at present conclusive but the evidence seems to be pointing not towards a destruction in the early fifteenth century, presumably by Glyndŵr, when the castle was occupied and still regarded as a military unit, but perhaps later in that century when military interest in it had ceased and when the castle and its lands were being exploited for their monetary returns only.

No doubt further excavation and research will enable us to expand this outline of the history and archaeology of Dryslwyn. However, with the inner ward excavations approaching their halfway stage, this seems an opportune moment to offer this interim attempt to combine these two elements in our knowledge of the site.

Acknowledgements. From the 1984 season, excavations at Dryslwyn have been directed by Mr C. Caple. The present account was largely written in 1983, but, as far as possible, the results of the 1984–85 seasons have been incorporated, and I should like to thank Chris Caple for much help and useful discussion concerning both the 1984–85 seasons and the excavations as a whole.

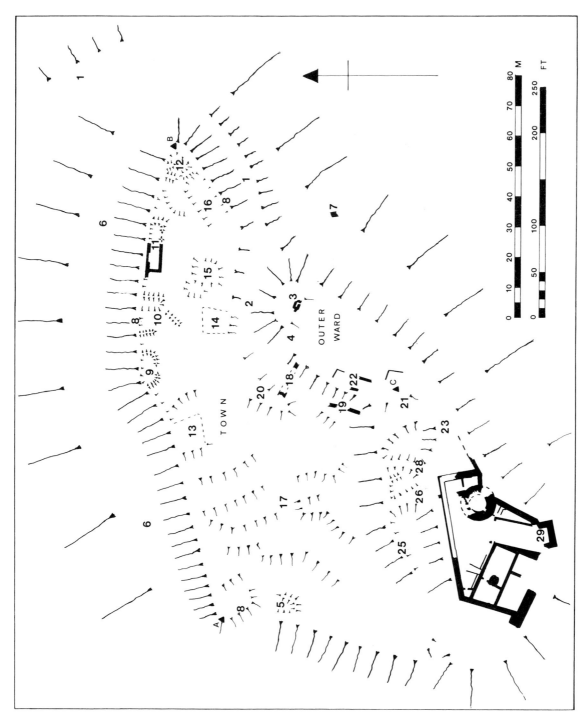

Fig. 19 Dryslwyn Castle and township.

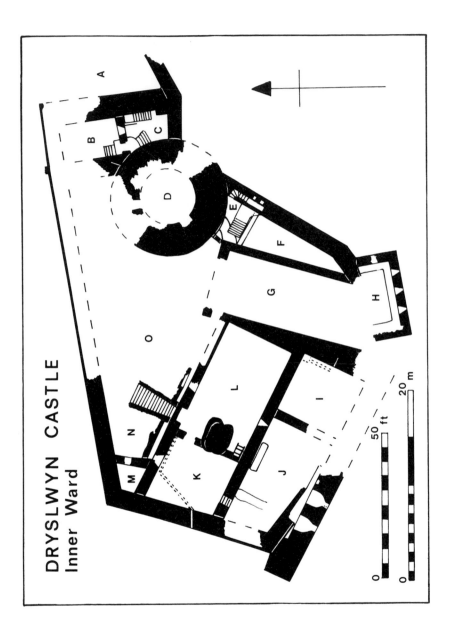

Fig. 20 Dryslwyn Castle: inner ward.

Holt Castle
John de Warenne and Chastellion

LAWRENCE BUTLER

T HE castle of Holt stands on an isolated boss of rock above the river Dee, formerly utilizing the Dee for its eastern defences. However, its remains are now slight and much overgrown; the traveller can pass through Holt without ever suspecting that the village possessed a castle or even aspired once to urban status. This essay is an attempt to throw new light on the castle of Holt by examining the historical circumstances of its foundation and the personal qualities of its founder. The ground survey is apparently the first undertaken for 360 years. It may be worthily offered to David Cathcart King, who has over the years so valiantly advanced the study of castles throughout Britain and particularly in Wales, who has scrambled upon so many overgrown mounds to discern their true character and who has inspired his disciples to undertake their own studies in siege weaponry and 'castellology'.

Holt is a problem castle.[1] The problems start with the name itself. Throughout the middle ages the name of the castle was Chastellion or Castrum Leonis—the castle of the lion. Only in the sixteenth century was the name Holt supplanting it.[2] Similarly the town was Villa Leonis (or Villa Castrum Leonis) and this Latin form also remained in use until the late sixteenth- and early seventeenth-century map-makers gave currency to the English form. Victorian antiquaries were certain that the name Lyons Castle was a direct translation of the Welsh Caer Lleon (*castrum legionis*) and this gained currency in Palmer's work and was repeated in the publication of the excavations at the Roman works depot by Grimes.[3] However, the equation is not proved. The Roman works were not obvious—they escaped discovery until 1906. The existence of a Welsh form rests on a misreading of a medieval document.[4] It is far more likely that this name is a Norman-French introduction by the Warennes and links directly to names such as Château Gaillard or Wolf's Castle. It may be a deliberate mocking

---

[1] The main sources have been given by King (1983), **1**, 103–04. In order of importance they are Palmer (1907), 311–33, 389–402; Taylor in Colvin (1963), **1**, 334–35; RCAM (1914), 74–75; Hemp (1935), 357–58.

[2] The earliest occurrences are 'chastellyon' or 'chastellion': PRO C 66/136, m. 6, and 'castro leonis': PRO C 66/150. The English 'The Holt' occurs in 1478 (*Worc. Itin.*, 68) and in 1539 (*Leland's Itin.*, **3**, 69).

[3] Palmer (1906), 220–22, 238; Palmer (1907), 10; Grimes (1930), 5–6; see also Lloyd (1874), 135. However, Caerleon in Gwent does derive its name from the Roman fortress: Nicolaisen *et al.* (1970), 75.

[4] *Ann. Rep. Dep. Keeper Public Rec.*, 21, 'the castles of Dinaslraw and Caerleon': this is an error, followed by Palmer. The actual document (C 66/150) reads *castra de dinasbran et castro leonis*. It is given correctly in *Cal. Pat. R. 1317–1321*, 264. Grimes (1930, 6) accepted Palmer's view without independent verification; I am grateful to Professor W. F. Grimes for this information.

contrast to John de Warenne's other castle in Wales—Dinas Brân—Crow's Castle. Another possibility is that this lordship was given in 1284 to John de Warenne's eldest son, William, and that he carried the nickname 'The Lion'.[5] Although the main gate was surmounted by a panel with a lion passant guardant, there seems to be no heraldic evidence to support the choice either in the Warenne family or in their marriage alliances (Lusignan, De Vere, Bar).

There seems to be no Welsh equivalent, such as Castell Llew, recorded in medieval times.[6] The settlement lay in Welsh Maelor, east of Offa's Dyke; most villages here in the lordship of Bromfield carried English names, e.g.,. Allington, Gresford, Marford, Hoseley, Acton, Abenbury, Wrexham, though Madog ap Llewelyn (of Eyton) had a *mansio* at Holt in 1315[7] and some village-names had Welsh equivalents.

The second problem concerns the castle's origins and its relationship to other defensive works. The earliest general reference is to the grant of the lordship of Bromfield to John de Warenne (7th earl of Surrey) on 7 October 1282.[8] He granted it to his son William on 1 August 1284 but the latter's early death on 15 December 1286 caused the lordship to revert to his father.[9] It remained in his possession until his death at Michaelmas 1304, after which it passed to his grandson John (8th earl of Surrey) on 7 April 1306.[10] The earliest mention of the castle at Holt is during the tenure by this earl.

The evidence for castle guard in 1304 claims to rest on a late testimony, though castle guard was required in a tenancy commencing in 1308.[11] The first mention in 1311 is in royal documents and the mention of the 'new castle' in 1315 is in a local survey.[12] This conjunction of documentary references might

---

[5] *Cal. Fine. R. 1272–1307*, 233. Charles of Anjou had built a Lion Tower at Lucera in the 1270s, while at the Tower of London Edward I had built the Lion Tower in the early years of his reign (name first recorded in 1532). Another possibility is that Holt was known as New Castle or as Eyton Castle or Hewlington Castle until John, the eighth earl, completed the work and placed over the gate a lion statue in honour of his wife's ancestral castle of Châtillon-sur-Sâone (Vosges), rather than the king's statue as at Caernarfon and Denbigh.

[6] Buck (1774), **2**, 386.

[7] Ellis (1924), 46–47; Pratt (1965), 21 and fns. 30, 31; 69, fn. 32.

[8] *Cal. Chanc. R.*, 240.

[9] *Cal. Fine R. 1272–1307*, 233; *Complete Peerage*, **12**, pt. 1, 507.

[10] *Cal. Close. R. 1302–1307*, 373.

[11] BL Add. MS 10013, f. 20, cited by Pratt (1965), 17. No date is given but the phrase 'given in time of good memory of the counts of Warenne and Arundell' should refer only to Richard (d. 1375/76) who was the first to hold both titles, but only after 1353. However, there is nothing inherently improbable in Pratt's suggestion that the 1391 rental is referring to the original land grants. It is therefore likely that all the tenancies commence under John, the eighth earl, probably in the summer of 1308 after he had returned from France. The only recorded land grant with castle guard is that to John de Wysham in 1308 (*Cal. Pat. R. 1307–1313*, 405). John de Wysham accompanied the earl on military service in 1327 (*Cal. Pat. R. 1327–1330*, 24).

[12] PRO C 66/136, m. 6. Confirmation on 6 December 1311 of a charter issued at Chastellion on 7 September 1308 (*Cal. Pat. R. 1307–1313*, 405); 'new castle' in Ellis (1924), 46–47. This 'new castle' may contrast with Oldcastle on the east bank of the Dee (SJ 434508): Dodgson (1972, 44) records this form as early as 1260. The argument that the ditches at Holt Castle were by 1315 'in a state of ruin' (Pratt 1965, 13) is based on an assumption made by Ellis (1924, 38–39). Ellis read a faulty text, *quia fossata sunt d... et nulla herba ibi cressit*, as if the missing word was *delapida*, but it could equally well read *decliva* (steep, precipitous).

suggest that the castle was only completed under the eighth earl, particularly if taken with the argument that in 1295 Edward I stayed at Wrexham because Holt castle was unfinished.[13] However, there is a strong possibility on historical grounds that the castle was started under John, the seventh earl, especially when his other castle-building activities are examined. It is unlikely that John, the eighth earl, who only came of age in 1307, would have initiated any new work. The reference in 1315 to the 'new castle' raises two further points: was there a Norman castle in the lordship of Bromfield as part of the eleventh-century advance under Robert of Rhuddlan, and was there an earlier choice by de Warenne for his castle? The evidence for an earlier castle is the earthwork at Erddig or Glyn.[14] This is a predominantly earthwork structure though with anomalies—possibly as a result of quarrying and eighteenth-century tree planting. The suggestion that the castle at Holt had a local predecessor, either 1277–82 or 1282–1304, depends upon the absence of any earlier documentary record and the (admittedly late) 1391 reference to Earl Warenne's castle at Glyn having been burnt.[15] This might suggest that Holt had an earlier commotal centre at Wrexham. The phrase 'new castle', as applied to Holt in 1315, may be in contrast to the then still identifiable Roman site, or in contrast to a Norman earthwork supplanted by or quarried away in constructing the new castle, or may be in recognition of a new site after a false start elsewhere in the lordship.

The evidence of the name and siting is inconclusive, but the evidence from family history points in only one direction. The three contenders for the construction of the castle are John, the seventh earl (from 1240 until his death in September 1304), his son William and his grandson John, the eighth earl (from 1304 until his death in 1347).[16] The first-named John is clearly the strongest claimant to be the originator and founder of the castle: he had a distinguished military career under Henry III and Edward I; he had military experience in Gascony and Germany as well as taking a prominent part in Edward I's wars in Wales and Scotland; he travelled with the Lord Edward in France in 1260–62 and was in close touch with his Lusignan relatives. He took a decisive part in the refashioning of Sandal Castle, including the new barbican; he may

[13] Fryde (1962), 2, 9, 18, 58, 146, 163. The suggestion that Holt was incomplete is from Pratt (1965). However, it is more likely that the line of march of 5,000 infantry from Chester crossed the Dee immediately on leaving Chester, spending their first night at Hope and their second night at Wrexham. They did not stop at Holt because this would mean a detour. There was also a lack of space and it would be of no advantage to keep close to the Dee at this point. It is uncertain whether Earl Warenne accompanied the army, although a knight in his service, Anselm de Gyse, died on campaign (Fryde 1962, 199).

[14] Evidence assembled by King (1983), **1**, 103, 105; the historical background to Edward's invasion of Powys Fadog and the Welsh loss of Bromfield is given in King (1974), 113–19.

[15] The evidence for a castle at Glyn is late: the mention in BL Add. MS 10013 (cited by Pratt (1965), 11, fn. 6) is ambiguous for no earl is named and it could equally well be referring to any one of the many fourteenth-century periods of unrest described by Pratt (1963, 26–40). The other reference to a castle at Glyn (BL Harl. MS 43, cited by Palmer (1903), 237–38) is of 1574 and is clearly describing the earthwork at Erddig.

[16] Their respective careers are given in *Complete Peerage*, **12**, pt. 1, 503–11 and Fairbank (1907), 193–264. For building work: Godfrey (1972) (Lewes), Hooper (1945), 44–49 (Reigate), Coad and Streeten (1982), 141–43, 193–94 (Castle Acre), Johnson (1980), 80–81 (Conisbrough) and Mayes and Butler (1983), 3–4, 12–17, 76–78 (Sandal).

have built the new barbican at Lewes, following the model of Harlech, and he was responsible for minor works and the chapel at Conisbrough. It is not known what work he did at his other two castles of Reigate and Castle Acre. By contrast, there is no work that can be attributed to William. The longer mature life of John, the eighth earl, was clouded by his continuing marital difficulties and his quarrels with Thomas and Henry, successive earls of Lancaster. He did campaign with both Edward II and Edward III in Scotland. There is no evidence that he initiated any building work at Castle Acre or at Sandal, though there may have been repairs at the latter. He was responsible for much refurbishing at Conisbrough. If the barbican at Lewes was started after 1305, then it must belong to the eighth earl's activity. If castle guard at Holt only commenced in 1308 when the castle was operational, then this might herald the start of building, but it is much more likely to mark the completion.

The balance of family and historical evidence points firmly to John, the seventh earl, acting in conjunction with Edward I. This was a marcher lordship, exactly comparable to those centred on the castles of Henry de Lacy at Denbigh and of Reginald de Grey at Ruthin. Whether the master of the king's works, James of St George, assisted in the choice of location or the distinctive plan is uncertain. The king was clearly aware that Chester needed a south-western defence post holding a crossing of the Dee in the lordship of Bromfield.[17] Dr Taylor's view can be fully supported: 'We should expect, in the light of what happened in the other lordships, that its foundation would have followed closely on the royal grant [of 1282] and would have had the king's full cognisance. Whether, in these circumstances, the services of the master of the king's works would have been made available, as it has been suggested they were in those cases [Denbigh and Ruthin], for laying out the castle site and 'ordaining' the works, can only be conjectured. All that can be said is that the precedents make it likely and the likelihood is strengthened by the evidently accomplished character of the resulting design.'[18]

The design was indeed unusual, but precedents for it and other influences upon it can be discerned (Fig. 21). However, it is first necessary to determine what the plan was before the major destruction after 1675 obscured the site.[19] The evidence must be assessed and depends principally on Tudor and early Stuart surveys and two plans and elevations.[20] Certain discrepancies exist between the earlier plan of *c.* 1562 and the later one of 1620, but much can be explained in that the earlier survey concentrates upon the ground floor apartments and the later one upon the first floor uses. These surveys have been

[17] *Cal. Anc. Corr.*, 84.

[18] Colvin (1963), **1**, 335.

[19] In 1586 it was stated 'that the castle was in better repair than it had been 48 years ago' (Palmer 1907, 318, giving actual spelling). In 1643 and 1646 it was captured in the Civil War (references in King (1983), **1**, 103–04). Between 1675 and 1683 the castle was demolished to provide building stone for Eaton Hall five miles downstream (Colvin 1963, **1**, 335).

[20] PRO LR 2/249, ff. 4ᵛ–5 (Tidderley's Survey); BL Harl. MS 2073, ff. 112–13 ('1562 drawings'), perhaps accompanying PRO LR 2/234 and SC 12/17, no. 93; BL Harl. MS 3696, ff. 5–6 (Norden's Survey).

published by Palmer and mentioned more briefly by RCAM, Pratt and in Colvin.[21] To some (e.g. Edward Owen, RCAM) the discrepancies seemed to be too great to be resolved,[22] but with the aid of an accurate, modern, measured survey considerable progress can be made. The only significant pre-Victorian print is that by the Bucks published in 1742; the castle was too ruinous and too bereft of dramatic impact to attract the artists upon tours in Wales. The discrepancies rest upon the presence of five circular towers and a rectangular chapel on the Tudor plan and the presence of four circular towers and a square one on the 1620 plan, together with the absence of the projecting chapel. All the other differences are minor.

The first survey is undated but there is no reason to doubt Palmer's assignment of it to the end of the reign of Henry VIII—probably 1538–47 would be its range.[23] It provides a description of the outer gatehouse and its attendant timber-built farm and court buildings which is supported by the evidence of the 1620 elevation and plan. It describes the isolated square tower (the outer ward) and this also accords with the later evidence of the 1562 plan and the 1620 plan. The third and major element is the castle proper or inner ward; this is carefully described,[24] its principal rooms at first floor level are identified and its state of repair indicated. The major discrepancy with the two later plans is the absence of any mention of a chapel (shown in 1562) and the insistence that all five towers are round (as in 1562, but not in 1620). The well and the secret passage are shown on the plan of 1562, but it is not clear whether the full extent of the passage or sally port is shown on the 1562 plan as this can hardly lead directly into the river Dee.

The evidence at two inquiries in 1586–87 describes the parts of the castle used by the constable, deputy constable and porter, and mentions the 'house towards the river of Dee' with an iron door.[25] This 'house' will be examined with regard to the Bucks' engraving.

The second survey was undertaken in 1562. Although this is principally concerned with the town and the lordship, the occasion of this survey is the most

[21] Palmer (1907), 311–14 (Tidderley), 393–96 ('1562 drawings'), 389–92 and 397–400 (Norden); RCAM (1914), 75; Pratt (1965), 16; Colvin (1963), **1**, 334.

[22] Palmer (1907), 396, fn. 1; the same writer in RCAM (1914), 75, '... the various plans being hopelessly discrepant... it is impossible to settle this point, as well as others, without a complete clearance of the site'.

[23] The earliest date is established by the return of the castle to royal possession after the death of Henry Fitzroy, duke of Richmond, in 1536 and the appointment of Thomas Byrde as chaplain of Holt Castle in 1538.

[24] The transcription given in Palmer (1907), 311–15, is generally accurate: on p. 312 it should be noted that the measurements in paces are inserted in a later hand; on p. 313 there are some errors in spelling but nothing of significance; on p. 314 there is one error (line 11, 'tower' to read 'lower'), and two qualifying phrases omitted.

[25] Palmer (1907), 317–19 (original source not located).

probable time when a plan and elevation were drawn (Pls. IV and V).[26] The parallel lies with the series of elevations which accompany the survey of Duchy of Lancaster castles in northern England.[27] The elevation is entitled 'the... side of Lion Castle al^s Holt' and shows a view from the north omitting the outer gatehouse, court house and farm buildings, diminishing the importance of the isolated tower and concentrating on the north and east faces of an impressive castle with towers strongly resembling Conwy. On a separate sheet is a plan with annotations identifying the rooms at courtyard or basement level and with dimensions of different parts of the castle. Within the main castle the plan shows close attention to detail with doorways, stairs, fireplaces and room divisions being shown; the isolated 'Chequer' tower is less carefully shown and the margin of the ditch and the outer gatehouse range is omitted. A summer house or arbour is shown in the ditch. Both plan and elevation are credible, though the chapel addition is unusual and militarily unsound.[28]

The third survey was prepared by John Norden in 1620.[29] The elevation ('uprighte') and plan ('platforme') accompany a detailed survey of the lordship. The elevation is a bird's-eye view on a double-spread page;[30] it is attractively drawn and also annotated, particularly as to the buildings of the outer gatehouse and the use of the grounds between the gatehouse and the moat. The plan in general tallies with the elevation, but shows more buildings in the outer court, west and north of the castle.[31] The detail of the main castle is less convincing; the doorways in the ranges are, with one exception, placed centrally, the doorways into the towers are also centrally placed as if this was the arrangement at parapet level, no internal divisions are shown and the towers are disproportionately large. The tower opposite the entrance is square not round. On the reverse of the plan (f. 6^v) is Norden's estimate of the lead still on the roofs and the need for timber and lead.[32] In the main body of the survey the jurors give an account of the castle, mainly concerned with the value of its materials and the evidence of ownership of the various leased portions in the outer court.[33]

[26] BL Harl. MS 2073, f. 112 (elevation), f. 113 (plan); this drawing is a copy made by a Randle Holme (probably Randle Holme I) in about 1640, using older material. The plan and its annotations are much more precisely drawn than his usual style. The pencil lines beneath the ink suggest that he was copying a measured survey. In the same volume is a poor thumb-nail sketch of the same elevation by Daniel King (f. 126). Palmer (1907, 393–96) gives an accurate transcript except on p. 396, line 2, last word, for 'with' read 'each', and line 9, insert 'The chequer house before the gate... foote broad and... foote longe'.

[27] PRO MPC 94–97 (Clitheroe, Melbourne, Tickhill, Sandal), MR 14–17 (Knaresborough, Lancaster, Pontefract, Tutbury).

[28] A chapel does occur in this position at Kidwelly, but at Conwy the chapel is placed in the wall thickness of one of the towers. At Conisbrough, Denbigh and Ruthin it was located within the courtyard. The fact that the chapel dimensions are given separately suggests that it was a free-standing building.

[29] BL Harl. MS 3696, f. 5 (elevation), f. 6 (plan), f. 6^v (estimates of repairs); illustrated and discussed by Palmer (1907), 397–400.

[30] Because of the deep fold in the double page this elevation is more usually reproduced from the engraving by Peter Mazell for *The London Magazine*, XVI (January 1779), 205.

[31] Palmer records all the annotations on the plan, except p. 398, line 8 to read 'come to the river at B', and p. 400, lines 16–17 to read 'Fish pondes, now streme land all worth per. ann. about xvi *li*'.

[32] Palmer (1907), 390, fn. 1 (copied without errors).

[33] BL Harl. MS 3696, f. 24^v; Palmer (1907), 389–91 is a careless transcription with spelling errors and six omissions of words or phrases.

It is clear that there are substantial discrepancies to be resolved if this body of evidence is to be reconciled. Some additional information is provided by two eighteenth-century views of the castle, the earlier by the Bucks of 1742 (Pl. VI and Fig. 23) and the other by an unknown artist (but probably Moses Griffith) at a later date.[34] These help resolve the matter of the tower shown square in plan on Norden's account but are more eloquent of the decay that this once substantial castle had suffered.

The outermost gatehouse and its attendant half-timbered buildings do not present a strongly defensive profile; they are shown in detail only on Norden's elevation and plan, though described in Tidderley's survey. These works require no further discussion in this paper. There is considerable agreement over the form and appearance of the isolated 'Chequer' tower, though the 1562 drawing tends to minimize its height and importance in contrast to Norden. The 1562 drawing shows two windows facing the outer bridge and a gabled roof; the Norden drawing omits the windows and has a flat (lead) roof. Since this tower was used to store records it must have had an upper floor.

The main castle was approached over a drawbridge: in Norden's elevation this is noted and shown partly raised; in the 1562 drawing the slots for the drawbridge chains are shown either side of the doorway. In both drawings there is an attempt to contrast the rock base with the masonry above it, though the 1562 drawing shows arrowslits cut in the rock below the towers flanking the entrance (T1, T5) perhaps intentionally deceptive, unless the artist has miscalculated and this lights the basement.[35]

The towers are all depicted as round on the 1562 plan and shown as such, where perspective allows, on the accompanying drawing; this also supports the evidence of Tidderley's survey. The 1562 drawing is not uniform in its treatment of the towers but the basic form (as in T2) is of three main stages, lit by windows and divided by string-courses, a fourth stage above the roof level of the adjacent range and a fifth stage only of battlements and a stair turret with pinnacle or finial. On the 1562 drawing the towers, the battlements with arrowslits, and stair turrets look convincing. On Norden's drawing the towers do not possess string-courses, their windows are disproportionately large arrowslits (crosslet or double oillet) or circular gunports, and the stair turrets end abruptly.[36] In the 1562 drawing Tower 2 has no turret; in the 1620 drawing Tower 3 has no turret. In the 1562 drawing and plan the towers are entirely outside the line of the ranges; in the 1620 plan they are partly within the ranges but on

---

[34] Samuel and Nathaniel Buck published their view of Holt on 9 April 1742. The best engraved version occurs in the *Antiquities* (Buck 1774). In the National Library of Wales are other versions, e.g. by Basire (P 3784), for Hogg (PD 2684), for a historical tour (CR 4672). The later drawing from a more southerly viewpoint (PA 4035) is in the 'Warwick Smith' collection and may be by Griffith. Palmer (1908, 162) uses a drawing based on the Bucks' print and a photograph (1905) from a similar viewpoint.

[35] On the original drawing these slits are smeared over as if drawn in error. On Palmer (1907), 393, they have been cleaned; Pratt (1965, 16) has redrawn this elevation. For ease of reference the towers are numbered clockwise, commencing north-east of the entrance with T1, etc. The ranges are numbered with reference to the towers between which they stand: R1/2, R2/3, etc.

[36] It may well be that Norden's drawing has been influenced by contemporary designs for gunports, e.g. at Upnor Castle of the late seventeenth century.

the drawing they seem to be outside the curtain walls. In the 1562 drawing the location of the stair turrets matches the position of the newel stair on the plan; on the 1620 plan no stairs are shown and there is no sound reason for the location of the turrets which might even be chimneys.[37]

The illustration of the ranges shows comparable discrepancies. On the 1562 drawing the entrance range (R1/5) is of equal height to its flanking towers. The heraldic lion is in a large semi-circular arch between small window slits; the range is divided by horizontal string-courses into three storeys. The doorway has a rectangular head. By contrast, the Norden drawing makes the entrance range one stage lower than the flanking towers, places the lion in an applied shield and has two two-light square headed windows. Less can be said of the other ranges: the 1562 drawing shows the north-west range (R1/2) with windows at regular intervals and a ground-floor doorway serving a path down the face of the rock (supported by evidence of the plan). The Norden elevation has none of these details but does show a corbelled oversailing parapet with plain battlements. The higher viewpoint of the Norden drawing shows also the exterior wall of R4/5, plain apart from a single gunport, and the interior walls of R2/3 and R3/4 have large two-light windows with transoms and a hood mould at the upper stage of each visible range.

In both of the elevations and plans there is the problem of the square tower. In Norden's elevation it is shown as part of the main circuit (T3), with a rectangular headed door at parapet level and two square windows in the uppermost storey; the plan supports this position. In the 1562 drawing the square tower is an addition to T2: it stands on a rock-hewn base, rises through four stages punctuated by string-courses and is lit by two-light pointed-headed windows with Y-tracery. The plan shows it directly attached to Tower 2, though without any doorway, and gives the dimensions as 12 ft broad and 15 ft long. There is one clue in the drawing, showing an additional diagonal line on the rock base, which throws doubt upon its proximity to the adjoining tower and upon its height. Similarly, in considering Norden's drawing, it may be that the surveyor did not enter the main court because of unsafe buildings but made his observations from the safety of the outer bank.

The views produced by the Bucks and ?Griffith furnish an explanation for the square tower. On both drawings there is a two-storey square tower standing away from, and lower than, the main castle. On the earlier drawing there is jagged masonry suggesting round-headed windows at two levels; on the later drawing there are no openings on the side face of the tower. In both drawings it is clear that the square tower stood close to the river beyond Tower 3. The Bucks show the lower stages of Tower 2 with a square-headed window, the back of Tower 3, the inner face of the gateway and fragments of Towers 1 and 5, together with some walls of the lodgings ranges. On the later drawing there is no evidence for any tower on the main castle, but straight lengths of

---

[37] However, these 'chimneys' do not correspond with known fireplaces, as in R5/1 or R4/5. The turret finials on the 1562 drawing seem rather improbable, but two-stage turrets are shown at Conwy on an early fifteenth-century drawing (BL Harl. MS 1319, f. 14ᵛ), while Caernarfon has finials in the form of statuettes as well as eagles.

walling upon the sandstone base are probably the interior walls of the ranges (R2/3, R3/4, R4/5).

The square tower can thus be identified as a water gate (comparable with Gillot's Tower at Rhuddlan), perhaps with a low curtain wall along the river front. It may have been placed on a rock outcrop, as the 1562 drawing shows, but this seems unlikely. It probably housed a chapel on an upper floor, from the evidence of the Bucks' engraving. It was so placed that, when viewed from the outer gatehouse, it appeared to be immediately beyond or part of Tower 3, as on the Norden drawing. Its ground floor was reached by the 'secret narrow way' of Tidderley's survey. Either the outer door of the passageway or the outer door of the Water Gate was of iron. In the 1586 survey there was 'one iron doore being belowe in the house towards the river of Dee'.[38] The gate was removed by Edward Hughes between 1569 and 1585. The description of the square tower given by Norden relies on hearsay evidence for the iron gate, which suggests his inspection of the castle was not entirely thorough.

This lack of thoroughness in Norden's work is emphasized when the two plans are examined in detail. The 1620 plan shows the five ranges with no internal divisions, while the 1562 plan shows all the dividing walls at basement level together with wall-stairs, passages and fireplace jambs. From this plan it would seem that there was no direct access to the circular towers at basement level. However, the stair leading up to the hall (mentioned by Tidderley) is shown on the 1620 plan in the correct position; the other doorways on the 1620 plan are placed centrally within each range and the evidence of the 1562 plan is preferred. In addition to the newel stairs within the towers, the 1562 plan shows three external stairs in the interior angles of the ranges; this is partly supported by the evidence of Tidderley's survey ('from the leadds two severall wyndyng steires downe to the lower p[ar]te of the courte').[39] None is shown on Norden's plan or elevation. These stairs may be a later addition to the fabric under the earls of Arundel.[40]

There is a discrepancy in the position of the well. In Norden's plan it is marked in a central position within the courtyard—suitable for a cistern, decorative fountain or horse-trough. In the 1562 plan the room on the left of the gate-passage is termed 'The Well House' and a circular well is shown. However, in Tidderley's survey there is mention of 'a ffaire kychen with a drawght well yn the same'. This should presumably be located in range 4/5; it could be the circular feature shown in the outer wall thickness of range 2/3 close to Tower 3, where Norden locates the kitchen in 1620. However, such a feature as on the 1562 plan could well be a garderobe chute.

It is surprising that so little attention has been paid to the visible evidence

---

[38] Palmer (1907), 314, 318 (evidence of Lancelot Bates), 398 and fn. 1. It may be termed a 'house' because it had not been used as a chapel after the 1550s.

[39] The discrepancy between the total of the courtyard stairs (two in Tidderley, three on the 1562 plan) might be resolved by assuming that the stair nearest the kitchen was a well shaft, although the well is not mentioned by Tidderley as being in the courtyard.

[40] The wealth of Richard, earl of Arundel (executed 1397) was considerable (Salzman 1953, 34–36). He could well afford to pay for new work at Holt.

at the castle itself. Antiquarians have preferred to take the illustrations as their guide rather than search out corroboration from the ruins. Edward Owen did not attempt this in the *Denbighshire Inventory* and his successor as Secretary to the Royal Commission on Ancient Monuments, W. J. Hemp, appears to have been the first to examine the ruins critically.[41]

It is not possible to say anything useful about the outer ward with its half-timbered buildings: the site of these is occupied by post-war bungalows and examination would now be difficult. The 'chequer tower' on its isolated column of rock can still be identified, though eroded and overgrown. It has rooted in its ruins a substantial beech tree whose growth can be charted in the photographs of RCAM and of Hemp. No stonework is now visible and the ditch has been filled with debris at this point.

The main castle has some problems that are now incapable of solution because of the nature of the destruction, other problems that might well be solved through excavation and yet others that can be resolved through close observation. It is not now possible to determine the height of any towers or ranges, nor is it possible to establish the diameter of the towers. It is unlikely that the isolated Water Gate can be found, though its general position is clear: however, the river may have altered its course. The problems best solved by close examination are the accuracy of the plans and elevations. The first point to establish is that Palmer's and Hemp's assumption that the walls now visible are the inner walls of the ranges is correct. What can be seen are the five interior walls. The evidence is, first, that the inner jambs of the entrance passage are visible, second, that the door jambs shown in Ranges 4/5 and 3/4 are visible, and, third, that the scars where the dividing walls were linked to the interior walls are visible near T3 and the gateway. There is the additional confirmation provided by Griffith's illustration that the inner wall stood directly on the rock and in places the footings within the basement rooms can be seen.

This combination of evidence suggests that the 1562 plan can be regarded as accurate (except for the chapel addition). Where the Norden plan differs from the 1562 plan (and this can be checked)—i.e. on the form of Tower 3 and on the mode of junction of the towers to the curtain wall—Norden is demonstrably incorrect. The only feature on the inner face of the interior wall not shown on the 1562 plan, but visible today, is the doorway at the north end of Range 2/3. This is reached by at least eight steps from the courtyard and entered a stone-vaulted sub-basement, perhaps leading to the 'secret narrow way' utilizing the dip in the bedding of the Bunter Sandstone rock. Other points concerning the courtyard features could be checked by excavation, particularly the position of doors and staircases, the location of the well and the existence of the courtyard spiral stairs. The topsoil and turf lie over the courtyard surface and the bedrock is covered by as much as two metres of rubble (Fig. 22).

Dr Taylor has stressed the accomplished design of Holt and it is now necessary

---

[41] Hemp (1935), 357–58; Palmer (1908, 162) identifies the 'lower part of the wall of the inner pentagon, the court within being filled with rubbish'. Palmer saw the castle before the heavy growth of ivy, bramble and sycamore saplings had rooted in the walls. Hemp presumably visited the castle during his period of service as Assistant Inspector of Ancient Monuments in Wales from 1915 to 1927.

to place this design within the development of military architecture in the late thirteenth century. There is no evidence that the plan of Holt was influenced by any pre-existing castle or promontory. In the majority of cases in Britain the shape of the rock dictates the line of the curtain and the intervals of the towers. Examples such as Chepstow, Richmond or Beeston show how diverse a plan might develop. By contrast the plan at Holt is a regular pentagon imposed upon the existing ground which is then fashioned to accommodate it. Parallels for the pentagonal plan with circular towers may be sought on the continent, for example at Bagnols near Villefranche-sur-Sâone (Rhône), Saint Maixent-l'Ecole, near Niort (Deux-Sèvres), and Saint Verain (Nièvre), though the latter has also an isolated circular tower in the courtyard as at Pembroke.[42] The quarrying of the rock to support the castle or to make it more impregnable is encountered at Bamburgh and Goodrich, and under Edward I at Conwy and Harlech. The evidence is not sufficiently clear to indicate whether the towers had a foundation course placed horizontally on a specially cut rock-shelf (as is the case with the inner wall of the ranges) or whether the footings wrapped round the base of the rock as at Conwy and Sandal (as the Bucks' engraving suggests). Certainly there were no spurs bringing the circular towers to a square base for greater protection, such as occur at Goodrich, Kidwelly and Chepstow. Perhaps the depth and width of the ditch gave sufficient security.

Even though the plan has no direct parallel in England, it may be regarded as a close derivative of Edward I's work at Aberystwyth and Rhuddlan in 1277. Both these have a trapezoidal plan with a twin-towered gatehouse facing the town, single towers at the points of the trapezoid and a further pair of towers opposite the gateway, protected by the sea at Aberystwyth and by the Clwyd at Rhuddlan. At both castles there was a protective outer ward which at Aberystwyth closely echoed the inner ward but which at Rhuddlan was more spaciously stretched around the main towers. The point of departure is that at Holt the twin towers of the gatehouse are placed more widely and the other towers, all single, are regularly spaced, giving the defenders in the towers a shorter length of wall to cover.[43] The gate, between widely spaced towers, occurs on the west front at Conwy (1283), and it is indeed with Conwy and Harlech that the nearest parallel occurs. In both cases the towers are thrust out from the curtain walls (as on the 1562 drawing) and at both castles the stair turrets rise a further ten feet above the wall-walk. However, in the planning of Harlech in May 1285 the emphasis was placed upon the compact gatehouse capable of withstanding a siege independent of the inner ward, and this theme was later developed at Beaumaris.

It is difficult to discuss the arrangements of the internal ranges when so little

---

[42] Salch (1979), 95, 1057, 1093 (note also La Hunaudaye (Côtes-du-Nord) of 1378 of pentagonal form: p. 909). Héliot (1947, 54) describes Veiel Hesdin (Pas-de-Calais).

[43] The plan at Holt could also be seen as a development from the plan of Goodrich, where the south wall is angled out to avoid the Norman keep. If the keep had not provided the additional high-level strength, then it would have been necessary to build a fifth corner tower to defend the angle and provide cover to the wall faces. Aberystwyth is not quite as regular in plan as Rhuddlan, having a single tower in the inner ward opposite the main gate and a double tower off-centre to the north in the outer ward.

evidence survives. The minimal provision of external windows (as shown by Norden) would accord with the arrangements at Rhuddlan and Harlech; the greater provision of windows (as shown on the 1562 drawing) would match the appearance of Conwy and probably Goodrich. The use of string-courses on the towers is also to be seen at Goodrich, while at Caernarfon a similar effect is produced by the use of bands of brown sandstone in contrast to the limestone ashlar.[44] The ranges provided the type of accommodation and the differentiation of function commonly encountered in royal and baronial castles. In general terms it is a duplicate of the west ward at Conwy, though there the Great Hall is on the right of the entrance while at Holt the hall is on the left of the entrance, but the sequence is very similar (Appendix). There is, however, a danger in trying to base too much argument upon evidence of use 250 years or more after the first planning, particularly when it was in royal hands but leased to minor gentry and occupied by constables and their deputies of the same rank or their attendants.[45]

The isolated chequer tower needs little further comment. It was set on a pinnacle of rock, about 30 ft square. Such stepping stones are particularly common in the Pyrenees, though the finest example is Sahyun in Syria.[46] Both Goodrich and Conwy have stone-built supports for the drawbridge, but a closer parallel is the Barbican Tower built by John de Warenne at Sandal. Here a semi-circular tower, similar in plan to the Lion Tower at the Tower of London and to the barbican at Goodrich, embraces a sandstone base. This rock is carved out of the bailey in a manner precisely similar to that in which Holt castle is carved out of the river cliff; in some places the walls sit on a rock-cut shelf, but usually a skirt of ashlar wraps protectively around the base of the barbican and around the flanking towers of the defended stair which climbs the slope of the motte at Sandal. It is tempting to see this not as the common currency of Edwardian military design but as the specific planning and design contribution of John de Warenne, the seventh earl. What was constructed in the 1270s at Sandal was developed in the 1280s at Holt. However, Earl John did not act alone; his extensive travels and campaigns had made him aware of continental military developments. His service with both Henry III and Edward I in Wales had shown him the nature of the terrain and the type of guerrilla warfare at which the Welsh excelled. His close contact with the king and presumably with his master of works, James of St George, meant that he could construct at Holt a castle of compact design yet of considerable strength. It rivalled in compactness the east ward at Conwy and had in appearance a family likeness to Conwy

[44] It is possible that the artist of 1562 was influenced by the gatehouse at Harlech or wished to indicate the storeys within the ranges and towers. No string-courses are shown by Norden or the Bucks.

[45] After the death of Thomas, earl of Arundel, in 1415 the castle was not inhabited by a noble or royal household until Richard III granted Holt to Sir William Stanley in 1484; he held it until his execution in 1495. It is not known if it was refurbished for Henry, duke of Richmond (1516–18). Some repairs were carried out for Bishop Roland Lee, as president of the Council in the Marches of Wales, in 1538 with six fothers of lead being sent from the dissolved abbey of Basingwerk (*L. & P., Henry VIII*, 13.1, 231, no. 624, item 3), and window glass being taken from Valle Crucis Abbey (PRO C 1/1108, mem. 25–27: case of 1544–47).

[46] Boase (1967), 48–51; see also Msailha (pp. 46–47).

and Harlech, just as Henry de Lacy's Denbigh and Richard de Burgh's North-burgh—i.e. Greencastle (Co. Donegal)—had a close relationship to Caernarfon.

This compactness may also be seen as a personal architectural development already being attempted on John de Warenne's other castles. There is no evidence from Reigate, but at Castle Acre the hall-keep was abandoned in favour of the ranges in the lower ward. At Conisbrough the keep received no alterations, but there was rebuilding of the hall and supporting domestic buildings in the bailey. At Lewes, there were additional polygonal towers added to the keep, but it was situated apart from the bailey. Finally, at Sandal there was consider-able rebuilding: the keep was completed in stone, the barbican was created in the bailey, new courtyard lodgings and a great hall were built and an impres-sive defended staircase rose from the barbican to the summit of the motte. Many of the ideas first seen at Sandal find their consummation at Holt.[47]

This account of Holt castle has attempted to make sense of conflicting informa-tion. If one examines only the early elevation drawings the problems seem insur-mountable, but by also using the later artists' views the relationship of the various buildings is made clear. The combination of the earliest plan and a modern survey has shown the accuracy of the former. It is by utilizing fully all the types of evidence, however diverse and apparently contradictory, that the castle at Holt can be seen as one of the innovative designs of the Edwardian period. Only clearance and excavation will reveal more of the structure, but the forces of destruction and decay have already reduced this once impressive edifice to a bramble-covered and ivy-shrouded ruin far removed from the splen-dour evoked by its proud name of Chastellion.[48]

APPENDIX (Fig. 24)

An attempt has been made to present the use of the ranges and the development of the units as in Faulkner.[49] However, there are many uncertainties on the upper floor. It may be assumed that each tower contained a lodgings room on the ground floor and on the upper floor, with a fireplace and a privy at each level. There may have been additional privies in the wall thickness in some of the major chambers. The external stairs in the courtyard ($\triangle \triangle \triangle$) may only have provided communication from the cour-tyard to the parapet roof for defensive purposes, but it is more likely that they served three distinct suites of lodgings. The only other recorded stair direct from courtyard to 'ground' floor led to the Great Hall.

---

[47] They also herald the inventive plans of Poitiers (Vienne) and Caerlaverock, based on a triangle, and the compact planning of Wardour, based on a hexagon (Morley 1981, 111–13).

[48] 'Vegetation has fastened all over the castle, its battlements and towers; large sycamores have taken root in the halls, and spread their broad arms above the ruined roof; creeping plants hanging in huge festoons, ivy clinging to the windows and doors, and lichens everywhere clothing the stones, give this fine monument of the middle ages the appearance of a castle of moss and ivy.' This description of Msailha in 1844 (Boase (1967), 41–42) could almost as well apply to Holt today.

[49] Faulkner (1963).

118

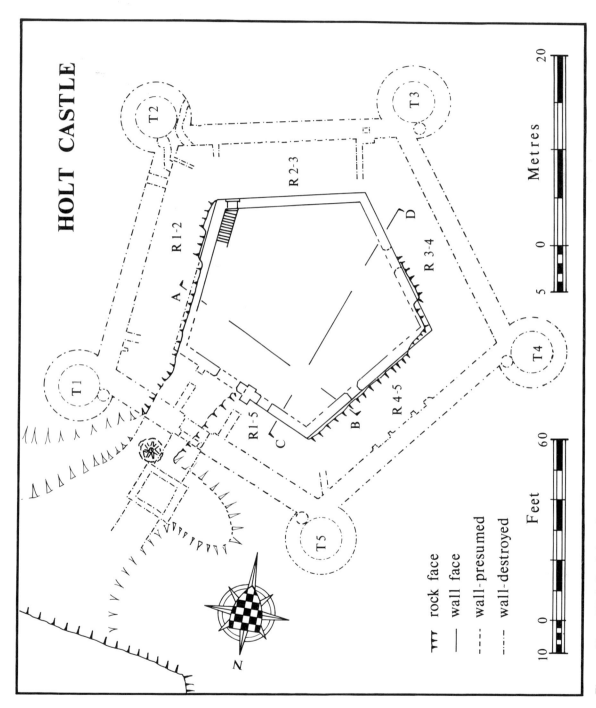

HOLT CASTLE

rock face
wall face
wall - presumed
wall - destroyed

Feet

Metres

N

Fig. 21   Plan of Holt Castle in 1983.

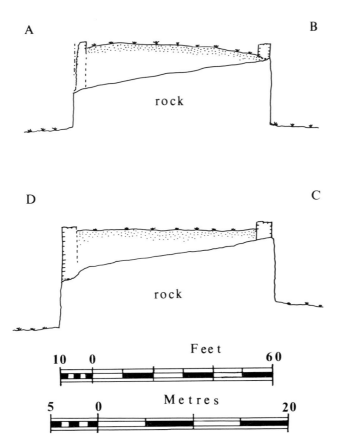

Fig. 22 Elevation (cross sections) of Holt Castle in 1983.

Fig. 23   Interpretation of walls shown on the Buck engraving of 1742.

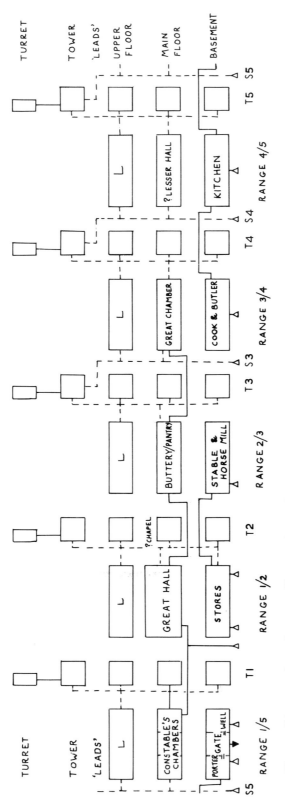

Fig. 24   Diagram of use of rooms to illustrate Appendix.

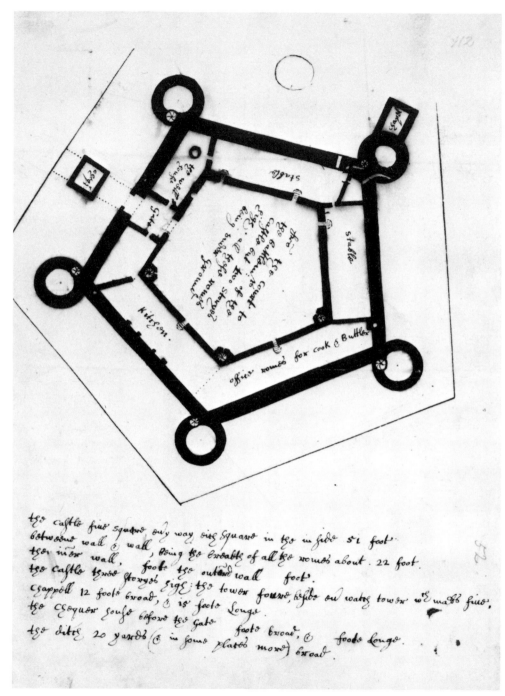

IV   Plan of Holt Castle in 1562 (BL Harl. MS 2073).

V   Elevation of Holt Castle in 1562 (BL Harl. MS 2073).

VI   Engraving of Holt Castle from the south-east in 1742 (NLW).

The Beaumaris Castle building account of 1295–1298

ARNOLD TAYLOR

THE building of Beaumaris, like the compilation of *Castellarium Anglicanum*, stands as the crowning achievement of a master. By 1295 James of St George had behind him a working lifetime of castle-building and, we may guess, was already in his sixties. It was only then that the defeat of Madog ap Llywelyn at last furnished the opportunity to carry into execution designs probably already long prepared and approved for the castle that would at once give Britain its most perfect example of symmetrical concentric planning and bring Anglesey into line with the other two shires of Gwynedd.[1] The supervision of its construction was henceforward to be Master James's principal preoccupation, interrupted only by the claims of serving the king in Scotland; though still sometimes referred to as 'master of the king's works in Wales', after 1295 he is more usually named simply as *magister operacionum de Bello Marisco*.

It so happens that there is preserved, on the Pipe Roll of the year 7 Edward II, a series of summary accounts for the first three-and-a-half years of the work, more detailed and more explicit than any that have survived for the corresponding initial phase of operations at either Conwy, Harlech or Caernarfon (Pl. VII). It is as if we had, which of course unfortunately we have not, a full record over a like period for one of the castles begun in 1283, giving the wages paid to the different categories of workmen, as well as details of the amount of money spent on plant and materials and their carriage to the site.

In the case of Caernarfon, for example, apart from a number of relatively minor payments recorded in surviving wardrobe books, almost all that we know, documentarily speaking, of the beginnings and earliest progress of the works is that their cost must in the main have been met from some unspecified share of the very large sum of £9,414 4s. 11d. issued by Master William of Louth, the keeper of the wardrobe during the period 22 March 1282–20 November 1284 'for the wages of masons, carpenters, diggers and others at Chester, Hope, Rhuddlan, Conway, Caernarvon, Criccieth, Harlech, West Wales and elsewhere',[2] and perhaps also from a share of other sums amounting to £1,756 13s. 4d. issued to William de Perton, Louth's deputy at Chester, *ad operaciones castrorum et villarum regis in Wallia*.[3] The importance of the Beaumaris account of 1295–98

---

[1] For the suggestion that the building may have been envisaged and the site chosen as early as August 1283, see Colvin (1963), **1**, 395; Taylor (1983), 57–58.

[2] Edwards (1946, 20), quoting PRO E 352/84, m.1.

[3] PRO E 372/136, m.33.

is that, when read in conjunction with details given in Walter of Winchester's and James of St George's progress report to the Exchequer in February 1296,[4] it shows, by analogy, just how much *could* be achieved in the opening ten months, not only summer but winter months as well, of a castle building campaign. The astonishing initial momentum revealed in the Beaumaris figures cannot but make one pause to consider once again whether the traditional location of the birth of Edward of Caernarvon in the Eagle Tower may after all not be as implausible as has lately been generally held.[5] The same interval of approximately ten summer and winter months separates the first mention (10 June 1283) of works being begun at Caernarfon and the prince's birth there on 25 April 1284, just two weeks after the king had regarded the castle as being already a fit setting for his ceremonial Easter crown-wearing. If it be accepted that the first thrust of the work was directed, as the evidence of the fabric suggests it may well have been,[6] to building the lower floors of the Eagle Tower to an occupiable standard, then it may be suggested, on the basis of what we know could be done in a comparable period at Beaumaris, that the attainment of this objective would surely not have been beyond the capability of a comparable labour force working under identical direction. May this not indeed perhaps have been the most laudable of the services yet performed by Master James, for which the king was rewarding him when, six months later, at Caernarfon, on 20 October 1284, his appointment as master of the works was confirmed for life and his wife Ambrosia was accorded the rare privilege of a future widow's pension.[7]

Thus, the Beaumaris account of 1295–98 seems to merit publication *in extenso*, not only because of its intrinsic interest for architectural and economic historians, but also because it gives rise to thoughts like these about other castles whose earliest beginnings lack similar documentation. In the light of it, Richard Coeur de Lion's seemingly incredible feat of building Château Gaillard in a mere two years perhaps begins to become a little less incomprehensible.[8]

The account is here given in translation only; except, however, for the omission of much of the 'common form' of the Latin original, it is given in full. Thus, expenditure on the naval patrol in the summer of 1295, and on other such non-works items as the pay of the castle garrison, is necessarily included, as Walter of Winchester saw fit to reckon it as part of his outlay of the moneys he received *ad constructionem castri de Bello Marisco in Wallia de novo facti*. The inclusion of such items here, in the text and in Table 4, as against their omission from the table of Beaumaris expenditure in Sir Goronwy Edwards's *Castle-building*

[4] PRO E 101/5/18/XI. Original printed in Edwards (1946), 80–81, and in translation in Colvin (1963), **1**, 398–99.

[5] Johnstone (1946), 8 and note; Peers (1915–16), 5; Taylor (1950); Taylor (1983), 14–15.

[6] *Alone of all the towers*, the Eagle Tower 'appears to have been built complete from front to rear (i.e. with its sides towards the courtyard and its external sides built contemporaneously) *from the first*' (author's italics), whereas the other first-period towers along the south and east sides of the castle had the lower portions of their outward-facing walls built before the parts facing towards the courtyard (RCAM (1960), 127).

[7] *Cal. Pat. R. 1281–1292*, 137.

[8] For the building of Château Gaillard, see Powicke (1913), 111–17 and 204–06.

in Wales and from the table in the official guide reproduced as Table 5, accounts for some of the discrepancies between the various sets of figures given in these several sources.

As is well known, the hopes and promise of 1295–96 were destined to be unfulfilled and Beaumaris was never completed. The great inner towers never rose to their proper height above the curtains, nor were the turrets which give the other castles their distinctive skyline ever built. Yet Master James must have seen them from the first as the culmination of his last grand design, a design we need not doubt was to be as majestic in elevation as it is striking on plan. Great, therefore, is our debt to Terry Ball for giving us so fair an idea of what must have been the vision of the master's mind (Pl. VIII).

TEXT:

> *PRO E 372/158 (Pipe Roll, 7 Edward II), rot. 48.*

ACCOUNT OF WALTER OF WINCHESTER, clerk, of moneys received from the wardrobe of the lord king by the hands of divers persons, and of other receipts by the same Walter in divers years, as appears below, both in supplies and money, for the construction of the castle of Beaumaris in Wales, newly made by command of King Edward son of King Henry, from the 18th day of April in the 23rd year of his reign [1295] to the feast of St Michael next following [29 Sept. 1295], and thenceforward to the same feast of St Michael in the 26th year [1298], viz. for half of the 23rd year and the whole of all the three years following, by writ under the great seal of the king that now is [Edward II], directed to the lieutenant of the treasurer and barons [of the Exchequer], in these words:

> Edward, &c., to the lieutenant of his treasurer and barons of the exchequer. Walter of Winchester, clerk, has shown unto us that when, long ago [*quondam*], the lord Edward our father, sometime king of England, had deputed the same Walter by word of mouth to make the payments for the works of the castle of Beaumaris in Wales, and for the wages of the men then dwelling together in the garrison of the same castle for the time in which they were in the garrison, and likewise for the wages of Henry de Lathom and of divers mariners assigned with the same Henry at the same time by our father himself to keep the sea between Snowdon and Anglesey, and also to build [*faciendum*] the walls of the town of Caernarvon, lately thrown down [*dirrutos*] in the Welsh war; and although the same Walter fulfilled the tasks thus enjoined to him, and offered himself before you in the said exchequer there to render to you his account thereof, nevertheless because the aforesaid Walter had no commission in writing from our father himself to do the premises you have hitherto deferred admitting him to render his account aforesaid before you in the said exchequer and have further postponed his doing the things pertaining to this account. And because we wish what is just to be done to the same Walter in this matter, we command you to hear before you in the said exchequer the same Walter's account of both the receipts and the expenses and liveries made by him by reason of the premises, and to cause the same Walter to have due allowance as of right and according to the law and custom of the exchequer aforesaid, notwithstanding that the same Walter did not have any commission in the premises from our said father. Witness myself at Westminster the 1st day of December in the

7th year of the reign of King Edward son of King Edward. Enrolled on the Memoranda Roll under the *communia* of Michaelmas Term in the 7th year of the reign of the present king [1 Dec. 1313].

I. LAST HALF OF 23RD YEAR [18 April–29 Sept. 1295]
  (a) *Received*

		£	s.	d.
(i) From the king's wardrobe:				
By the hand of Philip de Everdon, then cofferer		300	00	00
By the hand of the same Sir Philip		600	00	00
By the hand of William de Dancastr', citizen of Chester		1,000	00	00
By the hand of John de Burwell		1,330	6	8
By the hand of the said John	2,000 marks	[1,333	6	8]
By the hand of the same John	1,000 marks	[666	13	4]
By the hand of Philip de Douuegate		1,400	00	00
By the hand of the said Philip		120	00	7½
(ii) From the issues of Ireland:				
By the hand of Sir William de Sigons, constable of the castle of Aberconeway		500	00	00
By the hand of William de Sprotton, constable of the castle of Rotheland		[666	13	4]
Total received		7,917	00	7½

  (b) *Expended*
    (i) Wages of workmen:

	£	s.	d.
Wages of diggers [*fossatores*] digging trenches [*fossata*] and the moat [*motam*] for the site of the castle of Beaumaris and also for making an enclosing fence [*bretagium*] by precept of the king, and of other general labourers [*minuti operarii*] working there from 18 April in the 23rd year to Michaelmas next following, 164 days	1,468	12	00
Wages of quarriers breaking stone in the quarry	636	8	3
Wages of masons	1,004	16	10
Wages of carpenters	186	15	9
Wages of smiths	71	8	8
Wages of clerks and gangers [*vintenarii*] supervising the various workmen	99	6	2
Wages of shipmen [*marinarii*] carrying stone and timber from divers places by sea from 31 July	12	12	00
	3,479	19	8

    (ii) Purchase of materials, etc.:

	£	s.	d.
314 bends of iron bought for divers works	61	6	4
105,900 assorted nails	10	16	11
3,277 boards	7	2	9
Unworked timber [*in grosso meremio*]	31	14	6
8 carrats of lead	9	13	00
2,428 tuns of sea-coal for burning lime	60	13	00
640 quarters of charcoal bought for the king's forge fabricating iron there	5	11	2

	£	s.	d.
Hods, barrows, scaffolding and thatch for roofing the houses in the castle	11	00	10
4 barrels and 60 sheaves of steel	25	1	8
160 lbs. tin		18	5½
Cables, ropes and chains [*cynguli*]	2	12	6
Stone [*in petris grossis*] bought at divers times and places	443	14	3
Pitch		6	8
Brushwood [*busca*] for burning lime		18	2
Burnt lime		8	4
42 mason's axes for cleaving stone		15	2
	672	13	8½

(iii) Cost of carriage:

Carriage of stone, brushwood, sea-coal, etc. 2,128 11 8½

(iv) Naval patrol:

Wages of Sir Henry de Lathom and 95 sailors keeping the sea between Snaudon' and Anglesye in the king's barges 18 April to 17 July, 90 days, Sir Henry de Lathom taking 2s. a day for himself and 6d. a day for each of 4 master mariners in the aforesaid barges, and 3d. a day for each of 91 men in the said barges, with the wages of John Frere and 19 fellow crossbowmen, John Frere taking 6d. and the 19 others 4d. 151 2 6

(v) 'Task' work:

For divers operations worked *ad tascam* 221 9 4

(vi) Garrison:

Wages of William de Felton, esquire-at-arms and constable of the aforesaid castle, and of 22 fellow guards dwelling together with him, with their horses and arms, in the garrison of the aforesaid castle, 1 May to Michaelmas, 152 days @ 12d. a day each 129 00 8

Wages of Adam de Haskayt, esquire-at-arms, and of 100 foot archers dwelling with him in the garrison of the aforesaid castle, 12d. a day for himself, 4d. a day for each of 5 twentymen, and 2d. a day for each of 95 archers 194 5 00

Wages of Simon de Cremplesham and his 19 fellow crossbowmen staying together in the aforesaid garrison, 6d. a day for himself, and 4d. each for his 19 fellows 52 12 44

Wages of Master William the artiller and his servant, staying in the garrison aforesaid for making and repairing crossbows, quarells and other necessaries, 9d. a day for himself and his servant 5 15 6

	£	s.	d.
Wages of Master Richard the engineer and Master Thomas the engineer, esquires-at-arms, repairing engines as required [*reparancium ingenia per vices*], 1 May–10 July, 71 days inclusive, the one taking 12*d.*, the other 9*d.* a day	6	4	3
Total wages of garrison 18 April–29 Sept. 1295	387	17	9
Total of sums expended, 18 April–29 Sept. 1295	7,041	14	8½
And he owes	875	5	11

II. First half of 24th year [29 Sept. 1295–7 May 1296]

Account of the same Walter of divers receipts, payments made and expenses incurred on the works of the aforesaid castle for the 30 weeks from Michaelmas to 7 May 24 Edward I [1295–96], on which day the payments to the workmen partly failed [deficiebant in parte], as appears below.

(a) *Received*

	£	s.	d.
(i) From the king's wardrobe:			
By the hand of Roger de Walton, king's sergeant	400	00	00
By the hand of Geoffrey le Hurer 1,000 marks	[666	13	4]
By the hand of Peter de Aulton, king's clerk	400	00	00
By the hand of the same Peter	400	00	00
By the hand of John of Gloucester and Alan de Waleton', king's sergeants	1,000	00	00
(ii) From the issues of North Wales:			
From Sir Hugh de Leominster, then chamberlain of North Wales	300	00	00
Total received	3,166	13	4

(b) *Expended*

	£	s.	d.
(i) Wages of workmen:			
Wages of men making ditches round the castle, and of other labourers [*minuti operarii*], from Michaelmas to 7 May, viz. for 30 weeks	534	1	4
Wages of quarriers breaking stones in the quarry	89	16	10
Wages of masons	612	6	4
Wages of carpenters	63	19	2
Wages of smiths	65	12	8
Wages of shipmen carrying stone, timber and divers other necessaries by sea to the works	37	19	6
Wages of clerks and gangers supervising the workmen	49	18	00
Wages of a plumber and his mate working in the king's plumbery for 21 days @ 8*d.* a day		14	00
	1,454	7	10
(ii) Purchase of materials, etc.:			
Stone [*in petris grossis*] bought in divers places	105	15	8¼
1,343 boards bought for the works	3	15	6
Timber [*in grosso meremio*]	1	0	6
Scaffolds, barrows, hods, poles, straw, thatch	7	14	1¾
240 tuns of sea-coal for burning lime	6	0	0

	£	*s.*	*d.*
113 quarters of charcoal for the king's forge		18	10
4 barrels of steel, each containing 106 sheaves	21	7	6
Ropes, cables, chains and small cords	6	2	6
117,000 nails, bought at various prices	8	9	8
12½ bends of iron, each bend containing 24 pieces	1	13	9
24 carrats of lead	31	4	0
Pitch		5	7½
	194	7	8½

(iii) Cost of carriage:

Carriage of brushwood, timber, stone boards, lead, etc.   403 17 10½

(iv) Garrison:

Wages of William de Felton, esquire-at-arms, constable of the aforesaid castle, and of his 10 fellows in the garrison, @ 12*d.* a day each   118 16 00

Wages of William Moigne and his 19 fellow cross-bowmen in the garrison, @ 4*d.* a day each   72 00 00

Wages of Adam de Clogh and his 99 fellow archers in the garrison, 5 @ 4*d.* and 95 @ 2*d.* a day each   189 00 00

Wages of Master William the artiller and his assistant [*garcio*], repairing and manufacturing [*ad reparandum et de novo faciendum*] crossbows, bows, arrows, etc., @ 9*d.* a day   8   2 00

Wages of Adam the watchman and John his fellow, Thursday 1 April to 6 May, 36 days @ 8*d.* a day   1   4 00

                                                   389   2 00

Total of sums expended, 29 Sept. 1295–7 May 1296   2,441 15   5

III. Last half of 24th year [7 May–29 Sept. 1296]

Account of the same Walter de Wynton' of divers receipts, payments and expenses made by him about the construction of the castle of Beaumaris aforesaid from 7 May in the aforesaid 24th year to the feast of St Michael next following [29 Sept. 1296], within which time the payments to certain workmen were deficient [deficiebant], as is contained below.

(a) *Received*   £   *s.*   *d.*

(i) Moneys paid to divers workmen working about the works aforesaid in the same period   742   2   2½

(ii) Payments made to divers merchants for various necessaries purchased for the works for the construction of the aforesaid castle by the hand of the chamberlain of the wardrobe of the lord king Edward son of King Henry and of the lord king that now is, at divers times in divers years, as is contained in the book called 'le Peyll' in the treasury of the king's receipt   [No figure given]

Total received   742   2   2½
(*Summa recepte*)

	£	s.	d.
(b) *Expended*			
(i) Wages of workmen:			
Wages of divers diggers digging ditches around the aforesaid castle, from 7 May to Michaelmas, 21 weeks	789	17	4
Wages of quarriers breaking stone in the quarry	32	13	4
Wages of masons	29	13	10
Wages of smiths	54	5	0
Wages of boatmen carrying divers things by sea with the king's barges	25	14	6
Wages of clerks and twentymen guarding and supervising the aforesaid workmen	40	19	4
	973	3	4
(ii) Purchase of materials:			
446 tuns of sea-coal for burning lime	11	3	0
200 bends of iron @ 4s. each	40	0	0
35 carrats of lead @ 26s. each	45	10	0
700 scaffold poles	1	16	0
	98	9	0
(iii) Cost of carriage:			
Carriage and porterage of charcoal from Holston' to the castle by sea, and from the sea into the castle	36	4	9½
(iv) Garrison:			
Wages of William de Felton, esquire-at-arms and constable, and of his 7 companions staying in the castle with their horses and arms, @ 12d. a day each	58	16	0
Wages of William Pilard [*sic; rectius* 'Pikard'] and his 19 fellow-crossbowmen, @ 4d. a day each	44	00	0
Wages of Stephen of Worcester and his 99 fellow foot-soldiers, 5 @ 4d. and 95 @ 2d. a day each	82	5	0
Wages of Master William the artiller and his assistant, for making and mending crossbows and quarells in the castle, 9d. a day	5	10	3
	190	11	3
(v) 'Task' work:			
Robert of Preston and his fellow boatmen, for breaking and carrying flagstones [*petras velosas*] from the quarry by sea, taking 'at task' for the tun-load 2d., viz. for 19,706 tuns	164	4	4
Alan of Kirkeby and his fellow boatmen, for breaking and carrying maylloun stones [*petras de Maylloun*] from the quarry by sea to the castle, taking 'at task' for the tun-load 2d., viz. for 12,877 tuns of stone	107	6	2
Ralf of Ocleye, for firing and burning 6 kilns of lime, @ 40s. the kiln	12	0	0

	£	s.	d.
Reginald of Torvey [Thurueye], for burning 5 kilns of lime 'at task', @ 30s. the kiln	7	10	0
Walter le Grai, for burning 4 kilns of lime 'at task', @ 13s. 4d. the kiln	2	13	4
William of Sutton, for porterage of 6 kilns of lime *ut supra* from the kiln to the castle, @ 13s. 4d. the kiln 'at task'	4	0	0
To the same William, for porterage of 5 kilns 'at task', @ 10s. the kiln	2	10	0
William of Holywell and his associates for porterage of 32,583 tuns of stone from the sea to the castle 'at task', @ 1d. per tun	135	15	3
John of Denbigh, carpenter, for making a latrine projecting over the sea, 'at task', for the workmen	5	0	0
John Penne and John Fraunceys, for 6,000 free-stones hewn [*fractis*] at the quarry of Portwynge [?Porthaethwy] 'at task', @ 8s. a hundred	24	0	0
William de Hou and John Fraunceys, for 8,000 freestones hewn *ut supra* 'at task', @ 8s. a hundred	32	0	0
John of Alverton', for 2,200 freestones hewn *ut supra* 'at task', @ 8s. a hundred	8	16	0
William of Thornton [Thorinton'], for making 2 chimneys 'at task', @ 40s. the chimney	4	0	0
Total of sums expended, 7 May to Michaelmas in the abovesaid 24th year	2,323	8	5½

He has outstanding £1,581 6s. 3d. owed to divers merchants for various purchases for the aforesaid works, and also to divers workmen for their wages there for the same period, whose names appear in a roll which the same Walter has delivered into the treasury.

IV. 25TH YEAR [29 Sept. 1296–29 Sept. 1297]

(a) *Received*

	£	s.	d.
(i) From the king's wardrobe: By the hand of William de Felton	160	0	0
(ii) From the issues of the Twelfth of the county of Salop: By the hand of Sir Robert Corbet and Master Adam Gest, collectors of the Twelfth in the same year	460	0	0
Total received	620	0	0

(b) *Expended*

	£	s.	d.
(i) Wages of workmen: Wages of masons	123	10	11
Wages of carpenters	31	7	2
Wages of smiths	22	0	6
Wages of plumber and mate @ 8d. a day	8	15	4
Wages of labourers [*minuti operarii*]	70	11	0

	£	s.	d.
Wages of a man guarding sea-coal outside the castle at night		11	8
Wages of twentymen guarding the workmen	2	5	4
	259	1	11

(ii) Purchase of materials:

	£	s.	d.
Stone [*in petris grossis*] bought for the works	19	6	3
Scaffolding, poles, barrows, etc.		3	6
20 lbs. tin		3	4
Brushwood for lime-burning		2	8
Cables and ropes	1	1	7
1,000 nails		1	0
20 carrats of lead	25	0	0
	45	18	4

(iii) Cost of carriage:

	£	s.	d.
Carriage of brushwood, stone, etc.	25	12	8

(iv) Garrison:

	£	s.	d.
Wages of William de Felton, esquire-at-arms, and his 7 associates, @ 12d. a day each	100	0	0
Wages of Milo de la Haye and his 19 fellow cross-bowmen, @ 4d. a day each	96	11	5
Wages of an artiller and his assistant, repairing crossbows and making bolts for them, @ 9d. for them both	13	13	0
Wages of Adam the watchman and John his associate, keeping watch in the castle for 125 days from Michaelmas to 2 February, @ 4d. a day each, and for 239 days from 2 February to Michaelmas following @ 3d. a day each	10	2	10
	220	7	3

Total expended £552 8s. 1d.;* and he owes £67 11s. 11d. and he answers below.

*The total expenditure as recorded under the above four heads amounts to £551 0s. 2d., suggesting inadvertent omission by clerical error, during compilation of the enrolled account, of an item of expenditure amounting to £1 19s. 11d.

V. 26TH YEAR [29 Sept. 1297–29 Sept. 1298].

(a) *Received*

	£	s.	d.
(i) From the issues of the county of Chester, by the hand of Reginald de Gray, then justice of the same county	326	0	0
(ii) From the defaults of workmen at different times throughout the whole period	40	5	6
(iii) From Hugh de Leominster, then chamberlain of North Wales, in flour, ale and other victuals given to the workmen instead of their wages [*sic solutis operariis ibidem pro stipendiis et vadiis eorundem*]	18	15	9
Total received	385	1	3

(b) *Expended*

(i) Wages of workmen:

	£	s.	d.
Wages of masons throughout the year, sometimes many, sometimes fewer [*per unum annum integrum aliquando plures aliquando pauciores*]	80	9	1
Wages of carpenters	24	8	11
Wages of smiths	10	3	10
Wages of plumber and mate	5	12	4
Wages of diggers and other minor workmen	13	6	8
Wages of twentymen supervising and guarding the workmen		16	0
	134	10	10

(ii) Purchase of materials:

	£	s.	d.
Stone	21	7	$2\frac{1}{2}$
36,000 nails bought at varying prices	2	2	$0\frac{1}{2}$
23 planks and 112 boards	3	14	0
Timber bought at varying prices	5	4	0
Cables and ropes	3	5	3
30 carrats of lead	37	10	0
Brushwood for lime-burning		10	2
23 sheaves of steel	1	3	0
Scaffold poles	1	13	11
Tin and pitch		19	10
Hods and barrows		15	0
	78	4	5

(iii) Carriage and 'task' work:

	£	s.	d.
Carriage of stone, timber and the other things abovesaid by sea and by land	23	8	$10\frac{1}{2}$
120 joists felled in the wood, carried by sea and land to the castle, trimmed [*carpentatis*] and placed in position [*positis in opere in eodem castro*], @ 3s. 4d. per joist 'at task'	20	0	0
4 great beams [*magnis someris*], ut supra, @ 6s. 8d. each	1	6	8
54 large joists, felled as above, @ 4s. each	10	16	0
3 perches of planking, *ut supra*, @ 10s. a perch	1	10	0
	57	1	$6\frac{1}{2}$

(iv) Garrison:

	£	s.	d.
Wages of William de Felton, esquire-at-arms, with his associates in the castle garrison, sometimes more, sometimes fewer	36	2	0
Wages of Thomas le Warner and 19 fellow crossbowmen	56	15	6
Wages of William the artiller and his assistant	9	17	0
Wages of 2 watchmen	4	1	0
Wages of Richard of Westminster and his fellow engineer, @ 6d. a day each	4	17	0
	111	12	6
Total expended	385	15	$3\frac{1}{2}$

	£	s.	d.
And he owes	3	5	11½
And he owes of the remainder of his account for the last half of the 23rd year	875	5	11
And he owes of the remainder of his account for the first half of the 24th year	724	18	11
And he owes of the remainder of his account for the whole of the 25th year	67	11	11
Total sum owing	1,671	2	8½

Let him be allowed £170 10s. 4½d. which he laid out on the repair and making good of the walls of the town of Carnarvan, by virtue of the aforesaid writ as noted above, as appears below in his account of the costs and expenses of the aforesaid walls, leaving his debt at £1,500 12s. 4½d. Let him also be allowed £118 15s. 9d. which he says he paid to divers merchants for divers things bought from them for the construction of the aforesaid castle, and also to divers workmen there in money and in divers victuals, in part payment of a debt of £1,581 6s. 3d. in which the king was bound to them, as is contained in the account of the aforesaid sums allocated from 7th May to 29th September in the 24th year. And he owes £1,381 16s. 7¼d. And he answers (i.e. he renders account) for this on the 9th roll under 'London'.

Table 3. Summary of receipts and expenditure from the commencement of the works at Beaumaris Castle on 18 April 1295 to 29 September 1298, as recorded on the Pipe Roll of 7 Edward II (E 372/158, rot. 48).

	A 18 Apr.–29 Sept. 1295			B 29 Sept. 1295 –7 May 1296			C 7 May–29 Sept. 1296			D 29 Sept. 1296 –29 Sept. 1297			E 29 Sept. 1297 –29 Sept. 1298			A–E 18 Apr. 1295 –29 Sept. 1298		
	£	s.	d.	£	s.	d.	£	s.	d.	£	s.	d.	£	s.	d.	£	s.	d.
RECEIPTS	7,917	0	7½	3,166	13	4	742	2	2½	620	0	0	385	1	3	12,830	17	5
EXPENSES																		
(i) Wages of workmen																		
1. *Fossatores* (diggers)	1,468	12	0	534	1	4	789	17	4	70	11	0	13	6	8	2,876	8	4
2. Quarriers	636	8	3	89	16	10	32	13	4							758	18	5
3. Masons [9]	1,004	16	10	612	6	4	29	13	10	123	10	11	80	9	1	1,850	17	0
4. Carpenters	186	15	9	63	19	2				31	7	2	24	8	11	306	11	0
5. Smiths	71	8	8	65	12	8	54	5	0	22	0	6	10	3	10	223	10	8
6. Clerks and *vintenarii* (section leaders)	99	6	2	49	18	0	40	19	4	2	5	4		16	0	193	4	10
7. Plumbers					14	0				8	15	4	5	12	4	15	1	8
8. Boatmen	12	12	0	37	19	6	25	14	6							76	6	0
'shipping stone and timber											11	8	4	1	0	4	12	8
9. Watchmen																		
(ii) *Task work*	672	13	8½	194	7	8½	98	9	0	45	18	4	78	4	5	1,089	13	2
(iii) *Purchase of necessaries*	2,128	11	8½	403	17	10½	36	4	9½	25	12	8	23	8	10½	2,617	15	11
(iv) *Costs of carriage*	151	2	6													151	2	6
(v) *Wages of naval patrol*	387	17	9	289	2	0	190	11	3	220	7	3	107	11	6	1,195	9	9
(vi) *Wages of garrison*	221	9	4				509	14	1				33	12	8	764	16	1
I. Total of (i) 1–9	3,479	19	8	1,454	7	10	973	3	4	259	1	11	138	17	10	6,305	10	7
II. Total (ii)–(vi)	3,561	15	0	887	7	7	834	19	1½	291	18	3	242	17	5½	5,818	17	5
SUM TOTAL	7,041	14	8	2,341	15	5	1,808	2	5½	551	0	2	381	15	3½	12,124	8	0

9 Not including Master James of St George's wages of 3s. a day (cf. *Liber Quotid.*, 102).

Table 4. Summary of quantities and costs of building materials, plant, tools, fuel, etc., specified 29 September 1298.

	A 18 Apr.–29 Sept. 1295		A £ s. d.			B 29 Sept. 1295–7 May 1296		B £ s. d.		
I *Building materials*			£	s.	d.			£	s.	d.
a Stone		x	443	14	3			105	15	8¼
b Lime				8	4					
c Timber			38	17	3			1	0	6
d Nails		105,900	10	16	11	117,000		8	9	8
e Iron		314 bends	61	6	4	12½ bends		1	13	9
f Lead		8 carrats	9	13	0	24 carrats		31	4	0
Total I			564	16	1			148	3	7¼
II *Plant and equipment*										
a Scaffolding, hods, barrows, etc.			11	0	10			7	14	1¾
b Ropes, cords, chains, etc.			2	12	6			6	2	6
c Masons' axes		42		15	2					
d Steel		4 barrels	25	1	8	4 barrels		21	7	11
		60 sheaves				(each of 106				
e Tin		160 lbs.		18	5½	sheaves)				
Total II			40	8	7½			35	4	6¾
III *Fuel*										
a Seacoal		2,428 tuns	60	13	0	240 tuns		6	0	0
b Charcoal		615 qrs.	5	11	2	113 qrs.			18	10
c Brushwood				18	2					
d Pitch				6	8				5	7½
Total III			67	9	0			7	4	5½
Sum total			672	13	8½			190	12	7½

x Quantity not stated; on the basis of the price (£272 0s. 6d.) paid for 32,583 tuns of specified types of stone in the following year (column C'), it is likely to have been of the order of 50,000 tuns. For the relationship between 'tun' as a measure of shipping capacity and 'ton' as a measure of weight, see *Shorter O.E.D.*, *s.n.* 'ton'.

in E 372/158 as having been purchased for the Beaumaris works between 18 April 1295 and

	C 7 May–29 Sept. 1296			D Sept. 1296–Sept. 1297			E Sept. 1297–Sept. 1298			A–E Apr. 1295–Sept. 1298			
	£	s.	d.	£	s.	d.	£	s.	d.		£	s.	d.
Stone:	164	14	4	19	6	3	21	7	2½	**I**			
19,706										a	926	19	10¾
tuns *petrarum*							42	10	8	b	17	0	8
*velosarum**				1,000 1		0				c	82	8	5
12,877	107	6	2				36,000 2	2	0½	d	21	9	7½
tuns *petrarum*				20 crts. 25	0	0	30 crts. 37	10	0	e	103	0	1
*de Maylloun**				44	7	3	103	9	11	f	148	17	0
16,200	64	16	0							*Total I*	1,299	15	8¼
freestones													
fract' ad quarrer' de													
*Portwynge**	336	16	6										
Lime:	16	12	4										
Iron:										**II**			
200 bends	40	0	0		3	6	2	8	11	a	23	3	4¾
Lead:													
35 carrats	45	10	0	1	1	7	3	5	3	b	13	1	10
Total I	438	18	10							c		15	2
							23 sheaves 1	3	0	d	47	12	7
Scaffolding,													
etc.:	1	16	0	20 lb. 3		4		19	10	e	2	1	7½
Total II	1	16	0	1	8	5	7	17	0	*Total II*	86	14	7¼
Seacoal:										**III**			
446 tuns	11	3	0							a	77	16	0
										b	6	10	0
					2	8		10	2	c	1	11	0
										d		12	3½
Total III	11	3	0		2	8		10	2	*Total III*	86	9	3½
	451	17	10	45	18	4	111	17	1	*Sum total*	1,472	19	7

* Supplied 'at task' and cost therefore included under that head in Table 3.

Table 5. The rate of works expenditure at Beaumaris Castle between 1295 and 1330.

	Total recorded expenditure £ s. d.		Average weekly expenditure £ s. d.	
First 24 weeks, 10 Apr.–29 Sept. 1295	6,502 14 3		270 18 11	
Next 52 weeks, 30 Sept. 1295–29 Sept. 1296	4,185 10 7½		80 9 10	
Next 52 weeks, 30 Sept. 1296–29 Sept. 1297	330 12 11	(1295–96)	6 7 2	(140 12 8)
Next 52 weeks, 30 Sept. 1297–29 Sept. 1298	270 2 9½		5 3 10	
		(1296–98)		(75 1 11½)
Total, first 3½ years	11,289 0 9*	Average w.e., first 3½ years	62 14 4	
1306–1330, *Total, last 25 years*	3,055 8 1	Average w.e., last 25 years	3 2 8	
Total, 1295–1330	£14,344 8 10			

*excludes £100 allocated in 1300

VII   Beaumaris Castle. Expenditure by Walter of Winchester, clerk of works, 18 April–29 Sept. 1295 (Pipe Roll, 7 Edward II, E.372/158, rot. 48).

VIII   View of Beaumaris Castle drawn by Terry Ball as it might have looked if finished.

The chapel at Raglan Castle and its paving-tiles

J. M. LEWIS

TO see David King accoutred for a castle survey with clip-board, ranging-pole, and scaling-ladder (albeit collapsible and of aluminium) is to see castle-study brought to the verge of a military exercise, and to be reminded that its main aim must always be a greater understanding of 'the disciplines of war'. It is, therefore, with some diffidence that I offer him an essay on chapels and floor-tiles, topics that must appear hopelessly effete in military company. I take reassurance from the fact that he is a man of sound common sense, who will see that it is best to give what one is best able. This essay is offered him in sincere regard for his achievement in castle-studies, particularly in Wales.

Among the finds made at Raglan in the course of the clearance work carried out by the Ministry of Works in the years following World War II was a collection of fragmentary floor-tiles, which has recently been deposited by the duke of Beaufort on long-loan in the National Museum of Wales.[1] It appears that most if not the whole of the collection was found in the area of the chapel, where the original floor level was restored and turfed in the summer of 1947.[2] The tiles are of importance in several respects. In general they enable us to reconstruct in the mind's eye something of the internal furnishing of a building now almost completely destroyed. They also cast further light on a number of more specific questions: they suggest a continuity in internal planning between the thirteenth-century castle and the fortified fifteenth-century palace that replaced it; they indicate a date in the late 1450s or soon after for the internal decoration of the chapel belonging to this building; they illustrate the radical alteration in building-style that went with the building of the Long Gallery and the remodelling of the central range in the later sixteenth century. Before proceeding to

---

[1] Accession no. 83.32H.

[2] Cf. *Raglan Castle: chargehands' reports Dec. 1938–Dec. 1974* (Welsh Office: Ancient Monuments Branch W 118). Tile fragments did not count as reportable finds and consequently there is no mention of them in the reports, but a selection was clearly put aside. Workmen engaged in the work, when questioned in 1983, remembered finding quantities of tile fragments including the distinctive blue and white maiolica, and confirmed that these and the inlaid earthenware types came from the chapel area. One fragment of Malvern tile, however, bears an earlier adhesive label with an indecipherable inscription. This may come from nineteenth-century clearance of which there may have been a good deal; e.g. 'some curious specimens of encaustic tiles' are mentioned among the debris from 'the dungeons' recovered by Mr Cuxson, the new 'Keeper of the Castle' in 1858 (*The Merlin and Silurian*, 3 April).

these matters, however, it will be necessary to consider the surviving architectural remains of the chapel, such as they are.

THE CHAPEL

The chapel at Raglan Castle adjoined the hall on its south-west side, thus occupying an important site on the north-east side of the Fountain Court (Fig. 31, p. 168). Its remains exhibit little to identify it as a chapel, but its identity is not in doubt, resting on a seventeenth-century description of the castle which survives among the Beaufort manuscripts.[3] It was orientated south-east/north-west and measured approximately 40 ft (12.5 m) by 15 ft (4.5 m). Its north-east wall, which it shares with the hall, survives to full height, but the other three have been reduced to foundation level (Pl. IX). The chapel has been interpreted as belonging to the second period of building, carried out by Sir William Herbert, 1st earl of Pembroke, who held the castle from his father's death in 1445 until his execution after the battle of Edgecote in 1469.[4] Its entrance must have been from the hall porch. The principal surviving features are the two bays of four-centred vaulting ribs springing from corbel heads, which are built partly into the blocking of one of the original window-openings of the hall. These ribs are all that now remain of the chapel's vaulted ceiling, which, to judge by the spacing of the buttresses, three out of four of which survive (Fig. 31, p. 168), would have extended for three square bays, leaving a somewhat wider bay at the west end. It will be suggested below that from the first this end probably contained a gallery approached by stairs from the body of the chapel. Underneath the central bay is a shallow recess in the wall, its back wall having three rows of more or less regular gaps in its surface masonry; it retains patches of a tough, buff-coloured mortar rendering, which also survives in patches beneath the stair, as well as on the hall-side of the wall. It is most unlikely that this recess was intended to house the altar, as Bradney suggested;[5] it seems more likely that its purpose was to enable a pew (perhaps one of an opposing pair) to be set back slightly to gain some extra width in what was a very narrow building. At the south-east corner there is a narrow window through to the hall.

To the left of the recess there is evidence for an alteration in the planning of the chapel in the form of a curving stair in ashlar work, rising towards the west end, which is deeply recessed into the thickness of the wall and cuts through the projected level of the vaulting. This implies the adoption of a flat ceiling in the chapel, and must be associated with the construction of the Long Gallery, for which Raglan was famed,[6] the beam-holes for whose joists and roof-timbers punctuate the wall above as far as the door in the south-east wall, which gave

[3] 'At the entrance of the Hall straight forward by the Chapel, 40 ft long on the left hand, was a large court... very remarkable... for the pleasant marble fountain in the midst thereof'. ('Description of Raglan Castle, copied from an old MS which was written soon after the destruction of the Castle by the Rebel Army in the year 1646', HMC (1891), 2).

[4] Taylor (1979), 9–13.

[5] Bradney (1896), 73.

[6] Taylor (1979), 14–16, 35–36.

access to the dining-room and private apartments. This radical transformation of the central block was the work of William Somerset, 3rd earl of Worcester (1548–89), the great Elizabethan courtier. It gave a special glory to the last half-century of the castle's life, which can only be dimly apprehended from the existing remains.[7]

The small size of the chapel—though it is not very much smaller than those at some royal houses, which are rarely longer, but sometimes wider—has been commented on with some justification.[8] Its floor area, however, probably does not reflect its true seating-capacity, for in all probability it would always have had an upper storey or gallery at its west end, evidence for which survives only from its final phase in the form of the wall-stair. The fashion for two-storey chapels may have been begun by Henry III; it certainly appears that they became fashionable at court in his reign. After his marriage in 1236 the refurbishing of chapels for the queen's use at Winchester and Windsor included the insertion of upper storeys,[9] and the same plan was adopted for the new timber chapel at Kempton (which was very much smaller than the chapel at Raglan, measuring a mere 30 ft by 12 ft).[10] The tradition of providing separate accommodation in the chapel of a castle for the lord and his family may have sprung from this courtly fashion. As well as providing appropriate seating for the family when attending services with their households, this accommodation often came to be used for private devotions, so that it became enclosed and furnished with an altar. There are records of such provision being made in the fifteenth century.[11] Separate access by stair or gallery from the private apartments was frequently provided, a factor that may from the first have encouraged their location at first floor level. Such private gallery-rooms were known as *closets*.[12] They seem normally to have been placed at the west end, overlooking the body of the chapel, whose east end they could share with the worshippers at floor level. Access from the closet down into the chapel is sometimes mentioned, and may have been a normal arrangement.[13]

There is ample evidence from the royal accounts for the provision of closets in chapels in the sixteenth century.[14] That some such arrangement existed at Raglan in Elizabethan times is indicated by the existence of the wall-stair. This could not have given direct access to the Long Gallery, for the level at which it ends is too low for it to have mastered the vault of the south porch of the hall. It must, therefore, have given access to a closet in a gallery at the west end of the chapel. Whether further access was provided to the Long Gallery

---

[7] The view from the north-west of the great half-octagonal tower that formed the termination of the Long Gallery gives the best impression of its former majesty: see especially a fine pencil drawing by Edward Blore (1787–1879), BL Add. MS 42035, f. 44.

[8] Grose (1785), 163, quoting the account of the castle given in Gilpin (1782), 48; Gardner (1915).

[9] Colvin (1963), **2**, 862, 867.

[10] Ibid., 965.

[11] Ibid., 887, 1000.

[12] See *O.E.D.* s. closet, 1b, 2b.

[13] Colvin (1963), **1**, 517; Colvin (1982), 81.

[14] E.g. Colvin (1982), 14, 41, 97, 116–17, 125.

above must remain a matter of conjecture; this, if it existed, could have been along the south-west side, now completely destroyed.

This formal arrangement, making special provision for the earl and his family, would have been entirely appropriate to the impression gained from a surviving account of the dining arrangements for the household in the castle's heyday before the Civil War,[15] which provides a comprehensive list of household officials arranged in hierarchy. From this two things become clear: that the chapel establishment consisted of more than one chaplain (one of them at the time being Sir Toby Matthew, the son of the archbishop of York, who had turned papist) and a 'Gentleman of the Chapel'; and that the chapel, when used for anything more formal than private devotions, would have been required to seat, with due regard for precedence and in appropriate comfort, between twenty and thirty people at the very least. For the earl and countess's households were large and highly organized, containing functionaries with the kind of names familiar today only in the ceremonial titles of royal servants, from the Steward of the House to the Master of the Fishponds; the entertainment of guests would also have been a frequent requirement.

A report of 1574 on Petworth House contains a description of the closet in the chapel: 'There is a closet having the door to it from the second turning of the... stair, wherein is iii windows whereof one partly glazed, the other unglazed and the third looketh into the great chapel'.[16] Access was from the king's chamber. At Raglan one can only be certain about the access from the chapel, perhaps by a stair on each side, as seems to have been the case at Eltham.[17] Although the structural evidence at Raglan dates from only the sixteenth century, it is reasonable to suppose that a similar arrangement existed there a century earlier. A passage in the will of the 1st earl of Pembroke, drawn up in 1469, seems to imply such an arrangement: in giving instructions for work to be carried out at Abergavenny Priory, where he wished to be buried close to his parents, he orders that the windows are to be 'glazed with the stories of the Passion of Christ and of the Nativity and of the Saints of mine that be in my closet at Raglan'.[18]

This then was the building which contained the tiles, to which evidence we must now turn.

THE PAVING-TILES

In the following catalogue NMW numbers refer to accession numbers at the National Museum of Wales, and BM numbers to design numbers in the British Museum catalogue.[19]

---

[15] Printed in Percy (1905), 403.
[16] Batho (1957), 7.
[17] See note 13.
[18] Cardiff *Herbert. Pros.*, f. 56.
[19] Eames (1980).

The tiles are easily divisible into three groups as follows:

	Number of fragments	Number of designs represented	Number of tiles represented
Wessex group	8	7	7
Malvern group	117	20	95
Netherlands maiolica group	10	3	10

WESSEX TILES 1–7 (Fig. 25)

The tiles are $5\frac{1}{2}$ in (140 mm) square and about $\frac{7}{8}$ in (21–24 mm) thick, and decorated with white inlaid designs of about $\frac{1}{16}$ in (2 mm) depth. They are of a fine, reddish-buff fabric, tending to fire grey under the surface glaze. The undersides, which are smooth, sometimes with a slight gloss, have four scoops for keying. The edges are slightly bevelled and concave.

Some of the tiles belong to repeating 4-tile designs (nos. 1, 2, 5, 7), though in practice they may all have been laid in square blocks of four, separated by plain borders, although no plain tiles are represented among the preserved fragments.

1. Cf. Tintern Abbey (NMW 32.376/8, 11);[20] BM 2767.
2. Cf. Tintern Abbey (NMW 19.214/3; 32. 376/30–2); Cleeve Abbey no. 6.[21]
3. Unidentified.
4. Cf. Tintern Abbey (NMW 32.376/51, 53–5);[22] BM 1979.
5. Cf. Tintern Abbey (NMW 32.376/56–7); BM 1966.
6. Unidentified, but one of the numerous Wessex series of animals within circles, cf. BM 1866–1877; Tintern Abbey (NMW 32.376/46, 48–50).[23]
7. Cf. Tintern Abbey (BM 1619); Cleeve Abbey no. 5. The arms have not been identified with certainty, but probably have no local significance at Raglan.

The designs of these tiles identify them as belonging to the series widely fashionable in the south and west of England in the second half of the thirteenth century, having initially gained enormous prestige from their use at Clarendon Palace in 1250–52.[24] The Raglan tiles belong to a sub-group best known and dated at the Cistercian abbeys of Cleeve and Tintern. At Cleeve the occurrence of heraldic tiles with the arms of the abbey's royal benefactor, Richard, earl of Cornwall, with tiles bearing the arms of the de Clare family, indicates a date after the marriage in 1272 of Richard's son Edmund to Margaret, daughter of Richard de Clare, and before Edmund's death in 1300.[25] At Tintern they must belong to the rebuilding of the church, and may be dated sometime between 1272 and 1288, when Mass was first celebrated at the high altar, though building continued until 1301.

---

[20] Lewis (1976), 10, no. 7.
[21] The Cleeve Abbey numbers refer to Ward-Perkins (1941).
[22] Lewis (1976), 17, no. 15.
[23] Ibid., 12–13, nos. 10, 11.
[24] Eames (1957–58).
[25] Ward-Perkins (1941), 41–42; Eames (1980), 195–96.

Although the use of these tiles was not exclusively ecclesiastical, outside court circles it appears to have been almost entirely so. It is also reasonable to suppose that it was their use in the church at Tintern that had impressed the Bloet family and suggested their use at Raglan. Thus, they are likely to belong to a chapel. This raises the possibility that the fifteenth-century chapel might have been built on the site of a thirteenth-century—or earlier—predecessor. It has often been noted that the fifteenth-century layout at Raglan corresponds in general to a motte and bailey plan: the tile evidence suggests that this correspondence might have extended to the details of the planning within the bailey. Further, if the present chapel belongs, as it surely must, to the second phase of fifteenth-century building, one wonders whether the old chapel remained standing alongside the new hall until it was replaced late in the 1450s.

MALVERN TILES 8–27 (Figs. 26–29 and table 6)

These tiles are of a hard, sandy, brick-red fabric, the cut sections sparsely speckled with minute dark and white inclusions; the clay tends to be badly mixed in the thicker tiles. The undersides are sanded and flat, the edges bevelled. The inlaid designs are up to 1 mm deep, but sometimes a good deal thinner. Most of the fragments are well-worn, the design showing as a pale yellow against a light brown background, but a few retain a high gloss and tend to be a darker brown; in a few the glaze has a green tinge. With the exception of no. 8, all the tiles are $5\frac{1}{2}$ in (140 mm) square $\times$ $\frac{7}{8}$–$1\frac{1}{4}$ in (23–31 mm) thick.

One bears an old paper label and must be an older find than the 1947 clearance; a few have traces of a hard mortar, suggesting that they may have been reset, perhaps in some nineteenth-century repair of the ruins.

The fabric is the same as that of the Great Malvern and Gloucester series, and the tiles must come from the same source in the Malvern area.[26]

The floor-tiles would have been laid, as can still be seen in the presbytery of Gloucester Cathedral, in a regular scheme of 4-, 9- and 16-tile panels, separated by bands of plain tiles of dark colour, none of which are represented in the collection. The wall-tiles would have been set in vertical series, and presumably would have been used round the altar as a reredos, in the manner still to be seen at Great Malvern Priory. It will be convenient to consider them in three groups.

A. *Sebrok designs* 8–13

Tiles of these designs occur in 'Abbot Sebrok's pavement' in front of the high altar at Gloucester Cathedral, so called because it includes a design (not represented here) incorporating the words *Dominus Thomas Sebrok*, and the date AD 1455.[27]

8. $5\frac{3}{4}$ in (145 mm) square $\times$ $1\frac{1}{4}$ in (31 mm). Corner of a 16-tile design including the arms of Westminster, the mother house of Gloucester. BM 2897.
9. Corner tile of a 4-, 9- or 16-tile design with quartered arms of England and France. BM 1518.
10. Border tile used in conjunction with 9, with double M monogram (for St Mary the Virgin and St Mary Magdalene). BM 1421.

[26] I am indebted to Dr Alan Vince for this identification, arrived at from examining cut samples.
[27] Eames (1980), 237; Shaw (1858).

Table 6. Malvern tiles at Raglan and related sites.

	A.						B.										C.			
	8	9	10	11	12	13	14	15	16	17	18	19	20	21	22	23	24	25	26	27
Sebrok pavement	+	+	+	+	+	+														
Gt Malvern Priory	+	+	+	+	+	+	+	+	+	+	+	+	+	+	+	+	+	+	+	+
Raglan Castle	+	+	+	+	+	+	+	+	+	+	+	+	+	+	+	+	+	+	+	+
Monmouth Priory		+		+	+			+		+		+	+		+	+	+	+	+	
Llangattock Church		+		+				+						+						
Estimated number in Raglan Castle finds	4	6	1	5	3	4	2	7	11	11	4	1	2	3	9	3	4	3	5	5

11. 4-tile design with arms of de Clare (as earls of Gloucester). BM 1656. Cracked stamp, as at Malvern and Gloucester.
12. 4-tile design with the arms of Beauchamp. BM 1601. Cracked stamp, as at Monmouth.
13. 4-tile design. BM 2689.

B. *Great Malvern Priory designs* 14–23

This series is slightly later in date than the Sebrok tiles, for it includes a tile (no. 21) bearing the date AD 1456.

14. Repeating design with arms of England in cusped panel, probably used with 9 and 10 as the four centre tiles of a 16-tile design. The Sebrok pavement uses a different centre. BM 1519.
15. 4-tile design with arms of England and inscription: *Fiat voluntas dei*. A version of one of the principal tiles in the Sebrok pavement, with the arms of England here replacing those of the abbot. BM 1480. Cracked stamp at Monmouth and Llangattock, but not at Raglan.
16. 4-tile design. BM 1469.
17. 4-tile design with monogram as in 10. BM 1425.
18. 4-tile design, differing from the Great Malvern version in lacking a white border. Cf. BM 2688.
19. Centre of 9-tile design. BM 2533.
20. BM 2577. The Monmouth version may be a different stamp.
21. 4-tile design forming a quatrefoil within four squares, and including the date AD 1456. Inscription reads: *marc mathe: lucas: joh/a: d: mcccclvi/miseremini: mei: miseremini: mei/saltem . vos . amici . mei: quia: ma/nus . dn̄i . tetigit: / me*, the latter part being a quotation from the Book of Job, xix, 21. BM 1468. Found elsewhere in the county at Monmouth, Llangattock-nigh-Usk and Llanthony Priory.
22. Tile inscribed round sides and in centre circle: *mentem sanctam, spontaneū honorem deo, patrie liberacionem*. These words refer to St Agatha and occur in her *Life*; they were used as a charm against fire.[28] BM 1429.
23. Tile inscribed with a warning in verse against the evil of executors.[29]

C. *Great Malvern Priory wall-tiles* 24–27

These large tiles, measuring $6\frac{1}{4}$ in (160 mm) in width × $1\frac{1}{4}$ in (34–37 mm) thick (none of them survives to its full length), would have made up vertical wall-panels, of the kind still to be seen at Great Malvern Priory. Only four of the complete set of five are represented in the Raglan collection. The set is important as the uppermost tile (no. 24) bears the date *Henry VI 36* (i.e. 1458–59), presumably the date of their use at Malvern.[30] All four designs are known from Monmouth Priory.

24. Inscribed across the top: *anno r r h vi xxxvi* (i.e. *anno regni regis Henrici VI xxxvi*). BM 1321.

[28] Bollandius and Herschenius (1863), 640A; Griffinhoofe (1894), no. 26, p. 15.
[29] Griffinhoofe (1894), no. 3, p. 9. The transcription there given does not seem to be entirely satisfactory, but I cannot suggest a better one.
[30] Op. cit. note 27.

25. BM 1322.
26. BM 1323.
27. BM 1325. Window on left shows slight flaw in stamp.

If, as it is natural to assume, the Malvern tile series at Raglan belongs to a single phase of redecoration in the chapel, then this may be dated 1458–59 or soon after. The designs on the wall tiles bearing that date are sharp and their stamps undamaged, whereas two of the Sebrok designs first used in 1455 betray damaged stamps. The proposed date falls within the tenure of Sir William Herbert, later Baron Herbert and 1st earl of Pembroke, who as we have seen was responsible for the second phase of building at the castle. They can, however, add nothing to the debate on whether he began the rebuilding before or after 1461, when his rapid advancement in power and prosperity began under the patronage of Edward IV.[31] Certainly he may have commissioned Malvern tiles at Abergavenny Priory in the 1450s. Drawings of three tiles of Sebrok design from the Priory indicate that such a pavement existed there,[32] and it is highly likely that this would have been in the Herbert Chapel, where effigies of Sir William's father (d. 1445) and mother (d. 1454) still rest on a handsome contemporary table tomb. A date soon after 1454 would thus be likely there, but this need have no bearing on the date of the Raglan chapel pavement.

Whatever their date at Raglan, Sir William's use of Malvern tiles there seems to have had a considerable influence on local architectural fashions, for there is evidence that several other buildings in the region had pavements of Malvern design. Wakeman gives an account of the finding of a câche of tiles, including the Malvern wall-tile set, during alterations to an old building on the site of Monmouth Priory; this is supplemented by the existence of further examples at present built into the tower wall at St Mary's (formerly the Priory) church, and the series has been extended in recent years by finds of tile fragments from various parts of the town, all derived from rubble from the Priory site.[33] The church of Llangattock-nigh-Usk also has tiles of Malvern design,[34] as has Tintern Abbey[35] and Llanthony Priory.[36] The fabric of these tiles, however, differs from the Raglan finds: these correspond to tiles from the Great Malvern tilery, the other Gwent tiles do not, and were probably produced locally. A small fragment found in excavations in the town of Abergavenny differed from both groups.[37] In the case of one design (no. 12) there is clear proof that the same cracked stamp was used in making both groups; in the case of another (no. 15), that the Raglan version preceded those at Monmouth and Llangattock, the stamps

[31] Emery (1975), 167.

[32] BL Add. MS 29938, f. 40ᵛ includes three sketches by John Carter (1807) of tiles in Abergavenny Church. Two are designs present in the Sebrok pavement (no. 9 above; BM 2860, which occurs at Monmouth Priory and Llangattock Church), and the other a Malvern design similar to BM 1420.

[33] For the tiles at the church see Griffinhoofe (1894); for sight of the recent finds I am indebted to Mr Stephen Clarke; for the wall-tiles from the priory see Wakeman (1862).

[34] Rushforth (1924).

[35] Eames (1980), no. 7655 (BM 2792).

[36] Vince (1980).

[37] I am much indebted to Dr Alan Vince for examining and reporting on fabric samples.

being cracked in the latter two versions. What seems to be indicated is that sometime after the laying of the Raglan pavement a branch of the Malvern tilery began operating in Gwent, or (perhaps less likely) that ageing equipment had been sold off to some local enterprise.

To return to Raglan: the evidence supplied by the tiles for the internal decoration of the chapel gives a setting for the items of furnishing listed in an inventory taken in 1507:[38]

> 'A vestyment of violet velvet.
> Two fruntis of aulters of crymysen
>   velvet with flours of gold.
> A small frunte of cloth of gold.
> A lytell chales of silver.
> A prynted masboke.'

The reredos and pavement, gleaming with bright yellows and golden-browns would have provided a rich backcloth for these more exotic treasures.

NETHERLANDS MAIOLICA TILES 28–30 (Fig. 30)

These tiles are $5\frac{1}{8}$ in (132 mm) square $\times$ $\frac{3}{4}$ in (20 mm) thick, and of a fine off-white/buff fabric. Their surfaces have been worn to a smooth matt finish, except for some spots of high gloss that survive in surface hollows. There are small nailholes left by a template in each corner or in opposite ones. The designs are outlined in dark blue and filled with washes of dark and light blue, yellow and orange; they are composed of geometrical figures filled with stylised leaf ornament, which on the dark areas is reserved in white. All three designs are repeating patterns formed from single tiles.

28. Cf. Museum of London: unprovenanced (79.32/2 and 3) and from the site of the Bank of England (no. 14544);[39] also Manor of More, Rickmansworth.[40] Also found in the Netherlands.[41]

29 & These designs have proved difficult to parallel in England, but they belong
30. to types represented in continental collections.[42]

Stylised leaf patterns in reserve seem to have been adopted in Antwerp *c.* 1550, and it is suggested that the Raglan tiles were made in Antwerp or the south Netherlands *c.* 1550–80. If they are indeed imports—and there always remains a slight possibility that they could have been made by immigrant Flemish tilers in Aldgate—then one would expect them to date from before 1572, when Antwerp's trade began to decline in consequence of the war against Spain, which

---

[38] *Cal. Pat. R. 1494–1509*, 602 (quoted in Taylor 1979, 35).

[39] I am indebted to Dr Tessa Murdoch and Mr Frank Britton for their help and advice on the London tiles.

[40] Bernard Rackham in Biddle (1959), 187, Fig. 21.16.

[41] Cf. *Antwerps Plateel* (catalogue of an exhibition at the Fries Museum, Leeuwarden, 1971–72), especially nos. 104 and 108; de Jonge (1931), 2c (*c.* 1550); Korf (1963), 49, Fig. 44 (end of the sixteenth century); also Vis and de Geus (1978), Pl. 5. I am indebted to Dr J. D. van Dam, Curator of the Gemeentelijk Museum het Princessehof, Leeuwarden, for this last reference, and for his advice on the dating of the group.

[42] E.g. for 29, Berendson (1964), 129.

was followed in 1576 by the sack of the city.[43] This would put them within the first twenty years of the tenure at Raglan of William Somerset, 3rd earl of Worcester, the period which has already been suggested for his building work there.[44] He was a man of wealth and fashion, and a leading figure at court, with all the command of resources necessary for such a commercial transaction.

The transition in the chapel from the restless iconography of monogram and shield, the warm browns and yellows of reredos and floor, to cool Renaissance blues and whites must have been as dramatic a change as any in the castle as Raglan entered its final phase.

Acknowledgements. In addition to help specially acknowledged in the course of this paper, the author is indebted to the following for help or advice: Mr Michael Archer, Mrs Evelyn Baker, Mr Tarquinius Hoekstra, Mr Peter Humphries, Mr Jeremy Knight, Mr Jack Probert, Miss Yolanda Stanton, Dr A. J. Taylor and Mr Tim Wilson. Special acknowledgement is due to Mr Paul Hughes of the Department of Archaeology and Numismatics at the National Museum of Wales, who prepared the drawings for publication from the author's tracings.

---

[43] Davis (1973), 13–15.
[44] Taylor (1979), 15–16.

154

Fig. 25   Raglan Castle tiles: the Wessex series (1–7).

155

Fig. 26   Raglan Castle tiles: the Great Malvern series—Sebrok designs (8–13).

156

Fig. 27   Raglan Castle tiles: the Great Malvern Priory series (14–19).

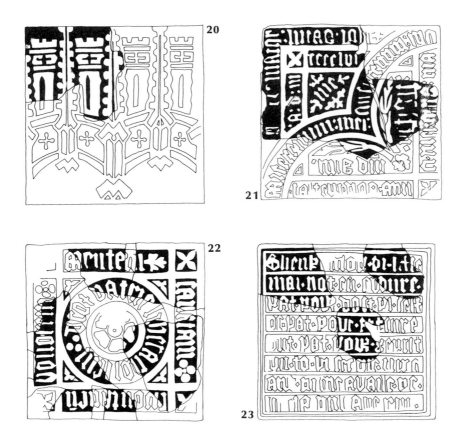

Fig. 28   Raglan Castle tiles: the Great Malvern Priory series (20–23).

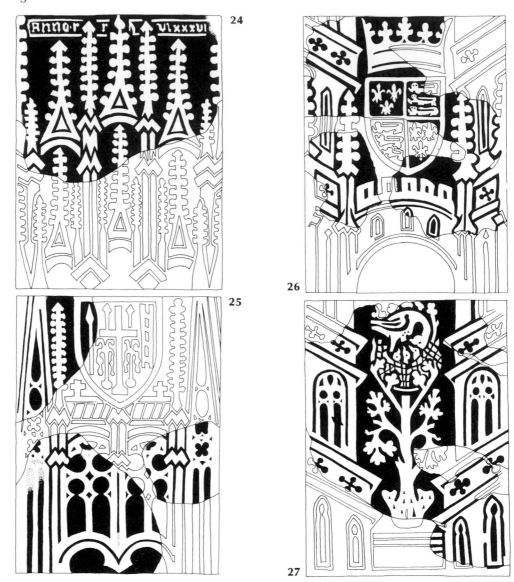

Fig. 29   Raglan Castle tiles: Great Malvern Priory wall-tiles (24–27).

KEY

Dark Blue   Light Blue   Yellow   Orange

Fig. 30   Raglan Castle tiles: Netherlands maiolica tiles (28–30).

IX   The chapel at Raglan Castle: composite photograph showing existing remains. (*Crown copyright reserved*).

The gunloops at Raglan Castle, Gwent

JOHN R. KENYON

IN a recent publication on early artillery defences the writer devoted little space to the gunloops at Raglan because of the intention of producing a 'paper on the Raglan gunports and seventeenth-century Civil War fortifi- cations at a later date'.[1] A note on the earthworks erected around the castle in the 1640s has since been published,[2] and I have taken the opportunity in this tribute to David King to examine the fifteenth-century gunloops at this castle, and thereby to acknowledge my debt to him for his advice and criticism given over the last few years. The study of Raglan's provision for guns in its defences is by no means an inappropriate subject for this volume, for David King's first publication was on a similar subject, the enigmatic little blockhouse known as Bow and Arrow or Rufus Castle on the Isle of Portland in Dorset,[3] which has loops with an external appearance similar to those under discussion in this contribution.

Raglan Castle is one of the finest late medieval buildings in Britain, a fact which not even the damage done during and after the 1646 siege can disguise. It is not my intention to give a detailed description of the castle's development as that has been done elsewhere,[4] although there are some differences of opinion in the two accounts. The castle is mainly a work of the fifteenth century with Tudor modifications. The earliest phases were the work of Sir William ap Thomas (d. 1445) and his son Sir William Herbert, earl of Pembroke (d. 1469). The official guide to the castle assigns to the former the construction of the South Gate and the Great Tower or keep, and to his son the Great Gate and the ranges of apartments, the Closet Tower and the Kitchen Tower.[5] This sequence has been challenged by Emery who has put forward the attractive theory that the keep was built by William Herbert.[6] Taylor has replied briefly to this sugges- tion,[7] and it is not my intention to add to the argument; either way the gunloops date to within a few years either side of 1450.

---

[1] Kenyon (1981), 216.
[2] Kenyon (1982).
[3] King (1947).
[4] Taylor (1979); Emery (1975).
[5] Taylor (1979), 10–11.
[6] Emery (1975).
[7] Taylor (1979), 52.

The distribution of the gunloops around the castle is impressive (Fig. 31).[8] Few sites can match the number, apart from walled towns, although if Kirby Muxloe in Leicestershire had been completed it no doubt would have had more. The loops are to be seen at Raglan wherever fifteenth-century masonry is still standing to some height, there being two areas where none occurs. These are the projecting range of buildings on the north-west side of the castle between the Fountain Court and the Kitchen Tower, dating to the early sixteenth century, and the northern side of the Pitched Stone Court where the original fifteenth-century Office Wing was replaced by a new range, also in the Tudor period. However, there may have been gunloops here originally as at least one of the vents at the back of a fireplace in the Office Wing is part of a circular gunloop.

Proceeding around the castle in an anti-clockwise direction from the keep, the distribution of the loops is as follows. There are four gun embrasures on the ground floor of the keep (Fig. 31, loops 1–4), this room being the kitchen serving the keep, and the circular openings are set below cross-slits (Pl. X). Due to the demolition of part of the wall of the keep after the 1646 siege, it is not possible to tell whether there was a fifth loop in the wall containing the fireplace. This is not as unlikely as it seems for as we shall see there are other gunloops set within fireplaces at Raglan. Nor is Raglan unique in this, for in the Tayside castle of Claypotts in Scotland there is a similar feature.[9] In the sixth face of the keep at this level there is simply a cross-slit lighting the entrance from the staircase into the kitchen. The keep's well is located in one of the embrasures, and unless the buckets were hauled up by hand the well apparatus would have hindered the positioning of a gun in that particular embrasure.

There are seven loops in both the ground and basement levels of the Great Gate and adjacent garderobe turret to the south-west, as well as four round openings in the drawbridge pit (Fig. 31, loops 5–15, A-G). The loops on the ground floor are set below windows except for one example (Pl. XI). There are two small openings in the ground floor rooms of the gatehouse flanking the entrance, similar to examples in the late fourteenth-century gatehouse at Carisbrooke Castle, Isle of Wight. They are not indicated on the plan but are immediately to the right and left of gunloops 8 and 13 respectively, as viewed from the bridge. They may be spyholes to give a view of the immediate vicinity of the entrance, but equally they could have been intended for handguns. Two smaller holes, about 100 mm wide, are set in the grooves of the outer portcullis; the purpose of these is not known.

The ground floor of the Closet Tower was the only room provided with gunloops (Fig. 31, loops 16–19), and again they are set beneath windows. The basement was evidently designed as a prison and is lit simply by a narrow shaft for ventilation. The embrasure in the tower which originally flanked the fifteenth-century Office Wing (loop 19) has been obscured by the outer wall of the Tudor rebuilding.

[8] The plan is based on the one to be found in Taylor (1979), with phasing deliberately omitted. I am grateful to Mr Paul Hughes, of the National Museum of Wales, for redrawing the plan.

[9] Apted (1980), 8. Mr Beric Morley has informed me that there is a possible gunloop in a fireplace of uncertain date to the east of the solar block at Ashby de la Zouche Castle in Leicesterhire.

The Kitchen Tower, like the gatehouse range, has gunloops at two levels: in the kitchen itself on the ground floor and in the basement, a room which is known as the Wet Larder (Fig. 31, loops 20–22, H-M). Two of the openings on the ground floor are set in the backs of the two fireplaces (Pl. XII), whilst the third is below a window. Later rebuilding may have obscure a fourth. In the Wet Larder there are six embrasures, with the external face of one blocked by the later Office Wing.

In the apartments ranged around the Fountain Court there are three loops (Fig. 31, loops 23, 28 and 32), one of which is in the east wall of the South Gate in what was the entrance passage until the gate was blocked to form a chamber during the work carried out by William Herbert. In another room a loop is set into the floor of the fireplace. At basement level there are seven gunloops in the two garderobe turrets (Fig. 31, loops 24–27 and 29–31; Pl. XIII). There may have been at least one more loop between No. 31 and the South Gate.

The circular openings for the cannon come in two main sizes.[10] The largest are those in the keep and in the South Gate, being 260 mm wide, although the chamfers of those in the keep are wider, 100 mm as opposed to 65 mm. The comparison of gunloops in order to date phases of buildings may seem highly tenuous, but the similar openings in these two buildings may suggest that they both date to William ap Thomas's time rather than that the keep came a generation later. It is of no matter that there are cross-slits above the openings in the keep as these were probably not so much for defensive purposes as to provide light in what would otherwise have been an extremely ill-lit kitchen. The remaining gunloops are smaller in size, all dating to the time of Sir William Herbert. They range from 230 mm in width, with a 30 mm chamfer, in the buildings around the Pitched Stone Court to 200 mm, with a similar chamfer, for those in the apartments and garderobes of the Fountain Court. The one accessible opening in the drawbridge pit, reached nowadays from under the inner arch of the bridge, is 160 mm wide, with a 40 mm chamfer.

Several of the embrasures are inaccessible today, but in the gatehouse range, and the Closet and Kitchen towers the average size of the embrasures at the internal face is 350 mm wide and 380 mm high, tapering down to the circular opening at the end of the embrasure; the length of each sill is approximately 1.2 m. The embrasures in the keep are higher and wider because of the combination of the cross-slits and the round openings, and the length of the sills is about 3.4 m, similar to the sill depths in the Wet Larder of the Kitchen Tower.[11] The similarity between the two sets ends here though, for without the cross-slits the width and height of the Wet Larder embrasures at the inner wallface are much smaller. The largest opening is 410 mm high and 870 mm wide, and the smallest 410 mm high and 480 mm wide. The lintels of the two widest are set beneath relieving arches.

---

[10] I am indebted to the Welsh Office works staff at Raglan Castle for their assistance which enabled me to examine several of the gunloops which are not usually accessible.

[11] I was not able to measure accurately the deep embrasures in the Wet Larder as they are blocked with birds' nests and other debris.

The original design for the castle would have been for the whole of the *enceinte* to be ringed with gunloops at ground floor and basement levels, but this was not carried out because of the break in the building of the castle following William Herbert's capture at the battle of Edgecote in 1469 and his subsequent execution. There is thus a close comparison between what happened at Raglan and the building history of Kirby Muxloe Castle. Lord Hastings's work at the latter came to a stop in 1484, soon after his execution by Richard III in 1483, but, as with Raglan, one can deduce from what was built that gunloops were intended for the whole circuit. The loops at Kirby Muxloe would have been more functional as they had short vertical sighting slits immediately above the gun openings.

The greatest concentration of loops at Raglan is, as one would expect, in the area of the Great Gate, with openings in this range and the keep covering the approaches to the castle's entrance. An improvement in the ability of the keep to cover this side of the castle more effectively would have been achieved if guns could have been mounted on the first floor, but the only openings at this level are small windows and cross-slits, although these could have been used by handgunners.

The Raglan gunloops are typical of the fifteenth century, simple circular openings, and one cannot get more basic than that. It was a period when the science of artillery fortification, such as it was, developed little in this country as opposed to what was beginning to happen on the continent. The writer has stated that 'Artillery fortification may even be said to regress after a *floruit* in the 1380–1420s'.[12] The majority of the earlier gunloops are of the inverted keyhole type with a sighting slit such as is to be found at Southampton and Canterbury, and the castles of Bodiam and Carisbrooke, although loops of the circular type do occur in fourteenth-century contexts. At Raglan only the gunloops in the keep have slits to the embrasures, and these, as mentioned above, were primarily intended to light the kitchen, but elsewhere in the castle there are windows above some of the loops. The long horizontal grooves in the keep embrasures may possibly have been designed to allow crossbow men to stand close to the cross-slits to fire their weapons, although Taylor argues against this.[13] If their prime function was to allow light into the keep from the oillets, this does not necessarily mean that the cross-slits could not have served a military function as well.

The effectiveness of the gunloops has been doubted, and certainly there are several which can be dismissed immediately as having no function other than to make the defences look impressive from the outside. Those in the garderobe towers around the Fountain Court could not have been used by gunners; in fact the only purpose they served, whether intended or not, was to provide some ventilation for these towers. It is possible to climb down and reach part of the cellars between the Great Gate and the hall range and see some of the lower tier of gunloops, and it is quite clear that these basement loops would also have been inaccessible to gunners as they are positioned too high up the

---

[12] Kenyon (1981), 216.
[13] Taylor (1979), 45.

wallface. The joist holes for the flooring are visible and it would only be possible for someone to look through the cross-slit in the cellar (Pl. XI). Presumably the other basement loops are similarly out of reach. If the openings in the draw-bridge pit were intended for guns then three would have been reached from the basement rooms or passages either side of and behind the pit, and they may also have been out of reach of a gunner, whilst the outer loop could be used from within the pit. A raised drawbridge, however, was not likely to have made any of the gunloops usable.

The ground floor embrasures in the keep, the gatehouse range, the Closet Tower and in the two levels of the Kitchen Tower appear at first glance to have been more practical. The lengths of the embrasures of some of the loops and the positioning of others just above the level of the floor implies that cannon mounted on wooden beds would have either been positioned on the sills or on trestles immediately behind the embrasures with the gun muzzles possibly resting on the sills; the loops are set too low for handgunners. As the mouths of the gunloops are at sill level, and as a gun would be slightly raised when in position because of the need for it to be set in a bed, this would have left very little margin of error for the gunner to ensure that the shot was fired cleanly through the loop. There was no room, therefore, for the gunner to traverse his weapon; all he could do was to fire along a line dictated by the alignment of the embrasure. This was a drawback to many a gun embrasure in the four-teenth and fifteenth centuries until the appearance of wider openings in the West Country blockhouses from the late fifteenth century, for example at Dart-mouth in Devon. The sheer length and the cramped nature of the embrasures in the Wet Larder would have severely hampered the operation of cannon in this room.

It has been seen from the above that the gunloops at Raglan Castle would have made it very difficult for gunners to defend the castle adequately. Gunnery was still in its infancy, as was the ability to design a building to make use of the full potential of the weapon. No doubt the type of gun that would have been found at Raglan was the wrought iron breechloader which would have been much easier to load than muzzleloaders, given the depth of the embrasures. One is left with the assumption that the main purpose of the gunloops was to look threatening to a potential attacker, to deter the small-scale attack. The defence of the castle would have rested primarily on more traditional methods, relying on the moats, the strong projecting towers and the main gate with its two portcullises, as well as the impressive range of machicolation that is still such a prominent feature of Raglan today. This is not to deny that the gunloops could have been used; it is just their effectiveness that is questionable.

It must be emphasized, however, that if the loops in the drawbridge pit were intended for guns then these would not have been visible from outside the castle until an attacker was literally at the door, and if the loops were just to impress why was none located in the basement prison of the Closet Tower? They would not have seriously weakened the security of the room.

Even if only a small percentage of the gunloops could have taken guns, the castle would still have required several pieces of ordnance, even more if cannon were mounted elsewhere in the castle such as on the tops of towers, where handgunners could also be positioned. It is not known whether Raglan had guns amongst its munitions in the fifteenth century, but it would have been surprising if it did not, representing as it did the seat of the premier Yorkist in Wales in the 1460s. A capable blacksmith would have been able to make wrought iron guns locally, as records from elsewhere confirm.[14] We know that the contemporary castle of Caister in Norfolk, which also has circular gunloops, was well equipped with ordnance. In an inventory of *c.* 1470, at the time when the castle had been forcibly taken from the Paston family by the duke of Norfolk, twenty guns are listed, placed in different positions about the castle.[15]

Thus the gunloops at Raglan fall into the pattern set by other examples of artillery defences around about the mid-fifteenth century in England and Wales, none of which is entirely convincing especially when compared with the buildings with keyhole loops built in the last two decades of the fourteenth century and in the early years of the following century, such as God's House Tower, Southampton. Although keyhole loops are to be found in later fifteenth-century buildings, for example at Baconsthorpe Castle, Norfolk, they are not common. This is in complete contrast to the fifteenth-century artillery works and town walls on the continent, where keyhole gunloops are very common, especially in such countries as France, Hungary and Italy.

This contrast in gunloop styles between examples in England and Wales, on the one hand, and those to be found on the continent, on the other, is particularly interesting in connection with Raglan, for the style of the fifteenth-century castle would fit better in the French countryside than it does in this country. Raglan has several characteristics common in French castles of this period, and it is no coincidence that both William ap Thomas and his son saw service in France. It may well be that the grandiose scheme undertaken at Raglan stems directly from fortifications that both may have seen during that service. One's immediate first impression of La Ferté-Milon (Aisne),[16] with its great gatehouse, albeit with towers *à bec* rather than polygonal, machicolations and carved stonework, is that here is a castle or fortress-palace that might have inspired the builders of Raglan. La Ferté-Milon was reconstructed from 1393 by Louis d'Orléans, the second son of Charles V, but the building campaign was interrupted by the assassination of Louis in 1407.

Another example of the French connection is to be seen at the original entrance to the keep which was via two bascule drawbridges, the vertical sockets for which are plainly visible. The bascule is an extremely common form of drawbridge in French castles, fortified houses and town defences in the fourteenth and fifteenth centuries, and this can be confirmed by even a cursory examination of Salch's 'dictionary' of fortifications. At the town of Vannes (Morbihan) one of the gates had two bascule drawbridges, one with two arms to carry heavy traffic, the other with a single arm for a narrower entrance, the pedestrian gate.

[14] Kenyon (1981), 230.
[15] *Paston Lett.*, 435 (No. 259).
[16] Salch (1979), 474–75.

This twofold arrangement occurs in other towns and outer gates of castles. Why it should be used in the keep at Raglan is a mystery, but it may simply be a piece of deliberate affectation; there is no evidence within the keep to suggest the reason, and certainly one would not expect to find in the keep an entrance for wheeled transport and one for those on foot! To the best of my knowledge, there is only one other castle in Britain where there is architectural evidence for a bascule bridge, and that is at Bothwell Castle, Strathclyde.[17]

In the light of these clear French parallels of the features to be seen at Raglan, it is therefore the more surprising that the more effective types of gunloops were not used. Admittedly, a variety of gunloop forms are used in France in the fifteenth century, although the larger rectangular types date from the latter part of that century, but the inverted keyhole loops were particularly common about the time William ap Thomas and William Herbert were in France. This, coupled with their use in England in the late fourteenth and early fifteenth century, should have led to the use of this type at Raglan, but it did not. However, it is also worth bearing in mind that when a solitary gunloop was added to give further protection to other buildings in Wales in the fifteenth century, it is in the style of the loops at Raglan. The isolated examples in the South Gate of Ewenny Priory's fortified enclosure in Mid Glamorgan and in the north-west tower at Carreg Cennen Castle in Dyfed were positioned to flank stretches of curtain wall, and clearly were intended to be used for active defence.

[17] Simpson (1978), Pl. 9. I am indebted to Dr Philip Dixon for bringing this example to my attention.

168

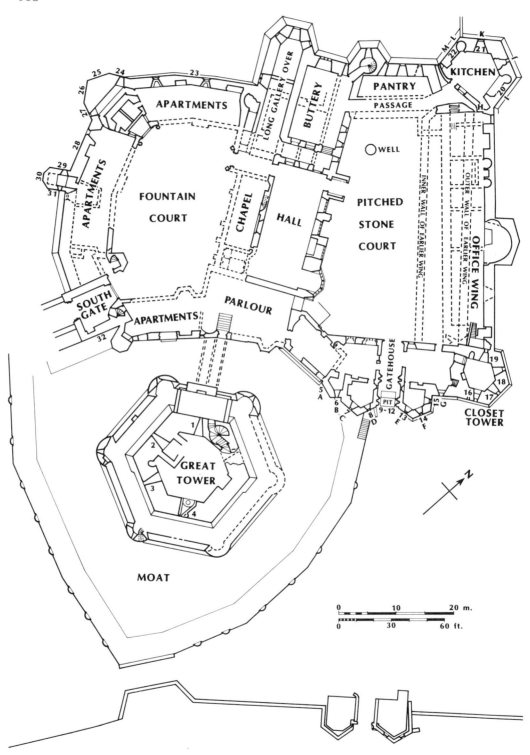

Fig. 31　Outline plan of Raglan Castle with the gunloops marked 1–32 and A–M.

X   Raglan Castle: the keep.
(*Crown copyright reserved*).

XI   Raglan Castle: the Great Gate.
(*Crown copyright reserved*).

XII Raglan Castle: gunloop set in the back of a fireplace in the Kitchen Tower.
(*Crown copyright reserved*).

XIII   Raglan Castle: the Fountain Court from the south.
(*Crown copyright reserved*).

The Herberts, the Mansells and Oxwich Castle

GLANMOR WILLIAMS

BY the reign of Queen Mary I (1553–58), the two most powerful of the resident landowners of Glamorgan were Sir Rhys (or Rice) Mansell (1487–1559)[1] and Sir George Herbert (?1498–1570).[2] They were distantly related to one another. Sir George Herbert's maternal grandfather, Sir Matthew Cradock, (d. 1531),[3] had married Alice Mansell, sister to Sir Rhys Mansell's father, Jenkin. In his day Cradock had been one of the leading figures in south Wales, in good standing with the Crown and on terms of close friendship with the highly influential royal favourite, Charles, earl of Worcester. He had exerted himself to give his grandson, George, and his nephew, Rhys, a good start in life. Both young men had taken advantage of the opportunities offered to them and had risen rapidly in the world. Each had his chief residence in west Glamorgan—Herbert at the 'New Place' in Swansea, and Mansell at Oxwich Castle, later at Margam Abbey. Both were powerful and ambitious figures in the badly-divided state of Glamorgan society.[4] In the disturbed climate of Mary's reign, with its deep rifts in politics and religion, they viewed one another with a degree of suspicion and envy. It was almost predictable that their rivalry should have burst open in an outbreak of violence. Late in the year 1557 a riotous affray erupted between the retainers of George Herbert and those of Rhys Mansell at the latter's castle of Oxwich. The litigation which ensued was taken to the Court of Star Chamber and led to a bitterly contested action.[5] It was, moreover, a quarrel sharp and serious enough to occasion the Privy Council itself considerable concern and was one which rumbled on in various forms for years after 1557.[6]

Sir George Herbert was the eldest son of Sir Richard Herbert of Ewyas, bastard son of William Herbert, 1st earl of Pembroke of the first creation (d. 1469). His mother was Margaret Cradock, daughter and heiress of Sir Matthew Cradock. George was, therefore, the elder brother and not the younger brother of William Herbert, 1st earl of Pembroke of the second creation, as has often

---

[1] Statham (1917–20); Clark (1886), 494–96; *DWB* (1959), *s.n.*; Williams (1962); *GCH* (1974), *passim*.

[2] Robinson (1977); Williams (1981); *GCH* (1974), *passim*.

[3] Jones (1919); *DWB* (1959), *s.n.*

[4] *GCH* (1974), ch. 3.

[5] PRO Star Chamb. Proc. 2/20/160, 2/24/365, and 4/1/26. See also transcripts from the Penrice and Margam collection of manuscripts published in Davies (1894), 165–95.

[6] See below, pp. 181–82.

been stated.[7] George Herbert was also related to George Nevill, Lord Abergavenny, to whose influence he may have owed his appointment as steward of the lordship of Abergavenny and his marriage to Elizabeth Berkeley. His main patron, nonetheless, was Charles, 1st earl of Worcester, who was probably responsible for securing his appointment as one of the gentlemen-waiters in Catherine of Aragon's household. In 1526 Herbert was appointed steward of the earl of Worcester's lordship of Gower in succession to his grandfather, Matthew Cradock. When Cradock himself died in 1531, Herbert inherited his large and valuable estates in the lordships of Glamorgan and Gower and added them to the lands he had already inherited from his father around Abergavenny. He took up residence in 'New Place' the handsome house his grandfather had built in Swansea. There he welcomed the poets of the region, to whom he was a generous patron.[8]

Under the new arrangements embodied in Henry VIII's statutes of 1536 and 1542–43 for administration and justice in Wales, Herbert acquired a number of important offices. He became the first sheriff of the new county of Glamorgan in 1540, was elected its first M.P. in 1542, and became a justice in eyre in 1536 and a justice of the peace from 1542.[9] Knighted in 1543, he was first of all *custos rotulorum* for Glamorgan, but later had to be content with acting as deputy to his younger brother, William. In 1549 he helped the latter to put down the dangerous rebellion against the Crown in the West Country.[10] From 1550 to 1558 he was vice-admiral for south Wales, with responsibility for the coastline between the rivers Wye and Loughor. During the 1550s he was included in the commission of the peace for no fewer than seven other counties besides Glamorgan—Flintshire, Radnorshire, Cardiganshire, Gloucestershire, Herefordshire, Shropshire and Worcestershire.

During these years Herbert had also profited markedly as the result of valuable and extensive estates which he acquired from the Crown. They included the manor of Llandough East, 1543, the manor of Cogan, 1544, the rectory of Cadoxton, 1545, the manors of Cardiff and Roath, 1545 (both had previously belonged to the abbey of Tewkesbury), a twenty-one-year lease of Dinas Powys, 1545, and the sites of the former Franciscan and Dominican friaries in Cardiff, 1546. Furthermore, in 1550 he acquired the site and property of the Hospital of St David, Swansea. He also diverted to his own possession many of the treasures of parish churches of Glamorgan, of which he had taken an inventory on behalf of the Crown.[11]

George Herbert did not make as many or as spectacular gains as did his younger brother, the earl of Pembroke. Nevertheless, he carved out an impressive niche for himself and his family in Glamorgan. What we know of him suggests that he had done so by a characteristic Herbert combination of energy, opportunism, and even plain ruthlessness. There is little doubt that he could be an

---

[7] This point has been made perfectly clear in Robinson (1977), 306–07.

[8] *GCH* (1971), 520.

[9] Phillips (1975), 285–88, 310.

[10] Rose-Troup (1913).

[11] *GCH* (1974), 217–18.

extremely forceful figure, not to say a downright blackguard. Some episodes in which he figured prominently shed a lurid light on the more unsavoury aspects of his character and his actions. An agreement drawn up in 1532 to regulate abuses in the lordship of Gower suggests that, as steward, Herbert must have borne considerable responsibility for them himself; similarly, he may well have been involved in financial malpractices in Glamorgan and other misdeeds in Ewyas Lacy. An incident of the 1520s or 1530s, relating to a dispute involving burgesses of Abergavenny being prosecuted in the city of Hereford, reveals his willingness to take reprisals against innocent visitors to his neighbourhood and the uninhibited way in which he expressed his intentions shows his 'predisposition to resort to forcible measures which was probably charactistic of him'.[12] Worst of all was his cold-blooded resort to judicial murder on one occasion when, having extorted from a young man a false confession of stealing sheep from his father, Herbert had him hanged in spite of explicit instructions from the Council in the Marches that he should do nothing until the Council had considered the matter.[13]

Rhys Mansell, born in 1487, was sprung from a family of lesser gentry in Gower, whose estates had been patiently built up in the fourteenth and fifteenth centuries mainly by a succession of judicious marriages. In 1464, the family's fortunes suffered a severe setback, when Rhys Mansell's grandfather, Philip, was attainted and his estates forfeited. Philip's son, Jenkin, was able to regain his family's position as the result of his solid and timely support for Henry Tudor in 1485. Owing much to his position of clientage to the outstanding Rhys ap Thomas (after whom he named his eldest son), Jenkin had his estates restored. His son, Rhys, was indebted to his uncle, Matthew Cradock, for his start in life when he put the young man in charge of some of his own ships. Mansell married three times. He took as his first wife Eleanor Bassett of Beaupré. After her early death he married Anne Brydges, by whom he had two daughters. His third and, as it turned out, much his most influential marriage he contracted in 1527, when he took as his wife Cecily Daubridgecourt of Solihull, a gentlewoman of the Princess Mary and one much in her favour. During the years 1534–35 Mansell performed 'right good exploits and acceptable service' for the Crown with the royal army in Ireland.[14] Though his wife was very anxious about his fate in Ireland and wrote to Thomas Cromwell asking for him to be allowed to return home, Mansell's services there may well have constituted an important turning-point in his career. They appear to have brought him to the favourable attention of the royal administration, and signal marks of the king's favour soon began to follow.

In 1536 Mansell became chamberlain of Chester, a member of the Council in the Marches, and was placed on the commission of the peace for more than one county. In 1538 he and George Mathew were commanded to take charge of a delicate and potentially dangerous inquiry into the accusations against the Herbert family of having stolen a ship. As well as being called upon to carry

---

[12] Robinson (1977), 305–06.
[13] Williams (1981), 51–52.
[14] Williams (1962), 39.

these administrative responsibilities, significant economic advantages also fell to his lot as a result of royal favour. He was allowed first of all to lease, and later on to purchase, the site and the bulk of the estates of Margam Abbey. The acquisition of these lands was in due course to turn him into one of the more substantial landowners of south Wales. It made him an altogether more consequential figure on the political and economic scene and hoisted his family to a perceptibly higher social plane on the social pyramid than it had ever enjoyed before. He seems to have determined to make the abbey his principal residence and began work on transforming it into his home not later than 1552,[15] if not before; and this in spite of the fact that in earlier years he must already have spent large sums on building work at Oxwich Castle.

During Henry VIII's wars of the years 1542–46 against the French and the Scots, Mansell was once more extensively employed as a commander of royal forces by sea and by land. In 1544 he served with distinction as knight marshal, i.e. quarter-master general, of the army against the Scots and in the following year raised 2,000 troops for service in his own county of Glamorgan. But, during Edward VI's reign, whereas the Herbert family had done very well for itself, Mansell seems to have been out of favour at that time. There are no indications of any important tasks being entrusted to him by the Crown, though he continued to perform routine administrative duties.

In Mary's reign, thanks not only to his own talents and experience, but even more to his wife's secure place in the queen's affections, he was restored to the royal favour. Both Lady Mansell and Sir Rhys were given a prominent place in the queen's coronation, and further indications of Mary's goodwill towards the Mansells were not long in following. In November 1553 Mansell was appointed to the important offices of chamberlain and chancellor of south Wales and the counties of Carmarthenshire and Cardiganshire. He was also appointed steward of many royal manors and lordships and custodian of royal castles. These positions made Mansell the most influential personage in the royal administration of south Wales. When his son was granted the right to succeed his father in these offices in October 1554 it appeared to set the seal on the family's position of authority. Given the successful way in which Mansell had been building up his estates, there seemed every possibility that his family would attain the peerage and might even come to rival in influence the Devereux, the Somersets and possibly the Herberts themselves.

In the meantime, Rhys Mansell's eldest son, Edward,[16] had also been emerging to take his place in county administration and society. A sign of his father's growing status and authority had been accorded when Edward married into the aristocracy, taking as his wife Jane, daughter of the 2nd earl of Worcester. His father's influence had also been sufficient to see Edward elected, as a very young man, as M.P. for the county of Glamorgan in 1554. In the following year he became a justice of the peace for the county. He was not, however, anything like as forceful or as talented an individual as his father.

---

[15] Ibid., 43.
[16] *DWB* (1959), *s.n.*; *GCH* (1974), 164–65.

The Mansells, father and son, must have spent considerable sums on Oxwich Castle in building a residence there appropriate to what they believed to be their dignity.[17] There had been a castle at Oxwich earlier, and a building specifically so named, in the possession of Philip Mansell, is referred to in 1459. The castle was rebuilt in the sixteenth century in two separate stages, leaving almost nothing in the way of remains of the earlier building. The handsome gateway and the South Block were put up during the first half of the century and are almost certainly to be attributed to Sir Rhys Mansell, whose initials appear on the plaque over the gateway (Pl. XIV). Though no evidence, other than that of building styles, survives by which the building can be dated, it would seem likely that it was undertaken between *c.* 1520 and *c.* 1538–40 (Mansell acquired the lease of Margam Abbey in 1538 and bought the site outright in 1540). The gateway figures prominently in the evidence given to the Star Chamber commissioners concerning the affray of 1557. The larger and more impressive East Block was built later in the sixteenth century by Sir Edward Mansell and is referred to by Rice Merrick, writing about 1580, who commented that Oxwich was 'latly re-edified or repaired by Sr. Ed. Mansell kt., lo[rd] thereof, whose ancient inheritance it was: Sr. Rhys Mansell built parte, and parte by Sir Edward his son.'[18] It is conceivable that it was the heavy expense sustained by him as the result of this building work that brought Sir Edward into severe financial difficulties in his capacity as steward of Gower.[19]

Oxwich Castle was to be the scene of a celebrated affray in December 1557 involving Sir George Herbert, Edward Mansell, and their retainers. The episode led to a Star Chamber suit, of which full and detailed records survive.[20] Like most Star Chamber documents which have been kept in full, they are unusually graphic and lively. On the basis of them, the action can be reconstructed in detail and even the actual words exchanged between the parties have been recorded. The account of the affray given below is drawn entirely from that evidence. Quotations of direct speech are included only where at least two witnesses confirmed that the words in question were used.

On St Stephen's Day, that is, 26 December 1557, Richard Cosin, rector of Oxwich, and his guests were sitting down to a midday meal at the rectory. They were a select little group of parish notabilities headed by Gruffudd ab Owen, steward to Sir Rhys Mansell. It was an extremely stormy day, with a violent westerly gale blowing. The convivialities were suddenly interrupted by a commotion outside and into the room came a straggle of five drenched and exhausted sailors. The words they gasped were mere gibberish to most of the company present, but by signs and dumb show they were given to understand that these unfortunates were members of the crew of a French vessel which had gone aground on Oxwich Point. No lengthy conference was needed to decide what was to be done. France was at war with England, and public

---

[17] RCAM (1981, 63–76) gives a superb description and excellent illustrations of the building.
[18] Quoted in RCAM (1981), 64.
[19] *GCH* (1974), 34.
[20] See note 5 above.

duty, not to mention private profit, demanded that the French sailors be taken into custody and the cargo of their vessel secured as a prize. Within a short space of time, every able-bodied man, woman and child in the parish was helping to unload the figs, raisins, almonds and wool with which the ship was laden. They also took away any of her timbers and fittings which could be conveniently removed. Naturally, the Mansell family, as lords of the manor, received a gentle-manly portion; their steward, too, was fittingly rewarded; and the rector was given what was due to his sacred calling. But most parishioners did well and all blessed this unwontedly seasonable benevolence of Providence.

Oxwich men were not the only ones to be interested in a mishap of this kind; others, too, had a lively concern—Sir George Herbert of Swansea, in parti-cular. As vice-admiral of the Crown and also as steward to the earl of Worcester, lord of the lordship of Gower, it was very much his business to learn what had happened in the event of there being a wreck anywhere along the coastline of Gower. Early on the next day, 27 December, one Jenkin Harry came up to Swansea post-haste with news for Sir George of the French vessel which had gone ashore at Oxwich. Suspecting what might happen unless he acted quickly, Sir George immediately dispatched two of his servants, Harry Franklin and William Hopkin Dawkin, to mount guard over the wreck, her crew and cargo until an inquiry should be held to determine the rightful ownership of the goods. When these two arrived at Oxwich they found that, prompt as Sir George had been, the men on the spot had forestalled him. High words passed between his emissaries and the villagers. Dawkin and Franklin demanded cus-tody of the goods in their master's name. The locals insisted upon seeing their warrants before they would even think of handing anything over. When thus pressed, Dawkin and Franklin had shamefacedly to confess that in his haste to get them down to Gower, Sir George had omitted to take the precaution of issuing them with warrants. Whereupon, with a great show of an affronted sense of legality, Mansell's tenants refused flatly to yield up the cargo. Persuasion having failed, and force at this stage being out of the question, there was nothing for Sir George's men to do but return to Swansea and report their discomfiture. They arrived back at their master's house in the small hours of 28 December.

The reactions of Sir George Herbert were predictable. Quite apart from his own normally irascible and domineering temper, setting aside even his indigna-tion that his official standing and the authority he had deputed to his servants had been flouted, the knowledge that the Mansells and their servants were at the back of it all had probably galled him most. When he heard what had passed at Oxwich he was furiously angry and resolved to go in person without delay to teach the Mansells and their men a lesson. Though it was only three o'clock in the morning, he roused his whole household. Pausing only to hear Vicar Price of Swansea sing mass, he set off with a considerable company of men, intending to give a clear demonstration that a Herbert's word was law in Gower. Near Nicholaston, he and his followers had more news of the French cargo, when they encountered four men riding to Swansea with some figs which they claimed to have found 'hidden in a bush' on the previous evening. Sir George seized the 'find' and pressed on to Oxwich.

Having arrived there, he made his way first of all to the rectory and knocked loudly on the door. A woman answered. (In the subsequent Star Chamber testimony, the witnesses on behalf of Herbert and his party conveyed dark hints that the relationship between her and the rector was more intimate than his vows of celibacy ought to have permitted.) The rector, however, made no mention of the lady's presence but testified only how, with him still in his doublet and hose, Sir George and his followers had burst unceremoniously into his bedchamber, demanding that he produce his share of the booty. 'I trust, Mr Herbert, that you will not take from us our own goods', he had remonstrated. Herbert, in turn, insisted that the rightful ownership of the cargo had not yet been established, and until that had been done it must be placed in custody. His men then broke into an outhouse and removed a quantity of figs and a horn of gunpowder. At the suggestion of Vicar Price of Swansea, who had accompanied Herbert's company, the French goods were placed in Oxwich Church for safekeeping.

From the rectory Herbert and his men next made their way up the hill to Oxwich Castle, the home of the Mansells, where they hoped to find the greater part of the cargo and the French prisoners. Marching into the hall, Sir George fiercely demanded to see the Mansells, only to be told that both Sir Rhys and his son, Edward, were away from home. Edward Mansell, he was informed, was not far away. He was either at Gruffudd ab Owen's house at Slade, only a short distance from Oxwich, or a few miles farther away over at his aunt's house at Llanddewi. Herbert determined to set off without further ado for Gruffudd ab Owen's house at Slade. Before he went, he ordered the removal of three French prisoners from the castle but did not take away any property in the owner's absence.

In the meantime, Gruffudd ab Owen had sent word of Herbert's coming to the young Edward Mansell, who was, in fact, at Llanddewi. He had also tried unsuccessfully to get one of his men to take two French prisoners over there as well. When Herbert arrived at Gruffudd ab Owen's house, the latter expressed surprise at seeing him there at all: 'How now, my lord, I had not thought to see you venture abroad at all in such foul weather.' To which Herbert replied with some vehemence: 'Hadst thou but done thy duty as a true steward, then had I no need to come', and once again demanded that the booty from the French ship be yielded up pending an inquiry. Gruffudd retorted with some spirit, 'Frenchman's goods it is, and our own, for such as took it ought to have it.'

Herbert abruptly cut short his protestations and insisted on knowing where Edward Mansell was. Gruffudd told him that he was at his aunt's house in Llanddewi, but urged Herbert not to quarrel with him over 'pilfry' goods taken from the wreck. His pleas served only to rouse Herbert to greater fury. Edward Mansell, he sneered contemptuously, was but a boy and would never be a man. He swore that he would send him to his father trussed like a bantam cock before he left Oxwich. Whereupon, his men pushed into Gruffudd ab Owen's premises and took away a barrel of raisins, a sack of wool and three 'toppetts' (an archaic word for 'basket', often used in connection with figs)[21] of figs, as

---

[21] *Oxford English Dictionary.*

well as two French prisoners. Then they proceeded to ransack other houses at Slade Cross and later at Oxwich Green. Having secured more of the French cargo, they obliged the Mansell tenants to undergo the further indignity of carrying it to the church on their own backs or those of their own horses.

While his men were thus occupied, Sir George remained on horseback at Oxwich Green waiting for Edward Mansell to return from Llanddewi. Mansell got wind of his intention and returned to Oxwich Castle by another route. It was his aunt, Anne Mansell, who encountered Sir George. She had ridden over to try to act as peacemaker and tried to persuade Sir George to agree to a drawing up of an inventory of the cargo. She urged him not to quarrel with her nephew over goods taken from the wreck. 'Tush, tush!', answered the knight testily, 'it is not for that. But I will not suffer my officers which are as good gentlemen as your nephew to be louted and misused at his hand.' And he added, in an outburst of indignation which provides us, perhaps, with the real clue to the reason for his anger, 'I will make him know the worst servant of my house that I send to do my commandment.' A Mansell must accept Herbert superiority.

Others tried to second the Lady Anne's efforts at mediation. Parson Cosin appealed to William Hopkin Dawkin, one of the two men originally sent by Herbert to Oxwich, to intervene. Dawkin only shrugged his shoulders and muttered fatalistically, 'Be as may be now; it is past my remedy.' Although some four or five houses remained still to be searched, Sir George called off his men and set off again for Oxwich Castle.

For all Sir George's threatening talk of trussing Edward Mansell like a bantam, he may have been somewhat hesitant about getting involved in open conflict. He was not entirely unwilling to listen to Anne Mansell's counsels of moderation, and particularly to her suggestion of compiling an inventory of all the French goods taken to the castle. So he decided to send his friend, William Griffith of Llancarfan, to parley with Mansell. Griffith, a principled and level-headed gentleman, who was to play an honourable role as an outstanding recusant leader in Elizabeth's reign,[22] was enjoying Herbert's hospitality for a few days. Not averse to assuming the part of arbitrator, he set off ahead for the castle. There he found Edward Mansell angry and defiant. Herbert, declared the young man hotly, had taken advantage of Rhys Mansell's absence from home to break into his tenants' houses, but sooner than let him rifle Oxwich Castle he would die at the gate. The placatory and well-intentioned Griffith managed to smooth down the young man's ruffled feathers, however, and succeeded in persuading him to consent to the taking of an inventory. He then returned to Sir George to report his success and the whole party moved off to Oxwich Castle.

When they got there they found Mansell standing resolutely a short distance outside the gate, sword and buckler in hand. Just behind him were four or five of his men, wearing armour and carrying swords and daggers. The rest of his company, armed with nothing more lethal than staves, waited just inside the gate. Mansell, far from being entirely pacified, brandished his sword and

---

[22] *GCH* (1974), 236–37.

cried out, 'How now, are ye come hither to rob and invade me?' At this, Anne Mansell dismounted and, taking her nephew's arm, begged him not to offer violence. He, fearing that she had been made a dupe for some trickery on the part of Herbert's men, slipped her quickly inside the gate. Rounding swiftly to face his enemies, he discovered that under cover of Anne Mansell's approach, William Herbert, George Herbert's bastard son, had quietly sidled up to the gate. Mansell turned on him furiously, 'Villain, whither comest thou?', he roared, and struck savagely at Herbert's arm with his sword. Two of Herbert's companions, Watkin John ap Watkin and Harry Watkin, came forward to protect him and reproached Mansell for not keeping the peace. Mansell, young and inexperienced, and possibly made all the more angry and confused by the consciousness of his duty to uphold his father's honour and his own in the face of the formidable Herbert and his company, would not now be restrained. The two sides quickly came to blows and in the skirmish that followed Sir George and Mansell tried to come to grips with one another.

The combatants were separated by the resourceful and quick-thinking William Griffith, who managed to get Anne Mansell's horse athwart the gate between them. There the fracas might possibly have ended and tempers cooled down, with the Mansell retainers inside the courtyard and the Herbert party outside. Unfortunately, Watkin John ap Watkin sought to vent his frustration by picking up a stone and hurling it into the midst of Mansell's people in the courtyard. By a sad irony the stone struck none other than the would-be peacemaker, Anne Mansell, on the forehead. She fell to the ground, bleeding profusely from a deep, narrow wound. The cry of 'Murder, murder' went up from inside the gate, and her plight seemed to sober both sides. Mansell and his men carried her carefully indoors, while Herbert and his company, dismayed by this turn of events and ashamed, perhaps, of having shed a woman's blood, withdrew to Swansea in discomfiture.

Within a short time, Anne Mansell died of her wound, and a coroner's inquest was held on her body at Oxwich on 3 January 1558. The jury found that her death had been caused by Watkin John ap Watkin having thrown a stone 'of no great bigness', which dealt her a wound 'of the breadth of two thumbs and the depth even to the brain'. News of the riot and the death of Anne Mansell was quickly brought to the Privy Council. The Council obviously thought that the event was more than a squabble of only local importance. With the country at war, one of the last things the Privy Council wanted to see was two major magnates in south Wales violently pursuing their own private vendettas. It acted promptly in an effort to put an end to the quarrel. As early as 8 January Sir George Herbert was summoned to appear before them to answer to the charge of causing a riot, and on 27–29 January he made his appearance.[23] A month later, on 23 and 27 February, the affair was referred to the Council in the Marches.[24] Shortly afterwards, on 10 March, George Herbert was ordered to

---

[23] *APC 1556–58*, 236, 251, 252–54.
[24] Ibid., 273, 276–77.

institute a search for his son William, described as servant to the earl of Worcester, and Watkin John ap Watkin, both of whom had gone into hiding, and to ensure that they appeared before the Privy Council.[25]

In the meantime, Sir Rhys Mansell had instituted an action against Sir George Herbert and his men in the Court of Star Chamber on a charge of riot and forcible entry. The court issued a commission to four Glamorgan gentlemen—Edward Lewis, William Bassett, John Carne and Richard Gwynne—to examine witnesses and take depositions. They did so during the month of April 1558. On the basis of the evidence, the Court of Star Chamber in May found Herbert and his men guilty of wrongfully entering premises and removing French goods and prisoners. A large fine was imposed, and in August William Herbert and Watkin John ap Watkin were committed to the Fleet.[26] In July it had already transpired that the five French prisoners, who were to have been handed over to Sir Rhys Mansell, had been ransomed by Sir George Herbert without Mansell's knowledge or consent. The Privy Council therefore ordered him to pay Mansell fifty crowns by way of compensation.[27]

Rhisiart Fynglwyd and other Welsh poets, alarmed and discountenanced by these dangerous quarrels between two of the leading families of patrons, had already tried to fulfil the traditional bardic role of acting as intercessors.[28] Later in the year 1558 no less august a body than the Privy Council came to the conclusion that it was time to bring pressure to bear on Mansell and Herbert to make up their differences. A weighty group of leading officers of state—the lord treasurer, Lord Montague, the controller and the master of the rolls—were instructed to bring Sir Rhys Mansell and Sir George Herbert together and reconcile them.[29] Three days later Sir George Herbert was released from the necessity of having to appear at intervals before the Court of Star Chamber.[30] Early in 1559 the names of George Herbert, William Herbert and Watkin John ap Watkin all appeared on the first pardon roll of Elizabeth's reign.[31] Such attempts probably came too late to do much good, for within a few months, in April 1559, Sir Rhys Mansell was dead. For long afterwards, however, the Mansells were always prominent in those groups of Glamorgan gentry that on a number of occasions did their best to thwart the Herbert interest in the county.[32] Old quarrels and intense inter-family rivalry died hard.

---

[25] Ibid., 282.
[26] Ibid., 316.
[27] Ibid., 347.
[28] Cardiff Hafod MS 20, ff. 42–43; Cardiff Reynolds, ff. 347–48.
[29] *APC 1556–58*, 385.
[30] Ibid., 427.
[31] *Cal. Pat. R. 1558–60*, 207, 236.
[32] *GCH 1974*, 175–91.

XIV   Gateway at Oxwich Castle with the arms of Sir Rhys Mansell. (*Crown copyright reserved*).

The siege of Laugharne Castle from 28 October to 3 November 1644

RICHARD AVENT

LAUGHARNE CASTLE in the south-western corner of Carmarthenshire lies in an area which could well be described as 'King Country' for it is flanked, on the east, by David King's Welsh Office guide to Llanstephan Castle and, on the west, by his and Clifford Perks's authoritative studies of Manorbier and Carew castles.[1] All three works have influenced my own understanding of the various phases of Laugharne's long and complex history. This paper, dedicated to David King, attempts to bring together contemporary written accounts and archaeological and topographical evidence to explain the last stormy event in that history.[2]

Either late in May or early in June 1644, Colonel Sir Charles Gerard landed with a Royalist army at Black Rock on the coast of Monmouthshire near Chepstow. By the second week in June he had entered Carmarthenshire on his westward march and captured Kidwelly Castle. The castles at Carmarthen, Cardigan and Newcastle Emlyn successively fell into his hands, followed by Laugharne and, in early July, Roch Castle.[3] Haverfordwest Castle was blockaded and Major-General Rowland Laugharne's troops withdrew into the last two surviving Parliamentarian strongholds of Tenby and Pembroke. Meanwhile, events in England had undergone a sudden change with the defeat of the king's army on 2 July at the battle of Marston Moor. Three weeks later Gerard removed his army to England, leaving troops only to maintain the blockade of Haverfordwest and scattered garrisons in the castles he had captured. One such garrison, that at Laugharne Castle, was described by the Parliamentarians as 'one of the holds from whence our forces and the country received the greatest annoyance'.[4]

During August a ship carrying infantry from London to join Sir Thomas Myddleton's forces in north Wales put into Milford Haven.[5] The troops were

---

[1] King (1963); King and Perks (1970); King and Perks (1962).

[2] This paper has greatly benefited from discussions I have had with Mr John Kenyon, although I alone am responsible for the views expressed herein. I am grateful to Miss Melanie Francis for preparing Fig. 33. I must also thank the Dyfed Archaeological Trust which, through its Sites and Monuments Record, drew my attention to the 1923 reference to the Glan-y-môr earthwork.

[3] TT E4.11; TT E4.12. TT is used throughout the text of this paper as the abbreviation for the Thomason Tracts.

[4] TT E256.44.

[5] Vicars (1646), 71.

commanded by Colonel Beale, with Lieutenant-Colonel Carter as his second-in-command.[6] In October the *Leopard*, a Third Rate with an armament of thirty-eight guns, then acting as the flagship of Admiral Richard Swanley, the commander of the Irish Guard, arrived with £991 worth of arms and ammunition.[7] Major-General Rowland Laugharne decided that the time had come to march against Laugharne Castle. He enlisted the help of Colonel Beale and his infantrymen and borrowed a demi-culverin ship's gun from the *Leopard*.[8] On 19 October, he sent out orders for all his troops to rendezvous at Carew.[9] However, this was delayed by bad weather and it was Monday, 28 October, before his army was finally assembled at a point about two miles from Laugharne Castle.

Two days earlier, on Saturday, 26 October, Laugharne with a detachment of sixty cavalrymen had gone on ahead of the main force to reconnoitre the castle. They were attacked by a similar number of horsemen who had ventured out from the castle. As a result of the encounter, one of Laugharne's troop, a Major Philips, was wounded and a lieutenant and a cornet from the castle were killed and another lieutenant, seven troopers and fourteen horses were captured. The army that Laugharne had assembled consisted of about 2,000 troops: three regiments of infantry under the command of Colonel Beale, Colonel Kilmady and the Major-General himself; two troops of horsemen, Laugharne's and the Major of Pembroke's (presumably John Poyer, the mayor and garrison commander at Pembroke) and a company of dragoons from Colonel Sheffield's regiment. That night (Monday) Laugharne's forces camped within a mile of the castle.

On Tuesday morning Laugharne's army was drawn up, 'on a plaine mountaine', facing the castle and Laugharne called upon the garrison to surrender, which they outrightly refused to do. He, therefore, ordered a party of 200 musketeers, under the command of Captain Sloman, to take possession of the town and church. This was completed in three or four hours and included the seizure of all the houses adjoining the castle. About one o'clock in the afternoon Laugharne sent down another party of about 200 musketeers to act as an escort for his guns, commanding his gunners to fire at the gatehouse of the castle. However, the guns were positioned too far from the castle to cause any serious damage. That night the rest of the army was ordered back to its quarters which were still about a mile from the castle.

[6] *Cal. State Papers, Dom. 1644–45*, 181.

[7] Leach (1937), 94.

[8] Powell (1962), 78. Powell refers to the gun as a *demi-cannon* and claims that another *demi-cannon* from the *Leopard* was used by Laugharne at the siege of Cardigan. However, it is quite clear from TT E271.22 and TT E25.1 that the two were, in fact, the same gun and that it was a *demi-culverin*.

[9] The following details of the siege are taken, unless otherwise stated, from the fullest account available in TT E256.44. Three other apparently quite independent accounts exist in TT E21.23, TT E20.5 and Vicars (1646), 71–72. The siege is also referred to in TT E256.35 which precedes TT E256.44 and in TT E258.1 which follows it. The accounts in TT E17.15 and TT E21.11 are directly derived from TT E256.35 and TT E256.44, respectively. TT E21.23 is directly preceded by a brief account in TT E21.8. Two other very brief references to the siege can be found in TT E21.1 and TT E21.3. Carew is mentioned as the place of rendezvous in TT E256.35.

On the following morning (Wednesday, 30 October), while Laugharne's troops were marching towards the castle, they saw two bodies of horsemen 'upon an high hill, in sight both of army, and the Castle'. Laugharne sent horsemen to intercept them and drew his infantry up in full view of the enemy. At this show of strength, they disappeared. That night the town gate was captured and, by mounting his guns in the gate, Laugharne was now close enough to the castle to damage the outer gatehouse. The appearance of the Royalists and their threats to raise the siege prompted Laugharne to take a party of horsemen on Thursday to the outskirts of Carmarthen, their principal stronghold in the area. By this further show of strength he hoped to dissuade them from attempting to relieve the castle. His guns fired continuously throughout Thursday and Friday and two accounts of the siege suggest that this caused a large breach in the castle gatehouse.[10] On Friday the Parliamentarians also unsuccessfully attempted to set it on fire.

On Saturday Laugharne decided that matters had to be brought to a head and, at a council of war, it was decided that a full frontal assault should be made that night against 'the gatehouse and a Forte: which two places was the strength of the castle and was answerably maintained by the Enemy'. Laugharne sent out orders that 200 chosen men, under the command of Captain Floyd, Captain Sloman and Captain-Lieutenant Srindy, were to make the assault while the rest of the army was to stand in reserve ready to assist if needed. Before mounting the attack, 'a strong work' was raised at the eastern end of the castle green.[11] The assault began in good clear weather at about 11 o'clock on Saturday night. After a short but fierce fight, both the 'Forte' and the outer gatehouse were captured. The inner ward of the castle, which had been transformed into a Tudor mansion in the late sixteenth century, was then besieged and Laugharne's men began to mine the walls.[12] After two or three hours, the defenders called out of the windows for a parley and sent out Major Alsworth to negotiate terms. They asked to be allowed to march away with bag and baggage and colours flying. Laugharne found these terms too high and offered more modest ones which, after some debate, the defenders accepted. These were:

'1. That the Governour and other Officers should march away with their Armes, to the next Garrison of the Kings.

2. That the common souldiers should leave their armes behind them in the Garrison, for the use of King and Parliament.

3. That so many of them as pleased should have liberty to go home to their own houses.

4. That the town should be secured from plunder, or any violence offered by the souldiers.

5. That they should leave their Artillery and Ammunition behind them in the Garrison.'[13]

[10] Vicars (1646), 72; TT E21.23.
[11] TT E21.23.
[12] Ibid.
[13] TT E20.5.

At 7 o'clock on Sunday morning (3 November) Laugharne took possession of the castle.[14] Descriptions of what was captured within the castle vary.[15] However, the three fullest accounts of the siege list 160 arms, four guns, three-and-a-half or four barrels of powder, along with other provisions.[16] The most detailed account describes the guns as being a saker, a minion and two (or three) smaller guns, loosely referred to as 'murthering peeces', and adds 5 cwt of small shot and a good store of butter, corn, cheese and beer to the list.[17] The common soldiery seem to have been disappointed by the lack of booty. Laugharne lost about ten of his men in the engagement and had another thirty or so wounded.[18] Thirty-three of the defenders were killed and an unspecified number wounded, including a Captain Ilinton.[19] The garrison was commanded by Lieutenant-Colonel Russell, who also owned the castle. His officers are listed as Major Alsworth, a citizen Captain Ilinton and Captain Fits. It is possible that there were other more junior officers who are not named. Russell had approximately 200 soldiers under his command. Under the terms of the surrender they were allowed to march away to Carmarthen, where the Royalists had a garrison of not more than 1,200 men.[20]

Laugharne's capture of the castle came not a day too soon as the garrison expected relief that Sunday, and indeed, shortly after they had departed, news reached Laugharne that a Royalist force was on the march towards him. He set out to meet them but, at the sight of his forces, they retreated. The nearest Royalist garrison to Laugharne Castle was at Clogaveraine, a well-fortified house just over four miles from Laugharne.[21] When they heard that the castle had fallen, they burnt the house, slighted its defences, blew up their powder and retreated, leaving behind one piece of artillery and a 'great store of bullets'.[22]

Laugharne placed a garrison in Laugharne Castle and then marched north towards Cardigan Castle with a force of about 500 cavalry and 300 foot. He arrived at Cardigan on 21 December and, upon receiving the garrison com-

---

[14] TT E21.23 gives the time as 8 o'clock.

[15] The much briefer accounts in TT E20.5, TT E21.3 and TT E21.8 differ from that given below. All list the number of guns captured as three and TT E20.5 is more specific: 'three peeces of Ordnance, a good quantity of powder and match, one Drake, some bundles of Pikes, two hundred muskets, besides other purchase'.

[16] Vicars (1646), 72; TT E256.44: TT E21.23.

[17] TT E256.44.

[18] Vicars (1646), 72 records fewer men as having been killed, 'and that only with the losse of not above 5 of our men'.

[19] Vicars (1646), 72 and TT E21.23 list the number of fatalities as thirty-three and include four captains amongst the wounded. TT E256.44 does not specifically mention the number of men killed and only Captain Ilinton, who is one of two captains listed when the garrison surrenders, is described as being wounded.

[20] TT E256.44. Captain Ilinton, who was left behind in the castle because of his wounds, gave this as the size of the Carmarthen garrison.

[21] The spelling of *Clogaveraine* and the distance from Laugharne Castle is taken from TT E256.44. In TT E21.23 *Cloggeverane* is about three miles from Laugharne and in TT E258.1 the spelling is *Clogavereigne*.

[22] The fullest account of the abandonment of Clogaveraine is given in TT E21.23. Lhwyd (1911, 58), writing not long after the Civil War, mentions a 'demolished & (hitherto) unrepaired House' at Clog y frân near St Clears. He further states that during the Civil War it 'was fenced with a Bulwark of earth' which 'bears already so little of ye face of what it was intended'. Clogyfran can be found on the map today at Ordnance Survey grid reference SN 240160.

mander's refusal to surrender, laid siege to the castle. After three days, realizing that it would be impossible to capture the castle without forcing a breach through its walls, and having no artillery with him, Laugharne issued orders that *the* demi-culverin should be brought from Laugharne Castle. With 'much difficulty and industry' it was brought to Cardigan[23] and, after firing for three days, a breach was created in the castle's defences and it was taken by storm.[24]

The main evidence for the siege and its aftermath that survives to the present day is to be found in the ruins of the castle and an earthwork to the north-east of it, which probably served as a Parliamentarian battery. The castle has been in State care and under repair since 1973 and the subject of archaeological excavations since 1976.[25] Of the other Parliamentarian gun positions and the town gate, nothing definite survives, although close examination of the country-side around Laugharne, and of the nineteenth-century history of the town, provides some indications as to their possible location.[26]

The medieval castle appears to have been in a fairly ruinous condition when Sir John Perrot, in the late 1580s and early 1590s, converted the inner ward into a Tudor mansion, restored the outer gatehouse and turned the outer ward into a garden.[27] Perrot served under Queen Elizabeth in Ireland as the first president of Munster from 1571 to 1573 and later as lord deputy of Ireland from 1584 to 1588. He is portrayed as having been a colourful and controversial character but also a man of great influence, with large landholdings in Pembroke-shire, the county of his birth.[28] His principal residence was at Carew Castle where, between 1588 and 1592, he built the imposing north range.[29] In March 1591 Perrot was removed to the Tower of London where, in June 1592, he was tried for treason and sentenced to death. However, he survived until September 1592 when, still in the Tower, he died of natural causes. Perrot's attainder resulted in all his land being seized by the Crown and an inventory prepared. The survey of the lordship of Laugharne is rather brief but it is clear that by 1592, which was presumably only shortly after Perrot's rebuilding of the castle had been completed, 'many of the windowes, as well wthin as wthout, doe moulder away by force of the weather, and badness of the stone. And the whole castle by reason of the bad buildings thereof (without excessive charges) is like wthin few yeares to run to utter ruin again'.[30] It is clear from the surviving remains that Perrot substantially altered the inner ward of the castle. All the medieval windows were replaced, the gatehouse was remodelled and a new hall-block was built against the south curtain. Although the outer ward appears to have been laid out as a garden, excavations to the east of the inner ward

[23] TT E271.22.

[24] TT E25.1.

[25] For a full list of references to the earlier interim reports on these excavations, see the latest report, Avent (1983b), 11.

[26] Curtis (1880).

[27] LCR 1592 Survey and, for a transcription of the section of the survey covering the castle, see Avent (1981), 27–28.

[28] Rawlinson (1728).

[29] King and Perks (1962), 294–95.

[30] LCR 1592 Survey, and Avent (1981), 27–28.

have shown that, at least on this side of the castle, the line of the medieval inner ditch was still preserved although the depth to which it would have been open is uncertain.

Over the next three decades or so, the castle was the subject of constant legal disputes, frequently changing hands and, on at least one occasion, being stripped of some of its lead and timber.[31] In April 1615 a special commission sent from the Court of Exchequer to survey the castle estimated that it would cost £2,000 to repair.[32] This change in the castle's fortunes can be seen in the upstanding masonry of the inner ward, where various windows and fireplaces and the postern entrance from the foreshore appear to have been blocked up during this period.[33] In 1627 the castle and lordship became the property of Sir Sackville Crowe, who later seems to have conveyed part of the lordship, including the castle, to Sir William Russell. On the basis of the foregoing, it seems reasonable to assume that the castle, although having a rather dilapidated air about it, was fully defensible at the time of the siege, with all the walls of both the inner and outer wards standing to their full height. However, total refenestration and the building of mock battlements during the Tudor period would have somewhat altered and weakened the medieval aspect and strength of the inner ward.

This, then, was the castle that Major-General Rowland Laugharne called upon to surrender on the morning of Tuesday, 29 October 1644, the first of six fateful days which were to bring to an end over five centuries of military occupation of this site. Taking the events in order, consideration must first be given to the location of Laugharne's main camp. This is described as being 'within a mile of the castle'.[34] Both the town and castle are located in a hollow, overlooked by low hills to the north, west and south, on the western shore of the estuary of the river Taf at a point where the small river Coran (today no more than a stream) enters the estuary (Fig. 32 and Pl. XV). At high tide the castle is enclosed by water on its southern and eastern sides. In the seventeenth century most of the town lay to the north of the castle. Laugharne's army, having assembled in Pembrokeshire, could have approached the immediate environs of the town from either the west, south-west or north-west. The main road from St Davids to London descended a narrow lane, known today as the Lacques, to enter the town square (the Grist) immediately south-west of the castle (Fig. 32). Travellers then crossed the river Taf by ferry and continued their easterly journey to Llanstephan.[35] Laugharne's army could have approached from this westerly direction but, instead of descending the hill into the Grist, cut across the fields onto the top of the hills to the south (above Orchard Park) or north (above Fern Hill) of the road. Either point would have provided a commanding view of the town. However, neither would have been anywhere near as much as a mile from the castle and both would have been

[31] PRO E 112/146/82.
[32] PRO E 178/5069.
[33] Avent (1981), 20–22.
[34] TT E256.44.
[35] Ogilby (1675), 33–34, Pl. 17.

in comfortable range of the castle's guns. The most probable approach would have been from the north-west along the road leading south from St Clears. This was also the route that would be chosen by any Royalist force coming to the relief of the castle from Carmarthen and it would, therefore, have made sound military sense for Laugharne to have established his camp on this side of the town. An ideal site, commanding a fine view of the town and about 1.3 kilometres (4/5 of a mile) from the castle, can be found on the southern side of a low hill just to the east of the road. This consists of two flat fields, covering an area of approximately 3.2 hectares (8 acres), just to the north of a house called Ants Hill, which form a level platform or shelf in the slope of the hill (Fig. 32, A, and Pl. XV). These fields are now occupied by the Ants Hill Caravan Park.[36] The two fields immediately to the north of the caravan site are called Cannons (Fig. 32, B) and Cannon Park (Fig. 32, C) on the 1842 tithe map and these names probably have their origins in the Civil War.[37]

On Tuesday, 29 October, Laugharne's army 'was drawne up on a plaine mountaine in the face of Langhorne Castle'. That night the army 'were commanded backe to their quarters, about a mile from the Castle'.[38] Taken together, these two statements make it clear that Laugharne moved his troops to a point which both overlooked and was nearer to the castle. If the above assumption, that the camp was to the north of the town, is correct, then it seems probable that Laugharne's forces would have been drawn up on the sloping ground facing the castle from the north-east. Today, this area consists of two fields above and to the west of Glan-y-môr (Fig. 32, D). Holiday 'chalets' have been built on the lower field while the upper is used for 'mobile' caravans. The north-east corner of the upper field is occupied by a semi-circular earthwork consisting of a bank with slight traces of a ditch on its north-west side (Fig. 32 and Pls. XV, XVII and XVIII). This is approximately 90 m (295 ft) long, faces uphill and defends an area of about 0.16 hectares (2/5 of an acre). The ground level on either side of the bank varies considerably from one end to the other. Along the north-eastern section, part of which is incorporated in a later field boundary, the top of the bank is almost level with the ground surface of the field above it but nearly 1.75 m (5 ft 9 in) above the interior to the south. At the other end, this is reversed with the bank standing to a greater height (about 1.25 m—4 ft 1 in) above the exterior (western side). At its highest, where it diverges from the field boundary, it stands over 2 m (6 ft 7 in) above the level of the interior. The overall width of 8 to 9 m (26 ft 2 in to 29 ft 6 in) is fairly consistent throughout, although it narrows towards both ends.

Today, there is a large gap between the southern end of the bank and the cliff edge to the east of it and a similar smaller one at the northern end of the bank. However, the earthwork appears to have extended right up to the cliff-edge until sometime before 1923, when J. P. Gordon Williams writes that

---

[36] The flat area was extended slightly further east when the Caravan Park was created to provide more space for parking caravans.

[37] NLW Laugharne tithe. Cannon Park is also shown on the Broadway estate map (BL Maps 137. c. 2(7)).

[38] TT E256.44.

'It was removed by the late Mr Weinholt for road mending and building'. He also records that 'The plough has been at work here. Fragments of the usual Coygan (?) ware, and a bronze button, have been thrown up by moles'.[39] Taken together, these two statements point to this having been a prehistoric and/or Romano-British hillslope enclosure with the cliff-edge providing a natural defence on the east. The earthwork is first referred to in 1839 as 'the battery of the Parliamentarians, of a semi-circular form'.[40] This is less than two hundred years after the siege and, at such a time span, it is quite possible that this interpretation is based on well-founded tradition. Viewed from the top of the castle, about 600 m (1,968 ft) away, the earthwork stands on the skyline above the cliff and overlooks a point on the river Taf which was used until thirty years ago as the ferry crossing from the east (Pl. XVII). This was a perfect site on which to position a gun battery aimed at the eastern side of the inner ward of the castle. It had the added advantage of controlling the ferry crossing, assuming that this was in approximately the same position in the seventeenth century as it was in the twentieth, and overlooked any traffic moving up and down the river. It, therefore, seems very probable that Laugharne took advantage of a pre-existing defensive enclosure as the site for a battery for his guns. Indeed, its very existence may have influenced his choice of this hillslope on which to draw up his army and call upon the garrison to surrender. The guns presumably began firing on the Tuesday morning as soon as Laugharne received the garrison's refusal to surrender.

About 1 o'clock that afternoon, having secured the town, Laugharne 'sent downe another partie of about 200 Muskets, and with them his Guns, commanding the Gunners, to make battery against the Gatehouse of the Castle, but it was at such a distance that the shot tooke little effect'.[41]

This reference obviously implies that Laugharne had more guns at his disposal than just the demi-culverin he had borrowed from the *Leopard*. It is impossible to say how many and of what calibre. So far, only demi-culverin balls and one, smaller, 4 lb cannon ball, probably from a minion, have been found during excavations within the castle. A minion is listed amongst the Royalist guns captured by Laugharne (p. 188). Another factor which should be borne in mind, when reading the following interpretation of the movement of these guns, is that the demi-culverin, as a ship's gun, would have been mounted on a truckle carriage with small wheels only intended for a ship's deck. This means that, assuming Laugharne did not have a field carriage at his disposal, both gun and truckle carriage would have to be moved around in a heavy cart.

On Wednesday night the town gate was taken, 'which did much pleasure us for battery against the castles gatehouse' and, on Thursday and Friday, 'our guns played hard this day, and night, the next day also'.[42] Taking all this evidence together, it is clear that the guns were located, at different times, in at least three places: the battery at Glan-y-môr, a position in or near the town from

---

[39] Williams (1922–23), 3.
[40] Kemp (1839), 353.
[41] TT E256.44.
[42] Ibid.

which it would have been possible to fire at the outer gatehouse of the castle, and the town gate. It would have been impossible to damage the outer gatehouse, in such a way as to effect entry to the castle, from the Glan-y-môr battery, although this would have been ideally situated to fire upon the eastern side of the castle and this will be returned to later. Curtis, in her history of Laugharne, mentions another battery on top of the hill behind Fernhill and claims that the castle was also fired upon from the field known as Orchard Park.[43] This latter field is above and to the south of the Grist and overlooks the castle from the south-west (Fig. 32, G, and Pl. XV). Guns sited here would have been well placed to inflict damage on the southern and south-western side of the inner ward and its gatehouse but not the outer gatehouse. However, the battlements on this side of the castle are in generally good condition and what damage there is to the upstanding masonry probably occurred in the 340 or so years since the Civil War (Pl. XVII). The only earthwork visible in Orchard Park on the aerial photograph (Pl. XV) is a short, straight stretch of bank constructed sometime shortly before the field was developed for housing in the 1960s. It, therefore, seems unlikely that a battery was ever established on this side of the castle. However, a battery located somewhere above Fernhill would have been well placed to fire at the western side of the outer gatehouse and two cannon balls were found embedded in the upper part of the masonry in its damaged north-west corner. Each weighed just over 4 kg (9 lb) and had a diameter of 110 mm ($4\frac{1}{4}$ in) and must have been fired from the *Leopard's* demi-culverin. With a point-blank range of just under 600 m (2,000 ft) and a random range of 3,650 m (12,000 ft), this would have been the smallest of the large cannon capable of causing major structural damage to masonry.[44] The top of the hill behind Fernhill is about 630 m (2,066 ft) from the outer gatehouse, which is out of sight, although the upper part of the inner ward can be seen. No evidence of a battery can be found and Curtis provides no further details. The only physical irregularity in the landscape is in the corner of a field (Fig. 32, E, and Pl. XV), where a boundary bank takes on a distinct curve facing the castle and is slightly higher than the adjoining length of field bank; but this is too ephemeral to be seriously considered as the remains of a battery. A much more suitable position can be found further down the hill, where a commanding view can be gained of the gatehouse from one of two almost level natural platforms in the hillslope (Fig. 32, F, and Pl. XIX). Either would have been within point-blank range but only capable of damaging the north-west corner of the gatehouse. Hence the need to relocate the guns, so that they could fire directly into the gate passage, and the capture of the town gate on Wednesday night.

There are a number of problems involved in identifying the location of the 'town gate' (Fig. 32). Nothing remains of the medieval defences of the town and no mention is made of a wall in the nineteenth-century accounts of Laugharne.[45] Curtis gives the location of four gates, none of which was standing

[43] Curtis (1880), 75.

[44] Eldred (1646), 15.

[45] Kemp (1839); Curtis (1880).

when she was writing in 1880. One was on Wogan Street immediately above Island House and, therefore, just outside the western corner of the outer ward of the castle. Curtis claims that part of the structure of this gate had been incorporated in a later chapel. She also states that gates once existed at the eastern end of Victoria Street, at the northern end of the town near the church gates and 'across the road just below the Mariner's Corner. It was taken down about eighty or one hundred years ago.'[46] This last is a puzzling reference as the Mariner's public house is on the south side of Victoria Street, on the corner where it joins King Street, and only about 85 m (280 ft) north of the outer gatehouse. The upper end of Newbridge Street is 'just below the Mariner's Corner' and there could have been a gate here controlling the western approach to the town, but this would not be in keeping with a gate on the presumed line of the defences, further down Newbridge Street. Nevertheless, the present building on the corner between this street and King Street is called 'The Gatehouse', although this may have been a later toll-house (Fig. 32, H, and Pl. XVI, H). There is a noticeable drop in level at the northern end of King Street, just beyond Great House and Moir House, and this may indicate the line of the filled-in medieval town ditch. Furthermore, the pattern of the medieval burgage plots cannot be traced to the north of this change in level (Pl. XV).[47] This suggests that there ought to have been a town gate at roughly this point (Fig. 32, I), which is less than 300 m (984 ft) north of the outer gatehouse of the castle, rather than further north near the church gates as suggested by Curtis.

It seems quite probable that, whilst the gates were built of stone, the town wall was no more than an earthen bank, surmounted by a timber palisade and with an external ditch. It is unlikely that these defences served any useful purpose by the time of the Civil War and, indeed, the ease with which the town was occupied by the Parliamentarians implies that this was the case. However, one gate was defensible and sufficiently sound to mount guns on it. This must have been either the Mariner's Corner or the northern gate. Several factors militate in favour of the latter. First, it seems unlikely that guns mounted so close to the castle would have taken two days to batter a breach in the gatehouse. Second, the gate would have been directly overlooked from the inner ward of the castle and in point-blank range. Finally, in order to locate his guns behind Fernhill, Laugharne must have sent them down from Glan-y-môr into the eastern side of the town, along Victoria Street, past the Mariner's Corner and out the western side via Newbridge Street. In so doing, they would have passed only 80 or 90 m (260 or 300 ft) to the north of the castle and would, for a short period, have been very vulnerable both to musket and cannon fire and an attempt by the defenders to capture them. This would account for Laugharne providing an escort of 200 musketeers. The location of the battery at Glan-y-môr also makes sense in the light of this action. Continuous bombardment of the castle throughout the morning would have not only drawn the defenders' attention away from the action of Laugharne's men in capturing the town but also caused

---

[46] Curtis (1880), 90.
[47] Soulsby (1983), 159.

havoc on this side of the castle just before Laugharne moved his guns across its north face. There was also always the outside chance that the defenders, suitably 'softened up', would have surrendered during the morning. It is quite clear that Laugharne would not have been able to move his guns across the town if the Royalists had still held a gate near the Mariner's Corner. However, a Royalist outpost in a gate at the northern end of the town, isolated from the main action near the castle, could have held out for another day-and-a-half and, presumably, along with the defenders in the outer gatehouse, have provided some form of cross-fire through which Laugharne's guns would have had to pass.

One final point can be made about the Glan-y-môr and Fernhill gun emplacements. Both are near old tracks or hollow ways which appear on the 1842 tithe map and may date back to the pre-Civil War period.[48] A demi-culverin was a heavy gun, weighing somewhere in the region of 1,630 kg (3,600 lb), and it would have been greatly to Laugharne's advantage if such tracks had existed.[49] Both still appear on the modern Ordnance Survey map (Fig. 32). A small by-road leads north-east from Ants Hill past Mapsland, where it turns south, past Hillside, to St Martin's Church. From here, it forms a 2 m (6 ft) wide unpaved track, enclosed on either side by hedges, running in a south-easterly direction between fields. Finally, it turns through 90° up to a gateway in the north-east corner of the field with the Glan-y-môr earthwork in it. The same track extends several fields north and uphill and, provided that the guns could have been brought over some fields at the top of the hill, it could have been used, as an alternative route, to bring them downhill from the direction of Delacorse Uchaf. The other track is in a deep, hedge-enclosed hollow running uphill on the north-eastern side of the field above Fernhill. Had it been as it is today, this would have provided good cover from the castle.

The outer gatehouse of the castle would have been in point-blank range of the demi-culverin mounted in the town's northern gate and yet, despite firing throughout Thursday and Friday, the gunners were unable to create a breach large enough to storm it. Nor were the Parliamentarians able to set it on fire. Today, all the masonry at the front of the gatehouse, including part of the vault over the passage, is missing (Fig. 33, Pls. XVI and XIX). Much of this damage must have been caused by gunfire and this is, presumably, the 'great breach' referred to in two accounts of the siege.[50] Some damage might also be the result of later slighting.

In addition to the gatehouse, the other stronghold of the castle is described as being a 'Forte'.[51] During the Saturday night attack, the gatehouse and fort were taken at the same time, suggesting that the fort may have been just outside the gatehouse. This whole area was greatly altered in the eighteenth century when the earliest part of Castle House was built. However, even today it is clear that there was a considerable drop in level between the gatehouse and

[48] NLW Laugharne tithe.
[49] Eldred (1646), 15.
[50] TT E21.23; Vicars (1646), 72.
[51] TT E256.44.

the area, bordering Wogan Street, to the south-west of it. The 1592 Survey of Laugharne mentions a garden, covering about an acre, outside the castle walls.[52] This must have been in the area at present occupied by Castle House and its gardens, outside and to the east of the gatehouse (Pl. XVI). One account of the siege mentions 'the Castle green'.[53] It, therefore, seems likely that there was an area of open ground between the castle and the town, although the exact extent of this is uncertain, particularly in the light of the earlier reference to Laugharne's troops, when they took the town on Tuesday, approaching 'very nigh the Castle, possessing all the houses adjoyning to it'.[54] Archaeological excavations outside the north-west corner of the outer gatehouse have revealed evidence to suggest that the castle ditch may have been at least partially open in this area at the time of the Civil War.[55] No excavations have, as yet, taken place in the immediate area of the entrance to determine whether a solid causeway or a bridge crossed whatever was left of the ditch at this point. The fact that Laugharne's forces were able to raise 'a strong work' at the eastern end of the castle green further suggests that the fort must have been at the other end, near the gatehouse. The most acceptable explanation is that it took the form of a *redan* placed as an extra line of defence in front of the gatehouse. The remains of similar structures are preserved at Carew and Manorbier castles.[56] This was probably an acute-angled salient, facing out to the field in front of the gateway, and comparison with those at Carew and Manorbier suggests that it may have been constructed of earth derived from an external ditch, with stone revetments at the front and rear. At Carew traces of a paved gun-platform could be detected within the V-shaped enclosure formed by the redan and one or more of the four Royalist guns captured at Laugharne could have been mounted behind their redan. Later alterations have destroyed any evidence that might have survived of this or the Parliamentarian 'strong work'.

The final act of the besiegers was to attempt, for two or three hours before the garrison called for a parley, to mine the walls of the inner ward. No evidence of this work survives in the castle remains, although it may have taken place on the eastern side of the inner ward. As well as the outer gatehouse, several other areas of the castle appear to have been damaged during the siege (Fig. 33). Today, the curtain wall on the north-eastern side of the outer ward ends just east of the outer gatehouse. The rest of its original line is marked by a later red brick wall acting as a boundary between the garden of Castle House and the castle grounds. The south-eastern corner and the entire eastern side of the inner ward is missing and the excavations have shown that the buildings standing against these walls were destroyed by fire (Pl. XVI).[57] Finally, the eastern face of the thirteenth-century north-east tower is in a very ruinous state. All this damage to the fabric of the castle could have been initially caused by

---

[52] LCR 1592 Survey. This section is transcribed in Kemp (1839), 356.
[53] TT E21.23.
[54] TT E256.44.
[55] Avent and Read (1977), 20–22.
[56] King and Perks (1962), 277–78, 305; King and Perks (1970), 92, 112.
[57] Avent (1981), 23.

bombardment from the battery above Glan-y-môr, particularly if Laugharne had retained one or two guns in the battery after he had sent his others down into the town. However, most of the damage must have resulted from subsequent slighting, perhaps including the use of gunpowder. Laugharne left a garrison in the castle and it is from here that he called for the demi-culverin to be sent to Cardigan on or about 24 December. It is possible that the garrison was supervising the demolition of parts of the castle. Alternatively, it may have been abandoned and slighted when Gerard swept back into Pembrokeshire in late April 1645 having routed Laugharne's forces at Newcastle Emlyn.[58] The only other area of masonry in the castle which may have been damaged during the Civil War rather than at a later date is the upper part of the north-west tower or keep. This was rebuilt in the early 1930s, but photographs taken before then and eighteenth-century prints show that, although the roof vault was intact, the battlements were very ruinous. As the principal look-out point in the castle, this could have been bombarded from the battery above Fernhill.

Finally, all the above arguments are based on the assumption that there was only one major siege at Laugharne during the Civil War. Gerard's campaign in the early summer of 1644 does not receive the coverage in the Royalist pamphlets that Rowland Laugharne's does in those produced by the Parliamentarians. Nevertheless, the fact that the castle was fully defensible in late October of that year and the lack of any evidence of repairs to its fabric during the Civil War suggest that Gerard took it without a struggle. The castle is not referred to again in the pamphlets after the end of 1644.

[58] Phillips (1874), **1**, 292–93.

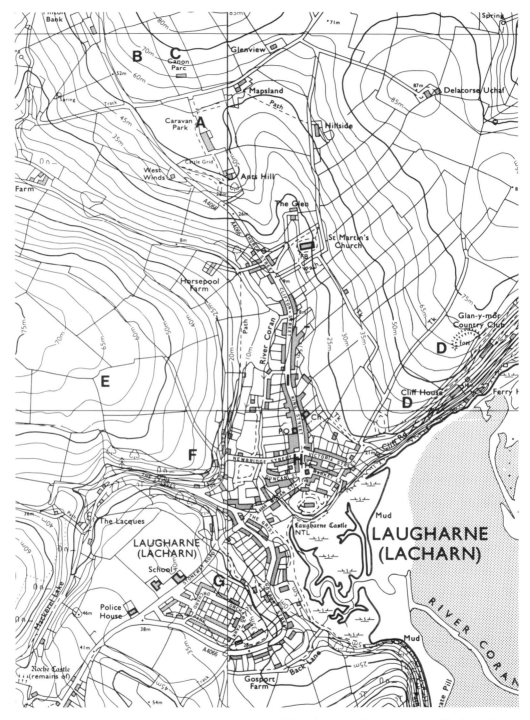

Fig. 32   6 inch (1:10,000) Ordnance Survey map of Laugharne and its environs with the various locations mentioned in the text indicated by the letters A-I.
(*Crown copyright reserved*).

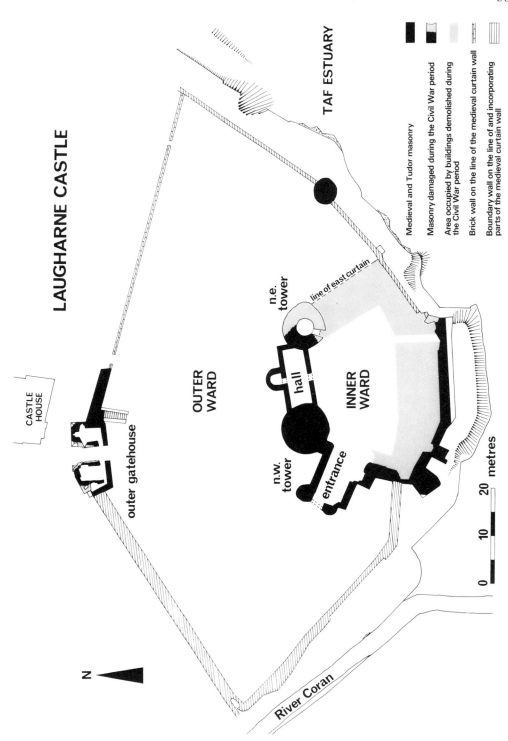

Fig. 33   Plan of Laugharne Castle showing the extent of damage during the Civil War period.

XV Vertical aerial photograph of Laugharne and the surrounding countryside taken in 1965. This should be compared with Fig. 32. North is at the top of the photograph and the castle is at the southern end of the town. The Glan-y-môr earthwork is two fields north-east of the edge of the town.

(Reproduced from an Ordnance Survey aerial photograph with the permission of the Controller of Her Majesty's Stationery Office, *Crown copyright reserved*).

XVI Aerial view of Laugharne Castle, taken from the south-west in 1986, showing the missing eastern curtain wall of the inner ward and the damaged outer gatehouse. The house known as 'The Gatehouse' near the Mariner's Corner is indicated by the letter 'H'. (*Crown copyright reserved*).

XVII   The southern aspect of Laugharne taken from Orchard Park. The Glan-y-môr earthwork can be seen above and to the right of the castle.

XVIII The eastern end of the inner ward of Laugharne Castle taken from the south, with the Glan-y-môr earthwork at the top of the photograph.

XIX   The western aspect of Laugharne taken from the hill slope just above Fernhill. The outer
gatehouse of the castle can be seen to the right of Castle House.

The abandonment of the castle in Wales and the Marches

M. W. THOMPSON

'I wittingly omit many Castles in this Country:
for 'twere endless to recount them all; since
'tis certain, that in the days of Henry the second,
there were 1,115 Castles in England.'[1]

THE scholar to whom we are dedicating this volume has done perhaps more than any other for the study of the castle in Wales. The lists of castles in Wales and the Marches that he published with Dr A. H. A. Hogg[2] provide the starting point for all general studies of the castle in the Principality. The present paper would not have been possible without them, and may indeed be described to some extent as merely a gloss on them.

It might reasonably be expected that the foundation of a castle would have attracted more attention than its demise. The dramatic physical changes caused by the construction, and its substantial costs in labour and materials, were likely to be recorded by the chronicler and clerk; the slow physical decay, often imperceptible in a lifetime, and the collapse of a ruin were hardly likely to be regarded as worthy of notice, especially as no costs were incurred. It is true that most castles were erected at a time for which surviving records are much scantier than those of the period of their abandonment, a compensating factor as it were. Yet it is probably fair to say that although the exact circumstances of the foundation of the majority of castles are not known, the general outline is better understood and grasped than the stages of abandonment.

The word 'abandonment' requires a more precise definition. If a castle was a 'fortified residence' (the normal definition) then, when there was no longer a resident owner, however infrequent his visits, it can said to be abandoned. An important exception in Wales was royal or Duchy castles, whose owner could not possibly visit all he owned, but where a garrison or administrative function made it necessary to keep a castle in good order. Otherwise, once occupation ceased mere neglect would cause it to become first derelict and then ruinous, unless secondary use for justice, for prison use or for estate management caused at least a part of it to be kept up. This was perhaps more likely to happen

---

[1] Camden (1695), col. 862. Since this paper was written I have dealt with the subject on a much broader scale, modifying to some extent the views expressed here; see Thompson forthcoming.

[2] Hogg and King (1963), (1967) and (1970).

in a town, particularly where the structure formed part of the defences of a walled borough, than in the country. Hence, on the whole castles tended to survive longer in towns than in the countryside, as we can see in Leland's *Itinerary*. There is, of course, no inviolate rule about this, as the disappearance of the castles at Hereford and Gloucester reminds us.

In the physical deterioration of a castle two very different rates of decay have to be recognized. Once water comes through a wooden roof, beams and floors will deteriorate quickly, so that failure to maintain the residential buildings in a castle would render it uninhabitable in quite a short time. It was a very different story indeed with massive defensive walls for, as George Owen of Pembrokeshire told us in 1603,

> 'all the buildinges of the auncient Castells were of lyme & stonne verye stronge & substancially built, such as our masons of this adge cannot doe the like: for althoughe all or most of the Castells are ruinated and remayne uncovered, some for diverse hundred yeres past, yet are all the walls firme and stronge, and nothing ympayred, but seeme as if the lyme and stonne did incorporate the one with the other & become one substance inseperable: so that yt ys more easie to digg stones out of the mayne Rocke, then to pull downe an old wall...'.[3]

It is very important to remember this when reading the word 'ruinous' in Tudor surveys. It probably means the castle was uninhabited but not that it was incapable of further use if its defences were required, as they no doubt were during the Civil War.

The foundation of a castle was often coupled with that of an abbey, but it is the contrast that is most instructive for our purpose. From its foundation to the Dissolution a monastery was in continuous use for worship by the religious in residence; a castle had discontinuous, possibly infrequent, use by its owner by whom it could be, and in the long run usually was, simply abandoned. In the quotation at the head of this paper Camden speaks of 1,115 castles in England (presumably excluding Wales) in the reign of Henry II, evidently implying that this was the peak period for castles. Hogg and King were able to list nearly 600 'early castles' in 1963 but only 209 'masonry castles' in their later list of 1967. The implication is clear: that there was a very high rate of abandonment of castles in the early middle ages, although it evidently slowed down when there was a major change of constructional material from wood to stone in the twelfth and thirteenth centuries. Hogg and King were able to mark on their maps castles already abandoned, but no doubt the written record can only give a very imperfect picture of this. The capital value, so to speak, of a stone castle was much greater than that of a wooden one, so abandonment was less frequent, though it continued. The essential point about the later middle ages is that the abandonment continued, or even accelerated, but replacement dropped to almost nil.

Our first reliable information on castles comes from Tudor topographers, but the emergency created by the rebellion of Owain Glyndŵr raised the question of the condition of castles. Hogg and King cite some twenty-eight references

[3] Owen (1892), 76.

of 1401–04 in the patent and close rolls which refer to castles in south Wales as being 'defensible', ranging from Manorbier in the west through Swansea, Usk and Goodrich, and Wigmore up to Montgomery. Although the destruction wrought by the rebels was very great, from the scanty information available it seems to have led to the permanent abandonment only of Criccieth Castle.[4] The town walls at New Radnor[5] and Montgomery[6] were apparently not rebuilt after damage by the rebels, whilst the construction of town walls at Beaumaris[7] was probably prompted by these events, as was the reconstruction of the gate-house at Carmarthen.[8]

We are ill-informed about events in the fifteenth century, but, although we may suppose that abandonment was very extensive, the massive works at Raglan are a fair indication that replacement had not stopped. Demolition of castles was frequent in early periods, notably of the 'adulterine castles' by Henry II, and was to recur later in the Civil War, but the most unusual case is from the later middle ages. In 1462 500 men with crowbars set about demolishing Carreg Cennen,[9] which was no longer occupied as a residence, to prevent it being used as a refuge for brigands. As a substantial ruin survives, the work cannot have been very thorough!

At the time of Leland's travels the monasteries were being dissolved and turned into ruins, but the traveller leaves us in no doubt that the landscape was already well-furnished with ruins; the ruined castle precedes the ruined abbey as a landscape feature (see appendix). It is not possible to produce statistics from Leland because of the ambiguity and laconic nature of his remarks, and the uncertainty as to whether his information was sometimes second-hand; but, as his special interest was castles, he provides a wealth of information on the castles in the areas he visited, which unfortunately excluded much of north and central Wales.

Some fifty castles in Wales and the Marches were in a bad state,[10] varying from 'down', 'partly standing', 'ruinous', 'somewhat ruinous', 'somewhat in decay', to 'tendithe toward ruine'. Clearly most were unoccupied, although few were total ruins. Many more are mentioned without definite information. Some are listed under 'ruinous castles', while in certain cases we know they were still in use, as at Ludlow. The remarks can be ambiguous: what de we make of 'It hath beene a notable thing', referring to Ewyas Harold? In some eighteen cases Leland is specific about the good condition of the castle, 'well maintained', 'repaired', for example: Abergavenny, Brecon, Builth, Carew ('repairid or magnificently buildid'); Chepstow, Chirk, Coity, Ogmore, Newcastle Emlyn ('repairid or new buildid'); Kidwelly ('meately wel kept up'); Bishop's Castle, Montgomery

[4] Johns (1984), 14–15.
[5] *Leland's Itin.*, **3**, 10, 41.
[6] Ibid., 11.
[7] RCAM (1937), cxlviii–ix.
[8] Colvin (1963), **2**, 601.
[9] Ibid., 602.
[10] I have culled the references from the index in vol. 5 of Toulmin Smith's edition of *Leland's Itin.*, vol. 3 of which is concerned with journeys in Wales. The index is not exhaustive.

('reedified'); Narberth ('preati'); Newport ('very fair'); Holt ('goodly'); Powis, Raglan, and Tretower. All these appear to have been in private occupation and it is noteworthy that several had undergone massive reconstruction.

The general implication from well over a hundred castles mentioned by Leland is clear. Only a minority, perhaps twenty-five to thirty, were still put to their intended use, that is, inhabited by an owner; possibly a similar number were totally ruinous beyond recovery, but the majority had ruinous or derelict living quarters, perhaps with limited use as a prison (as at Caerphilly) or a courthouse.

We have two other sources from the Tudor period, both based on closer observation than Leland's and fortunately covering areas omitted by him. The royal sources have been summarized by Colvin.[11] The famous castles of Edward I, Caernarfon, Harlech, Conwy and Beaumaris, no longer had garrisons after the early sixteenth century, and in a survey contemporary with Leland's journey they were said to be 'much ruynous and ferre in decay for lacke of tymely reparacons'; abandonment took place in Elizabethan times. Beeston Castle had been abandoned in the fifteenth century. Maintenance had stopped at Flint and Rhuddlan, Aberystwyth and Cardigan by the middle of the sixteenth century. Carmarthen was maintained until Elizabethan times. Chester Castle was kept up for its judicial function, and Ludlow, as the seat of the Council in the Marches of Wales, was well maintained; indeed, as the residence of the Council's president, new buildings were erected in it. Works are also recorded at Montgomery, Brecon, Wigmore, Chirk and Holt, where the castles benefited from being near the seat of the Council's activities at Ludlow.

In Pembrokeshire, from the end of the Tudor period we have very specific information from George Owen.[12] Of the nineteen ancient castles in the county, only three were in repair, Carew, Picton and Stackpole, which tallies well enough with the estimated figure of 25 per cent in Leland sixty years before, but now reduced to 15 per cent. Owen[13] does not for a moment write off the uninhabited castles as indefensible, for they are 'places of greate strength, and easly to be fortifyed by the Enymye, some of which are so seated naturally for strength, as they seeme Impregnable'. When speaking of the defences of Milford Haven, Owen saw the value of Pembroke Castle: 'All the Castle walles are standing verye stronge without any decaye onely the rooffes and leades have been taken downe'.[14] Events forty-five years later during the Civil War siege amply justified this confidence.

Owen was not sentimental about castles, but at the other end of south Wales, in Gwent, Thomas Churchyard, in his long, rambling, doggerel poem *The Worthines of Wales*, dedicated to Queen Elizabeth, hoped that 'the castles (that stand like a company of fortes) may not be forgotten, their buyldings are so princely, their strength is so great, and they are such stately seates and defences of

---

[11] Colvin (1975), 169–76. Since writing this, a third source is now available for castles in Glamorgan which had largely been abandoned by Elizabethan times—see Merrick (1983).

[12] Owen (1897), 401–02.

[13] Ibid., 564–65.

[14] Ibid., 558.

nature'.[15] He lamented their decay. The general decay of castles in Tudor times was a matter of common observation, but Churchyard was unusual in making this a theme of patriotic regret. They had decayed because they had ceased to be occupied, and the advanced state of decay described by Leland can leave no doubt but that abandonment had taken place in the previous century and sometimes even in the fourteenth century.

No two castles had the same history and there must have been apparent different causes of abandonment in each individual case. For example, the failure of male heirs, which led to the subdivision of the associated property, seems to have been a major cause of the astonishing decline of Richard's Castle near Ludlow between the fourteenth century and the time of Leland's visit.[16] Detailed study of individual cases would certainly throw light on matters of this kind, but a phenomenon that was so general and widespread deserves some more general explanation. It is tempting to invoke the kind of general economic recession in the later middle ages favoured by the late Professor Postan, but one may feel that, as so often, George Owen's view comes closest to the truth. He had no doubt that the castle had performed a function that was no longer required: '. . . and thereof grew that so manye Castles, and townes were in Ancient tyme built in Wales and wch nowe are fallen ruinouse, for every man that conquered a Countrey was forced to build a Castle for himselfe, and a towne for Receipt of such garrison . . .'.[17] The surprisingly rapid abandonment of the great Edwardian castles, and the evident confidence of the authorities that they would no longer be required, suggests that the accession to the throne of a Welshman meant that the troubles of a century before were thought not likely to recur.

Our best clue to the immediate cause of the abandonment of the majority of castles is to look at the minority that were not abandoned. As a rule the latter underwent massive reconstruction, as at Carew, Laugharne, Chirk, Powis and Picton. The accommodation of the early medieval castle was quite unsuitable for later medieval life, with its emphasis on privacy and individual chambers and suites, so either it had to be reconstructed, or, more usually, it was abandoned and a fresh start made. The replacement of Penrice Castle in Gower by Oxwich Castle, a manor house, is an example of this.[18] Inaccessibility, discomfort, lack of lodgings and private accommodation, so sought after in the later middle ages, were probably the main reasons for abandonment. The two notoriously inaccessible castles of Carreg Cennen and Beeston were abandoned in the fifteenth century, the former being deliberately pulled down (p. 207). The surviving castles were normally accessible, of moderate size, not huge like Caerphilly, and were capable of adaptation to a changed way of life.

The subject of castles in Wales during the Civil War deserves a paper, or rather a book, devoted to it. The sequence of events in Wales and the Marches

---

[15] Churchyard (1776), vi. I am indebted to Mr J. K. Knight for informing me of this work and lending me his copy of Churchyard.

[16] Curnow and Thompson (1969), 107.

[17] Owen (1892), 205

[18] RCAM (1981), 63–76.

was studied over a century ago by Phillips,[19] and an exceptionally valuable account of the course of the war in Pembrokeshire was published in the 1930s by Leach.[20] From these we can draw some general conclusions.

Both Wales and the Marches were predominantly Royalist territory, apart from Pembroke and Tenby in the first Civil War. Although bodies of troops did move around, even more so than in England, it was a battle of sieges, or very often of threats of sieges. Success was measured by the strong-points, castles but more particularly towns, that were taken. The great majority of castles and manor houses that were capable of defence were pressed into service, as a map of Pembrokeshire with its fortified places shows.[21] There was normally ample time for the construction of earthen defences for the disposal of artillery. Indeed, it was artillery rather than the numbers of fortified places that distinguished the fighting of this period from that of 500 years before. Clearly the possession of artillery gave the attackers a considerable advantage because of the opportunities for making a breach, as happened at Raglan and Chepstow. Nevertheless, for a determined and well-led garrison medieval walls could provide adequate protection, as was shown at Pembroke.

Our concern, however, must be with the extent to which the Civil War led to the abandonment of castles. The first effect in the early part was quite the reverse, with extensive re-occupation, refurbishment and repairs to many structures that were derelict or ruinous. As the war proceeded, the damage inflicted by sieges or, far more important, the deliberate 'slighting' or rendering of a castle unusable by demolition on the orders of Parliament, greatly reduced the numbers of castles that were usable. Unfortunately, it is quite impossible to quantify the destruction; probably the sources would not allow it and certainly no one has attempted the laborious task of trying to work it out.

It was as difficult to demolish a castle in 1648 as it had been in 1603, when George Owen had put this forward as the main reason for the survival of the carcasses of castles (p. 206). The stripping of lead roofs and timbers of monasteries in Tudor times, or of the bishop's palace at St Davids, still left the main ruin. More thorough-going was the demolition at Builth Castle, traditionally assigned to Elizabethan times, where virtually all masonry has vanished.[22] In the slighting of the Civil War in Wales we can distinguish two degrees of demolition: the reduction of the structure to a few fragments, probably with the use of explosives, as at Abergavenny, Aberystwyth,[23] Montgomery and Ruthin; and the impairment of the defences by the removal of a length of curtain wall or a side of the keep, as at Flint, Raglan,[24] Rhuddlan, Carew, Hawarden,[25] Laugharne, Oystermouth and Pembroke. In either case total abandonment normally

[19] Phillips (1874).
[20] Leach (1937).
[21] Ibid., 60.
[22] Colvin (1963), **1**, 299.
[23] Spurgeon (1975), 13.
[24] Taylor (1979), 21–22.
[25] Gladstone (1974), 3–4.

followed, although a prison might be later contained within the reconstructed walls, as at Carmarthen and Haverfordwest castles, or just outside as at Flint.

It is impossible to quantify the casualty rate among castles as a result of the Civil War, but it was clearly very high. Of the eighteen castles mentioned by Leland as being in good condition or rebuilt, only two, Chirk and Powis, are not in ruins today, and in nearly all other cases the abandonment took place at the time of the Civil War. A few struggled on before succumbing in the eighteenth century. The Council in the Marches of Wales was re-instituted and lasted until 1689 so its seat at Ludlow was needed, but the castle became a picturesque ruin soon afterwards. Chepstow was required as a prison for the regicide, Marten, and had its breach repaired, remaining in use for as long as Ludlow.[26]

Continuity of residential use from the middle ages to the present day is very rare; I can only think of Powis, Chirk, Picton, Penhow and St Donats in Wales and Croft Castle in Herefordshire. Re-occupation could take place by the erection of a later building on the site, as at St Fagans and Fonmon, more or less ignoring what was there already. At Penrhyn the original castle was swept away in the 1820s to allow the present 'Norman' pile to replace it. More care was taken to respect the original in the works of Telford at Shrewsbury or the 3rd marquis of Bute at Cardiff. The climax of Romantic reconstruction was by Burges at Cardiff and Castell Coch, with its curious mixture of archaeological accuracy and complete fantasy. The re-occupation of Roch Castle, after massive reconstruction in the present century, is the last of such expensive projects, but this has taken us outside the subject of abandonment.

Before closing the discussion, it may be useful to mention the normal adjunct of a castle in a walled borough, the town walls. In England construction of town walls was still in progress in the fifteenth century, for example at Coventry,[27] and, although walls may have suffered from neglect in Tudor and Stuart times, demolition is only recorded from the Restoration, curiously enough first at Coventry.[28] Demolition no doubt took place over the next century, although it is worth recalling that the walls at York were put in a state of defence at the time of the Young Pretender's incursion into England in 1745.[29] The period of greatest destruction was in the late eighteenth and early nineteenth centuries when increasing population and vehicular traffic generated by the Industrial Revolution made the walls appear a constriction to growth and the gates an obstruction to traffic. Colt Hoare mentioned how between visits to Hereford in different years he found a gate of the town had disappeared.[30]

In Wales some thirty-four sets of town walls or banks have been recorded by Hogg and King in their lists. As we have seen, those at New Radnor and Montgomery are said to have been damaged by Owain Glyndŵr and not rebuilt (p. 207), and fear of repetition of such events may have led to the construction

[26] Perks (1967), 10–11.
[27] Turner (1971), 118–19.
[28] *VCH* (1969), 23.
[29] RCHM (1972), 28–29.
[30] Hoare (1983), 200.

of the wall at Beaumaris, now virtually vanished. Some walls, like those at Cardigan, seem to have disappeared early, and Leland's remarks about those at Aberystwyth ('hath bene waullyd') and Hay ('sheuith the token of a right strong waulle')[31] indicate that others were in a bad way by Tudor times.

Between Leland and the Civil War we have very little information about the maintenance of town walls in Wales. One imagines that as with castles it was very much a story of neglect, although it is clear from the fighting during the Civil War that defence of the town had assumed a greater importance in relation to its castle. Sizeable earthwork defences were constructed at Carmarthen during the war. In Pembrokeshire Leach drew the distinction between the two boroughs where the medieval walls were capable of defence, Pembroke and Tenby, which indeed gave a good account of themselves in their respective sieges, and by contrast Haverfordwest where the walls were too ruinous to be capable of independent defence, although the castle underwent attack.[32]

The region contains some of the most impressive surviving town walls in the country, at Chester, Shrewsbury, Ludlow, Denbigh, Conwy, Caernarfon, Chepstow and Tenby. In areas acutely affected by the Industrial Revolution like Swansea, Cardiff and Newport (Gwent), they have vanished, but, in areas where these pressures did not exist, the picturesque character of the walls, which has attracted visitors since the eighteenth century, has afforded them a large measure of protection.

APPENDIX

Comments in Leland's *Itinerary* on the condition of castles in Wales and the Marches.

I have used the index in Toulmin Smith's edition of the *Itinerary* to identify remarks by Leland on the condition of castles and town walls listed in Hogg and King, 'Masonry castles in Wales and the Marches'. Where the castle is merely mentioned I have omitted it from the list below.

Aberedw	**4**, 165, ?ruin implied.
Abergavenny	**3**, 45, '... a faire waulled town ... a fair castel.'
Aberystwyth	**3**, 56, '... hath bene waullyd ...'
Alberbury	**4**, 1, '... the ruines ...'
Barry	**3**, 24, '... and most of it is in ruine.'
Bishop's Castle	**3**, 50, '... of good strenketh ...'; **5**, 15, '... well maintenid ...'
Blaen-Llyfni	**3**, 107, '... a veri fair castel now dekeiyng, and by was a borow now also in decay.'
Boughrood	**4**, 165, ?ruin implied.
Brecon	**3**, 105, '... welle waulled, and hath a fair castel yoining to hit ... iiii. gates ... the castel, the wich is very large, strong, welle mainteynid; and the keepe of the castel is very large and faire.'
Bronllys	**3**, 111, '... the great ruines of the castel ...'

---

[31] *Leland's Itin.*, **3**, 56, 110–11.
[32] Leach (1937), 20.

Builth	**3**, 109, '… a fair castel …'; **4**, 165, ?ruin implied.
Bwlch y Ddinas	**3**, 108, '… ruinus almost to the hard ground.'
Caergwrle (Hope)	**3**, 73, 'Ther stonde yet greate walles of a castel set on hylle, wher be diggid good mille stonis of a blew girthe.'
Caerleon	**3**, 44, 'The ruines of the walles of the town yet remayne, and also of the castel.'
Caerphilly	**3**, 18, '… ruinus waulles of a wonderful thiknes, and toure kept up for prisoners …'
Cardiff	**3**, 34, '… well waullid, and is by estimation a mile in cumpace. In the waulle be 5. gates … The castelle … is a great thing and a strong, but now in sum ruine.'
Carew	**3**, 115, '… repairid or magnificently buildid by Syr Rhese ap Thomas.'
Carreg Cennen	**4**, 179, '… fawlynge still to ruyn was at the last *spelunca latronum*, and therapon a 50. or 60. yeres syns almost totaly defacyd by men of Kydwely …'
Castell Bychan	**3**, 12, '… in ruine.'
Castell Coch	**3**, 18, '… al yn ruine no bigge thing but high.'
Castell Tinboeth	**3**, 11, 'In Melennith apere greate ruines of 2. castles. The one is cawllid Tynbot …'
Cefnllys	**3**, 11, 'In Melennith apere greate ruines of 2. castles … The othar is caulyd Keuenlles … now downe …'
Chepstow	**3**, 43, '… the castel, the which yet standeth fayr and strong not far from the ruin of the bridge.'
Chirk	**3**, 72, '… and there is on a smaul hille a mighty large and stronge castel with dyvers towers, a late welle repayred by Syr Wylliam Standeley …'
Clun	**3**, 53, '… sumewhat ruinus. It hath bene bothe strong and well builded …'
Clyro	**4**, 165, ?ruin implied.
Coity	**3**, 33, 'This castelle is maintainid …'
Criccieth	**3**, 88, 'There hath beene a franchisid toune, now clene decayed.'
Degannwy	**3**, 89, '… great ruines …'
Denbigh	**3**, 97, 'The castelle is a very large thing, and hath many toures yn it. But the body of the worke was never finishid.'
Dinas Brân	**3**, 90, 'It is now al in ruine …'
Dinas Powys	**3**, 23, '… al in ruine …'
Dinefwr	**3**, 57, '… now ruinus.'
Dolbadarn	**3**, 84, 'There is yet a pece of a toure …'
Dolforwyn	**3**, 54, '… ruinus …'; **3**, 125, '… ruinus …'
Ewloe	**3**, 93, '… a ruinus castelet, or pile …'
Ewyas Harold	**2**, 69, 'It hath beene a notable thinge.'
Fonmon	**3**, 24, 'This castelle yet stondith …'
Grosmont	**2**, 71, 'Moste parte of the castle wauls stand.'
Hay	**3**, 110–11, 'The Hay … yet sheuith the token of a right strong waulle, having in hit iii. gates and a posterne. Ther is also a castel, the which sumtime hath bene right stately … the toun within the waulles is wonderfully decaied. The ruine is adscribid to Oene Glindour.'

Hereford	**3**, 47, '. . . large and strongely walled, also having a mayne castel hard by the ripe of Wy. I take the castel to be as great circuite as Windesore. The dungyn of the castel is hy and stronge . . .'; **2**, 64–65, '. . . but now the hole castle tendithe toward ruine. It hath bene one of the fairest, largest and strongest castles of England . . .'
Holt	**3**, 69, '. . . goodly castel . . .'
Kenfig	**3**, 29, '. . . in ruine and almost shokid and devourid with the sandes that the Severn Se ther castith up.'
Kidwelly	**3**, 59, 'The old toun is pretily waullid, and hath hard by the waul a castel. The old town is nere al desolatid, but the castel is meately wel kept up.'
Knockin	**5**, 14, '. . . now a ruinus thing . . .'
Llanblethian	**3**, 31, '. . . yet partly standing . . . kept as the prison . . .'
Llandew	**3**, 109, '. . . sumtime a veri place of the bisshops, now no thing but an onsemeli ruine.'
Llandough	**3**, 31, '. . . a castelle much in ruine . . .'
Llanmaes (Llanfaes)	**3**, 27, '. . . almost al doun.'
Llantrisant	**3**, 21, '. . . ys in ruine. It hath beene a fair castel . . . at this castelle is the prison for Miskin and Glin Rodeney.'
Ludlow	**2**, 76, 'The towne of Ludlow . . . is well waullyd . . . There be in the waulls 5. gates . . . The castle hemithe in one parte of the towne . . .'; **3**, 50, '. . . a fair castel.'
Montgomery	**3**, 11, '. . . the castell, now a-late reedified . . . Great ruines of the [town] waulle yet apere . . .'; **3**, 41, 'Montgomerike deflorichid by Owen Glindour.'
Morlais	**3**, 18, '. . . in ruine . . .'
Myddle	**5**, 13, '. . . veri ruinus.'
Narberth	**3**, 62, '. . . a litle preati pile of old Syr Rheses . . .'
Newcastle Emlyn	**3**, 57, '. . . repairid or new buildid by Syr Rhese ap Thomas.'
Newport (Gwent)	**3**, 45, '. . . I marked not whyther yt were waulled or no. There is a very fair castel . . .'
New Radnor	**3**, 10, '. . . hathe be metly well wallyd, and in the walle appere the ruines of iiii. gates . . . The castle is in ruine, but that a pece of the gate was a late amendyd. The towne was defacyd in Henry the fowrthe dayes by Owen Glindowr.'
Ogmore	**3**, 28, '. . . ys meatly welle maintainid.'
Oswestry	**3**, 74–75, 'The cumpace of the towne withyn the waulle is about a mile. There be 4 gates . . . There is a castelle sette on a mont be likelihod made by hand . . .'
Oystermouth	**3**, 127, '. . . there remaine ruines of a castel . . .'
Pembroke	**3**, 115–16, 'The toune is welle waullid and hath iii. gates . . . The castel stondith hard by the waul on a hard rokke, and is veri larg and strong . . .'
Penlline	**3**, 32, 'This castelle yet stondith . . .'
Peterston	**3**, 26, '. . . almost al in ruine.'
Pontesbury	**2**, 26, 'On the south side of the chirche yarde appere greate tokens and stones faullen downe of a great manor place or castelle . . . In the midle way betwixt the chirch of Ponsbyri and this wood appere certen ruines of a castel or pile apon . . .'

Powis	**3**, 53, 'Walschpole had 2. Lorde Marchers castles within one waulle, the Lord Powis namid Greye, and the Lord Dudley caullyd Sutton; but now the Lord Powys hathe bothe in his hond... The Lord Duddeles parte is almoste fallen down. The Lord Powys parte is meatly good...'; **3**, 125, 'Castel Cough, in English Redde Castel, standith on a rokke of dark, redde colorid stone. It hath ii. separatid wardes, wherof the one was the Lord Duddeleys. Now both long to the Lord Powys.'
Raglan	**3**, 45, '... a very fair and a pleasant castel...'
Red Castle (Shropshire)	**5**, 13, '... now al ruinus. It hath bene strong and hath decayid many a day.'
Richard's Castle	**2**, 76, 'The kepe, the waulls, and towres of yt yet stond but goynge to ruyn. [There is a poore house of tymbar in the castle garth for a farmer...]'
St Fagans	**3**, 25, '... a part of it yet standith.'
Shrewsbury	**2**, 82, 'The towne is strongly waulyd... 3 gates. The castle hathe bene a stronge thinge, it is now muche in ruine.'
Skenfrith	**2**, 70, 'Muche of the uter warde of this castle yet standithe, the site of it is sumwhat low.'
Snodhill	**5**, 176, '... somewhat in ruine.'
Tal y Fan	**3**, 33, 'It is clerely in ruine...'
Tenby	**3**, 116, 'The toune is strongeli waullid, and welle gatid, everi gate having his portcolis *ex solido ferro*.'
Trecastle	**3**, 112, '... yet apperith the ruines of a castel.'
Tretower	**3**, 108, '... a prety castel...'
Troggy (Striguil)	**3**, 42, '... very notable ruines of a castel cawlled Trogy...'
Usk	**3**, 44, 'The castel ther hath bene great, stronge and fair.'
Wenvoe	**3**, 23, 'Al the buildinges of this Wenuo Castelle stonding on a litle hille is downe saving one toure and broken waules.'
Weobley (Herefordshire)	**2**, 69, '... a goodly castell, but somewhat in decay.'
Wrinstone	**3**, 23, '... al in ruine saving one high tower.'

The published works of David James Cathcart King[1]

Compiled by JOHN R. KENYON

1947

'Bow and Arrow Castle, Portland', *Proc. Dorset Natur. Hist. Archaeol. Soc.*, **69**, 65–67.

1949

'The taking of Le Krak des Chevaliers in 1271', *Antiquity*, **23**, 83–92.

1951

'Castell Nanhyfer, Nevern (Pemb.)' (with J. C. Perks), *Archaeol. Cambrensis*, **101.2**, 123–28.
'The defences of the Citadel of Damascus; a great Mohammedan fortress of the time of the Crusades', *Archaeologia*, **94**, 57–96.

1956

'Llangibby Castle' (with J. C. Perks), *Archaeol. Cambrensis*, **105**, 96–132.
'The castles of Cardiganshire', *Ceredigion*, **3.1**, 50–69.

1958

'The donjon of Flint', *J. Chester N. Wales Architect. Archaeol. Hist. Soc.*, **45**, 61–69.

1959

'Beeston Castle, Cheshire' (with M. H. Ridgway), *J. Chester N. Wales Architect. Archaeol. Hist. Soc.*, **46**, 1–23.

1960

'Penrice Castle', *The hundred and seventh annual meeting at Swansea, 1960.* CAA, 16–17.

1961

'Penrice Castle, Gower' (with J. C. Perks), *Archaeol. Cambrensis*, **110**, 71–101.
'The castles of Breconshire', *Brycheiniog*, **7**, 71–94.

[1] This bibliography does not include the later printings or impressions of King's guide to Llanstephan Castle which was published in 1963.
The abbreviation CAA has been used throughout for Cambrian Archaeological Association.

1962

'Moat Lane [Llandinam]', *The hundred and ninth annual meeting to be held at Newtown, 1962*. CAA, 23.
'Carew Castle, Pembrokeshire' (with J. C. Perks), *Archaeol. J.*, **119**, 270–307.
'The castles of Pembrokeshire', ibid., 313–16.
'Manorbier Castle', ibid., 319–20.
'Wiston Castle', ibid., 326, 328.

1963

Llanstephan Castle, Carmarthenshire, London.
'Early castles in Wales and the Marches: a preliminary list' (with A. H. A. Hogg), *Archaeol. Cambrensis*, **112**, 77–124.

1964

'The Norman invasion & the building of castles', in D. Moore (ed.), *The land of Dyfed in early times*. Cardiff, 23–26.
'Castell Aber Lleiniog', *The hundred and eleventh annual meeting at Llangefni, 1964*. CAA, 18–19.
Review: A. W. Lawrence, *Trade castles and forts of West Africa*, *Antiq. J.*, **44**, 265–66.

1965

'Goodrich Castle', *The hundred and twelfth annual meeting at Hereford, 1965*. CAA, 30–31.
'The mottes in the Vale of Montgomery' (with C. J. Spurgeon), *Archaeol. Cambrensis*, **114**, 69–86.
'St Briavels Castle', *Archaeol. J.*, **122**, 230.
'A castle of Llywelyn ap Gruffydd in Brycheiniog', *Brycheiniog*, **11**, 151–53.
'Henry II and the fight at Coleshill', *Welsh Hist. Rev.*, **2.4**, 367–73.

1966

'Ewloe Castle', *The hundred and thirteenth annual meeting at Chester, 1966*. CAA, 26–27.
'Hawarden Castle', ibid., 28–29.
'Beeston Castle', ibid., 32–33.

1967

'Llanstephan Castle', *The hundred and fourteenth annual meeting at Carmarthen, 1967*. CAA, 18–19.
'Laugharne Castle', ibid., 21–22.
'Dryslwyn Castle', ibid., 24–25.
'Llandovery Castle', ibid., 29–30.
'Masonry castles in Wales and the Marches: a list' (with A. H. A. Hogg), *Archaeol. Cambrensis*, **116**, 71–132.

1967/68

'Excavations at Castell Bryn Amlwg' (with L. Alcock, W. G. Putnam and C. J. Spurgeon), *Montgomeryshire Collect.*, **60**, 8–27.

1968/69

'Two further castles in Breconshire', *Brycheiniog*, **13**, 155–57.

1969

'Ringworks of England and Wales' (with L. Alcock), *Château Gaillard*, **3**, 90–127.

'Degannwy Castle', *The hundred and sixteenth annual meeting at Vale of Conway, 1969*. CAA, 13–15.

Review: M. Fixot, *Les fortifications de terre et les origines féodales dans le Cinglais*, *Antiq. J.*, **49**, 427–28.

Review: D. F. Renn, *Norman castles in Britain*, *Archaeol. Cambrensis*, **118**, 163–64.

1970

'Manorbier Castle, Pembrokeshire' (with J. C. Perks), *Archaeol. Cambrensis*, **119**, 83–118.

'Castles in Wales and the Marches: additions and corrections to lists published in 1963 and 1967' (with A. H. A. Hogg), ibid., 119–24.

1971

'Lidelea Castle—a suggested identification' (with D. F. Renn), *Antiq. J.*, **51**, 301–03.

1972

'Newcastle Emlyn', *The hundred and nineteenth annual meeting in Lampeter and district, 1972*. CAA, 42–44.

'The field archaeology of mottes in England and Wales: eine kurze Ubersicht', *Château Gaillard*, **5**, 101–12.

1973

'Dodleston Castle', *The hundred and twentieth annual meeting in Wrexham and district, 1973*. CAA, 15.

'Whittington Castle', ibid., 24–25.

'Erddig motte and bailey', ibid., 34.

'Tomen y Rhodwydd', ibid., 41.

1974

'Clifford Castle', *The hundred and twenty first annual meeting in south Brecknock, 1974*. CAA, 36–37.

'Two castles in northern Powys: Dinas Brân and Caergwrle', *Archaeol. Cambrensis*, **123**, 113–39.

1975

Castles and abbeys of Wales. London.

1976

'Llawhaden Castle', *The hundred and twenty third annual meeting in south Pembrokeshire, 1976.*
CAA, 11.
'Narberth Castle', ibid., 13–14.
'Carew Castle', ibid., 16–17.
'Pembroke town walls', ibid., 19.
'Pembroke Castle', ibid., 19–21.
'Manorbier Castle', ibid., 23–24.
'Upton Castle and chapel', ibid., 33–34.
'Haverfordwest Castle', ibid., 37–38.
'Wiston Castle', ibid., 38–39.
'Picton Castle', ibid., 39–40.

1977

'The defence of Wales, 1067–1283: the other side of the hill', *Archaeol. Cambrensis*, **126**,
1–16.
'Pembroke Castle: derivations and relationships of the domed vault of the donjon, and
of the Horseshoe Gate', *Château Gaillard*, **8**, 159–69.

1978

'St Briavels Castle', *125th annual meeting in Gwent and the Forest of Dean, 1978.* CAA,
10.
'Caldicot Castle', ibid., 13–14.
'Chepstow: castle', ibid., 15–16.
'Llangybi (Llangibby) Castle', ibid., 26–27.
'Monmouth: castle', ibid., 34.
'Pembroke Castle', *Archaeol. Cambrensis*, **127**, 75–121.

1979

'Dolbadarn Castle', *126th annual meeting: Lleyn and Snowdonia, 1979.* CAA, 26–27.
Review: W. Ubregts, *Le Château de Corroy*, Antiq. J., **59**, 457–58.

1980

'Neath Castle', *127th annual meeting: Swansea, Gower and West Glamorgan, 1980.* CAA,
30–32.
'Castles and the administrative divisions of Wales: a study of names', *Welsh Hist. Rev.*,
10.1, 93–96.

1981

'Flint Castle', *128th annual meeting: Chester and north east Wales, 1981.* CAA, 10–11.
'Beeston Castle', ibid., 12.

'Castles in England and Wales: their very varied character and purposes', in T. Hoekstra *et al.* (eds.), *Liber castellorum: 40 variaties op het thema kasteel.* Zutphen, 81–96.

'The old earldom of Pembroke', *Pembrokeshire Hist.*, **7**, 6–15.

Review: Somerset Archaeological and Natural History Society, *Steep Holm—a survey*, *Casemate*, **9**, 7.

1982

'The town walls of Pembroke' (with M. Cheshire), *Archaeol. Cambrensis*, **131**, 77–84.

'The trebuchet and other siege-engines', *Château Gaillard*, **9–10**, 457–70.

1983

Castellarium Anglicanum: an index and bibliography of the castles in England, Wales and the islands. 2 vols. New York.

'Ystradowen', *130th annual meeting, Vale of Glamorgan, 1983.* CAA, 21.

'Caerphilly Castle', ibid., 22.

'Llanblethian Castle', ibid., 27.

'Notes on the castle of Saint Clears', *Carmarthenshire Antiq.*, **19**, 5–7.

1984

Review: A. Châtelain, *Châteaux forts: images de pierres des guerres médiévales*, *Antiq. J.*, **64**, 181–82.

1984/85

'Camlais and Sennybridge castles', *Brycheiniog*, **21**, 9–11.

1985

'Château-Gaillard XII, 1984: Oostduinkerke & Floreffe', *Casemate*, **15**, 4.

'Llanstephan Castle', *132nd annual meeting, Old Carmarthenshire, 1985.* CAA, 9–10.

'St Clear's motte and bailey', ibid., 15–16.

'Carreg Cennen Castle', ibid., 19.

Bibliography

PRIMARY SOURCES: UNPUBLISHED

BL — British Library.

Add. MS 10013 — Additional Manuscript 10013, survey of Bromfield and Yale, 1391.

Add. MS 29938 — Additional Manuscript 29938, a collection of sketches by John Carter in 20 vols., of which this is vol. 14.

Add. MS 42035 — Additional Manuscript 42035, miscellaneous sketches: drawings of towns, castles, etc., in England and Wales.

Harl. MS 1319 — Harleian Manuscript 1319, *Histoire du Roy d'Angleterre Richard II*.

Harl. MS 2073 — Harleian Manuscript 2073, a collection of drawings made by Randle Holme of Chester *c*. 1650.

Harl. MS 3696 — Harleian Manuscript 3696, John Norden's survey of Holt and Bromfield, 1620.

Maps 137. c. 2(7) — Plan of the Broadway estate, Laugharne, Carmarthenshire, with sale particulars, 1867.

Royal MS 12C XII — Royal Manuscript 12C XII, *Fouk le Fitz Waryn*.

Cardiff — Cardiff Central Library.

Hafod MS 20 — Hafod Manuscript 20.

Herbert Pros. — Sir Thomas Herbert of Tintern, *Herbertorum Prosapia*. (MS 5.7).

Reynolds — Llyfr Hir Llywarch Reynolds.

LCR 1592 Survey — Laugharne Corporation Records: *A Booke of Survey of the Castle, Lordship, and Manor of Tallaugharne, alias Laugharne, the Second Day of October, in the XXXIIIIth Yeare of the Raigne of our Soveraigne Lady Elizabeth.*

NLW — National Library of Wales.

Add. MS 455D — Additional Manuscript 455D, a collection of documents illustrating the history of the castle, town and lordship of Dryslwyn from the earliest time to the close of the reign of Henry VIII. Compiled for Sir John Williams by E. A. Lewis, July, 1907.

Laugharne tithe — Tithe map of Laugharne, 1842.

PRO   Public Record Office.
  C 1/1108   Chancery Proceedings.
  C 66/136, m. 6   Charter of 2 Edward II: Lordship of Brom-
                           field.
  C 66/150   Licence of 12 Edward II: Lordship of Brom-
                           field.
  Court R.   Court Rolls.
  E   Exchequer Accounts: E 101, Account Var-
                           ious; E 112, Proceedings; E 178, Special
                           Commissions of Inquiry; E 352, Chancellor's
                           Rolls; E 372, Pipe Rolls.
  LR 2/234   Survey of Bromfield and Yale, 1562.
  LR 2/249   Survey of Bromfield and Yale, *c.* 1538–47
                           (Tidderley's survey).
  Minist. Acc.   Ministers' and Receivers' Accounts.
  Orig. R.   Originalia Rolls.
  Rent. Surv.   Rentals and Surveys.
  Star Chamb. Proc.   Star Chamber Proceedings.
  Welsh R.   Welsh Rolls.
SA   Society of Antiquaries of London.
  Ludlow   Nineteenth- and early twentieth-century
                           plans of Ludlow Castle, some published in
                           Hope 1908. (Roll Room).
  MS 785   Manuscript 785, notebooks of Sir William
                           St John Hope.
SRO Walcot   Shropshire County Record Office, Walcot
                           Estate Office papers, Box 682.

PRIMARY SOURCES: PUBLISHED

Ann. Camb.   *Annales Cambriae*, ed. by J. Williams ab Ithel. Lon-
                           don. 1860. (Rolls Series 20).

Ann. Marg.   *Annales de Margan (AD 1066–1232)*, in *Annales Monas-*
                           tici, **1**, ed. by H. R. Luard, 1–40. London, 1864.
                           (Rolls Series 36).

Ann. Rep. Dep. Keeper Public Rec.   *The thirty-first annual report of the Deputy Keeper of*
                           the Public Records. London, 1870.

APC   *Acts of the Privy Council of England.* London,
                           1890–1964.

Brenhinedd   *Brenhinedd y Saesson, or, The Kings of the Saxons*, trans.
                           by T. Jones. Cardiff, 1971.

Breviate of Domesday   'Chronicle of the thirteenth century: MS Ex-
                           chequer, Domesday', *Archaeol. Cambrensis*, 3 ser., **8**
                           (1862), 272–83.

Brut (Hergest)   *Brut y Tywysogyon, or, The Chronicle of the Princes: Red*
                           Book of Hergest version, trans. by T. Jones, 2nd edi-
                           tion. Cardiff, 1973.

Brut (Peniarth)   *Brut y Tywysogyon, or, The Chronicle of the Princes:*
                           Peniarth MS 20 version, trans. by T. Jones, Cardiff,
                           1952.

Cal. Anc. Corr.	*Calendar of ancient correspondence concerning Wales*, ed. by J. G. Edwards. Cardiff, 1935.
Cal. Chanc. R.	*Calendar of Chancery Rolls, Various, 1277–1326.* London, 1912.
Cal. Chart. R.	*Calendar of Charter Rolls.* London, 1903–27.
Cal. Close R.	*Calendar of Close Rolls.* London, 1892–1963.
Cal. Fine R.	*Calendar of Fine Rolls.* London, 1911–63.
Cal. Pat. R.	*Calendar of the Patent Rolls.* London, 1891—.
Cal. State Papers, Dom.	*Calendar of State Papers, Domestic.* London, 1856–1972.
Chron. John Worc.	*The Chronicle of John of Worcester 1113–40*, ed. by J. R. H. Weaver. Oxford, 1908.
Hathaway, E. J. *et al.* (eds.) 1975	*Fouke le Fitz Waryn.* Oxford, 1975.
Henrici Hunt.	*Henrici Archidiaconi Huntendunensis, Historia Anglorum*, ed. by T. Arnold. London, 1879. (Rolls Series 74).
Hist. Cart. Glouc.	*Historia et Cartularium Monasterii Sancti Petri Gloucestriae*, **1**, ed. by W. H. Hart. London, 1863. (Rolls Series 33).
Hist. Guill. Mar.	*Histoire de Guillaume le Maréchal*, ed. by P. Meyer, 3 vols. Paris, 1891–1901.
HMC 1891	*Twelfth report, appendix, part IX. The manuscripts of the Duke of Beaufort, K.G., the Earl of Donoughmore, and others*, Historical Manuscripts Commission. London, 1891.
Hunter, J. (ed.) 1844	*The Great Roll of the Pipe for the first year of the reign of King Richard the First, 1189–90.* London, 1844.
L. & P., Henry VIII	*Letters and Papers, Foreign and Domestic, Henry VIII.* London, 1864–1932.
Leland's Itin.	*The Itinerary of John Leland in or about the years 1535–1543*, ed. by L. T. Smith, 5 vols. London, 1964. (Reprint of 1906–10 edition).
Lhwyd, E. 1911	*Parochialia, being a summary of answers to parochial queries*, **3**, ed. by R. H. Morris. London, 1911. (Supplement to *Archaeol. Cambrensis*).
Liber Landavensis	*The text of the Book of Llan Dâv, reproduced from the Gwysaney manuscript*, J. G. Evans. Oxford, 1893.
Liber Quotid.	*Liber Quotidianus Contrarotulatoris Garderobae.* London, 1787.
Matth. Paris	*Matthaei Parisiensis, Historia Anglorum*, ed. by F. Madden, 3 vols. London, 1866–69. (Rolls Series 44).
Orderic Vitalis	*The Ecclesiastical History of Orderic Vitalis*, **4**, ed. by M. Chibnall. Oxford, 1973.
Paston Lett.	*Paston letters and papers of the fifteenth century*, **1**, ed. by N. Davis. Oxford, 1971.
Rhys, M. 1936	*Ministers' accounts for West Wales, 1277 to 1306. Part 1.* London, 1936. (Cymmrodorian Record Series 13).
Stevenson, J. (ed.) 1875	*The Legend of Fulk Fitz-Warin, in Radulphi de Coggeshall Chronicon Anglicanum, 275–415.* London, 1875. (Rolls Series 66).

TT	*Thomason Tracts. Catalogued in Catalogue of the pamphlets, books, newspapers and manuscripts relating to the Civil War, the Commonwealth and Restoration, 1640–1661*, collected by G. Thomason, 2 vols. London, 1908.
E4.11	*The True Informer*, **41**, 27 July–3 August 1644.
E4.12	*Mercurius Aulicus*, 20 July 1644.
E17.15	*The London Post*, **12**, 19 November 1644.
E20.5	*Perfect Passages*, **7**, 27 November–4 December 1644.
E21.1	*A Diary, or an Exact Journall*, **30**, 28 November–5 December 1644.
E21.3	*The Parliament Scout*, **76**, 28 November–5 December 1644.
E21.8	*Mercurius Britanicus*, **60**, 2 December–9 December 1644.
E21.11	*The London Post*, **15**, 10 December 1644.
E21.23	*Mercurius Britanicus*, **61**, 9 December–16 December 1644.
E25.1	*A Letter from Captaine Richard Swanley, to the Right Honourable, the Earl of Warwick*, January 1, 1645.
E256.35	*Perfect Occurrences of Parliament*, **14**, 8 November–15 November 1644.
E256.44	*Perfect Occurrences of Parliament*, **17**, 29 November–6 December 1644.
E258.1	*Perfect Occurrences of Parliament*, **18**, 6 December–13 December 1644.
E271.22	*God appearing for the Parliament, in sundry late victories bestowed upon their forces*, 10 March 1644.
Vicars, J. 1646	*The Burning-Bush not Consumed or, the Fourth and Last Part of the Parliamentarie-Chronicle.* London, 1646.
Vitae Sanctorum	*Vitae Sanctorum Britanniae et Genealogiae*, trans. by A. E. Wade-Evans. Cardiff, 1944.
Worc. Itin.	*William Worcestre: Itineraries*, ed. by J. H. Harvey. Oxford, 1969.

Secondary Sources

Aitken, M. J. 1970. 'Dating by archaeomagnetic and thermoluminescent methods', in Allibone *et al.* 1970, 77–88.

Aitken, M. J. 1974. *Physics and archaeology*, 2nd edition. London, 1974.

Aitken, M. J. and Hawley, H. N. 1966. 'Magnetic dating—III: further archaeomagnetic measurements in Britain', *Archaeometry*, 9 (1966), 187–97.

Aitken, M. J. and Hawley, H. N. 1967. 'Archaeomagnetic measurements in Britain—IV', *Archaeometry*, 10 (1967), 129–35.

Alcock, L. 1963. *Dinas Powys: an Iron Age, Dark Age and early medieval settlement in Glamorgan.* Cardiff, 1963.

Alcock, L. 1966. 'Castle Tower, Penmaen: a Norman ring-work in Glamorgan', *Antiq. J.*, 46 (1966), 178–210.

Alcock, L. 1967. 'Excavations at Degannwy Castle, Caernarvonshire, 1961–6', *Archaeol. J.*, 124 (1967), 190–201.

Alcock, L. 1975. 'Dry bones and living documents', in J. G. Evans *et al.* (eds.), *The effect of man on the landscape: the Highland Zone*, 117–23. London, 1975.

Alcock, L. 1980. 'The Cadbury Castle sequence in the first millennium BC', *Bull. Board Celtic Stud.*, 28.4 (1980), 656–718.

Allibone, T. E. *et al.* (eds.) 1970. *The impact of the natural sciences on archaeology*. London, 1970.

Apted, M. R. 1980. *Claypotts Castle*, 2nd edition. Edinburgh, 1980.

Astill, G. and Lobb, S. 1982. 'Sampling a Saxon settlement site: Wraysbury, Berks. 1980', *Medieval Archaeol.*, 26 (1982), 138–42.

Austin, D. 1979. 'Barnard Castle, Co. Durham. First interim report: excavations in the Town Ward, 1974–6', *J. Brit. Archaeol. Ass.*, 132 (1979), 50–72.

Avent, R. 1981. 'Laugharne Castle 1976–80', in R. Avent and P. Webster, *Interim reports of excavations at Laugharne Castle, Dyfed, 1976–80, and Dryslwyn Castle, Dyfed, 1980*, 1–33. Cardiff, 1981.

Avent, R. 1983a. *Cestyll tywysogion Gwynedd/Castles of the princes of Gwynedd*. Cardiff, 1983.

Avent, R. 1983b. 'Laugharne Castle 1981–2', in C. Arnold *et al.*, *Interim reports on excavations at three castles in Wales 1981–1982*, 2–11. Cardiff, 1983.

Avent, R. and Read, E. 1977. 'Laugharne Castle 1976: introduction, historical summary and excavations', *Carmarthenshire Antiq.*, 13 (1977), 17–41.

Baillie, M. G. L. 1976. 'Dendrochronology as a tool for the dating of vernacular buildings in the north of Ireland', *Vernacular Architect.*, 7 (1976), 3–10.

Baillie, M. G. L. 1982. *Tree-ring dating and archaeology*. London, 1982.

Baillie, M. G. L. forthcoming. 'Tree-ring and radiocarbon dating for bridge timbers at Caerlaverock', *Proc. Soc. Antiq. Scot.*, forthcoming.

Barker, G. 1978. 'Dry bones? Economic studies and historical archaeology in Italy', in H. McK. Blake *et al.* (eds.), *Papers in Italian archaeology I: the Lancaster seminar*, 35–49. Oxford, 1978.

Barker, P. 1964. 'Pontesbury castle mound emergency excavations 1961 and 1964', *Trans. Shropshire Archaeol. Soc.*, 57.3 (1964), 206–23.

Barker, P. 1977. *Techniques of archaeological excavation*. London, 1977.

Barker, P. and Higham, R. 1982. *Hen Domen, Montgomery: a timber castle on the English-Welsh border*. [London], 1982.

Barker, P. and Lawson, J. 1971. 'A pre-Norman field-system at Hen Domen, Montgomery', *Medieval Archaeol.*, 15 (1971), 58–72.

Barnetson, L. 1981. 'Animal bone', in G. L. Good and C. J. Tabraham, 'Excavations at Threave Castle, Galloway, 1974–78', *Medieval Archaeol.*, 25 (1981), 131–36.

Barton, K. J. and Holden, E. W. 1977. 'Excavations at Bramber Castle, Sussex, 1966–67', *Archaeol. J.*, 134 (1977), 11–79.

Batho, G. 1957. 'The Percies at Petworth, 1574–1632', *Sussex Archaeol. Collect.*, 95 (1957), 1–27.

Berendson, A. *et al.* 1964. *Fliesen*. Munich, 1964.

Berger, R. (ed.) 1970. *Scientific methods in medieval archaeology*. Berkeley, 1970.

Berger, R. *et al.* 1971. 'Can German tree-ring curves be applied in France and England?', *Vernacular Architect.*, 2 (1971), 3–6.

Biddle, M. *et al.* 1959. 'The excavation of the Manor of the More, Rickmansworth, Hertfordshire', *Archaeol. J.*, 116 (1959), 136–99.

Binding, G. 1977. 'Holzankerbalken im Mauerwerk mitterlalterlicher Burgen und Kirchen', *Château Gaillard*, 8 (1977), 69–77.

Boase, T. S. R. 1967. *Castles and churches of the crusading kingdom*. London, 1967.

Bollandius, J. and Herschenius, G. 1863. *Acta sanctorum . . . Editio novissima*, vol. 4. Paris, 1863.

Boon, G. C. 1986. *Welsh coin hoards 1979–1981*. Cardiff, 1986.

Boüard, M. de 1964. 'Les petites enceintes circulaires d'origine médiévale en Normandie', *Château Gaillard*, 1 (1964), 21–35.

Bowen, D. Q. 1977. 'The land of Wales', in D. Thomas (ed.), *Wales: a new study*, 11–35. Newton Abbot, 1977.

Bradney, J. A. 1896. 'Raglan Castle', in Monmouthshire and Caerleon Antiquarian Association, *Papers on Monmouth Castle and Priory. The Raglan Castle. [Etc.]*, 69–80. [S.l.], 1896.

Braun, H. S. 1935. 'Notes on Newark Castle', *Trans. Thoroton Soc. Nottinghamshire*, 39 (1935), 53–91.

Brears, P. C. P. 1983. 'Post-medieval pottery', in Mayes and Butler 1983, 215–24.

Brooke, C. 1963. 'St Peter of Gloucester and St Cadoc of Llancarfan', in K. Jackson *et al.*, *Celt and Saxon: studies in the early British border*, 258–322. Cambridge, 1963.

Brooke, G. C. 1916. *A catalogue of English coins in the British Museum: the Norman kings*, 2 vols. London, 1916.

Buck, S. and N. 1774. *Buck's antiquities*, 3 vols. London, 1774.

Burleigh, R. 1980. 'Dating and dating methods', in A. Sherratt (ed.), *The Cambridge encyclopaedia of archaeology*, 416–32. Cambridge, 1980.

Camden, W. 1695. *Camden's Britannia, newly translated into English: with large additions and improvements. Published by Edmund Gibson*. London, 1695.

Campbell, J. A. *et al.* 1979. 'Radiocarbon dates for the Cadbury massacre', *Antiquity*, 53 (1979), 31–38.

Carlyon-Britton, P. W. P. 1905. 'The Saxon, Norman and Plantagenet coinage of Wales', *Brit. Numis. J.*, 2 (1905), 31–56.

Carlyon-Britton, P. W. P. 1911. 'A penny of Llywelyn, son of Cadwgan, of the type of the second issue of William Rufus', *Brit. Numis. J.*, 8 (1911), 83–86.

Chaplin, R. E. 1971. *The study of animal bones from archaeological sites*. London, 1971.

Charles, B. G. 1934. *Old Norse relations with Wales*. Cardiff, 1934.

Charlton, P. *et al.* 1977. *Llantrithyd: a ringwork in South Glamorgan*. Cardiff, 1977.

Cherry, J. F. *et al.* (eds.) 1978. *Sampling in contemporary British archaeology*. Oxford, 1978.

Churchyard, T. 1776. *The worthines of Wales, a poem. A true note of the auncient castles, famous monuments, . . . that I have seen in the noble countrie of Wales*. London, 1776. [Reprinted from the edition of 1587].

Clapham, A. W. 1934. *English Romanesque architecture after the Conquest*. Oxford, 1934.

Clark, G. T. 1884. *Mediaeval military architecture in England*, 2 vols. London, 1884.

Clark, G. T. 1886. *Limbus patriae Morganiae et Glamorganiae*. London, 1886.

Clark, R. M. 1975. 'A calibration curve for radiocarbon dates', *Antiquity*, 49 (1975), 251–66.

Clarke, D. L. 1972. 'Models and paradigms in archaeology', in D. L. Clarke (ed.), *Models in archaeology*, 1–60. London, 1972.

Clarke, D. V. 1978–79. 'Excavation and volunteers: a cautionary tale', *World Archaeol.*, 10 (1978–9), 63–70.

Clwyd-Powys 1982. 'The structure of an early castle', *Review of projects*, Clwyd-Powys Archaeological Trust, 11. Welshpool, 1982.

Coad, J. G. and Streeten, A. D. F. 1982. 'Excavations at Castle Acre Castle, Norfolk,

1972–77: country house and castle of the Norman earls of Surrey', *Archaeol. J.*, 139 (1982), 138–301.

Cokayne, G. E. 1910–59. *The complete peerage*, edited and revised by V. Gibbs *et al.*, 12 vols. London, 1910–59.

Coles, J. 1973. *Archaeology by experiment*. London, 1973.

Coles, J. 1979. *Experimental archaeology*. London, 1979.

Colvin, H. M. (gen. ed.) 1963. *The history of the king's works. 1–2. The middle ages*. London, 1963.

Colvin, H. M. (gen. ed.) 1975. *The history of the king's works. 3. 1485–1660 (part I)*. London, 1975.

Colvin, H. M. (gen. ed.) 1982. *The history of the king's works. 4. 1485–1660 (part II)*. London, 1982.

Complete Peerage. See Cokayne, G. E. 1910–59.

Conant, K. J. 1959. *Carolingian and Romanesque architecture 800 to 1200*. Harmondsworth, 1959.

Conzen, M. R. G. 1968. 'The use of town plans in the study of urban history', in H. J. Dyos (ed.), *The study of urban history*, 113–30. London, 1968.

Craster, O. E. 1967. 'Skenfrith Castle: when was it built?', *Archaeol. Cambrensis*, 116 (1967), 133–58.

Craster, O. E. 1970. *Skenfrith Castle, Monmouthshire*. London, 1970.

Curnow, P. E. 1980. 'Some developments in military architecture *c.* 1200: Le Coudray-Salbart', in R. A. Brown (ed.), *Proceedings of the Battle Conference on Anglo-Norman Studies II, 1979*, 42–62, 172–73. Woodbridge, 1980.

Curnow, P. E. 1981. 'Ludlow Castle', *Archaeol. J.*, 138 (1981), 12, 14.

Curnow, P. E. and Thompson, M. W. 1969. 'Excavations at Richard's Castle, Herefordshire, 1962–1964', *J. Brit. Archaeol. Ass.*, 3 ser., 32 (1969), 105–27.

Curtis, M. 1880. *The antiquities of Laugharne, Pendine, and their neighbourhoods*. London, 1880.

Davies, J. D. 1894. *A history of west Gower, Glamorganshire*, **4**. Swansea, 1894.

Davies, W. 1979. *The Llandaff charters*. Aberystwyth, 1979.

Davis, R. 1973. *English overseas trade 1500–1700*. London, 1973.

Davison, B. K. 1969–70. 'Aldingham', *Current Archaeol.*, 2 (1969–70), 23–24.

Davison, B. K. 1971–72. 'Castle Neroche: an abandoned Norman fortress in south Somerset', *Proc. Somersetshire Archaeol. Natur. Hist. Soc.*, 116 (1971–72), 16–58.

De Jonge, C. H. 1931. *Dutch tiles*. London, 1931.

Dodgson, J. McN. 1972. *The place-names of Cheshire*, **4**. Cambridge, 1972. (English Place-name Society vol. 47).

Dolley, M. 1962. 'The 1962 Llantrithyd treasure trove and some thoughts on the first Norman coinage of Wales', *Brit. Numis. J.*, 31 (1962), 74–79.

Dolley, M. and Knight, J. K. 1970. 'Some single finds of tenth- and eleventh-century English coins from Wales', *Archaeol. Cambrensis*, 119 (1970), 75–82.

Donaldson, A. M. *et al.* 1980. 'Barnard Castle, Co. Durham. A dinner in the great hall: report on the contents of a fifteenth-century drain', in D. Austin, 'Barnard Castle, Co. Durham. Second interim report: excavation in the inner ward 1976–78: the later medieval period', *J. Brit. Archaeol. Ass.*, 133 (1980), 86–96.

Drury, P. J. (ed.) 1982a. *Structural reconstruction: approaches to the interpretation of the excavated remains of buildings*. Oxford, 1982.

Drury, P. J. 1982b. 'Aspects of the origins and development of Colchester Castle', *Archaeol. J.*, 139 (1982), 302–419.

DWB 1959. *The dictionary of Welsh biography down to 1940*. London, 1959.

Eames, E. S. 1957–58. 'A tile pavement from the Queen's Chamber, Clarendon Palace, dated 1250–2', *J. Brit. Archaeol. Ass.*, 3 ser., 20–1 (1957–58), 95–106.

Eames, E. S. 1980. *Catalogue of medieval lead-glazed earthenware tiles in the Department of Medieval and Later Antiquities, British Museum*, 2 vols. London, 1980.

Eastham, A. 1977. 'Birds', in B. Cunliffe, *Excavations at Portchester Castle. III. Medieval. The outer bailey and its defences*, 233–39. London, 1977.

Edwards, J. G. 1946. 'Edward I's castle-building in Wales', *Proc. Brit. Acad.*, 32 (1946), 15–81.

Edwards, J. G. 1956. 'The Normans and the Welsh March', *Proc. Brit. Acad.*, 42 (1956), 155–77.

Eldred, W. 1646. *The gunners glasse*. London, 1646. (Information taken from H. L. Blackmore, *The Armouries of the Tower of London: I. Ordnance*. London, 1976, p. 396).

Ellis, C. 1952. *Hubert de Burgh: a study in constancy*. London, 1952.

Ellis, T. P. 1924. *The first extent of Bromfield and Yale, AD 1315*. London, 1924. (Cymmrodorion Record Series 11).

Emery, A. 1975. 'The development of Raglan Castle and keeps in late medieval England', *Archaeol. J.*, 132 (1975), 151–86.

Evans, J. G. 1972. 'The environment of the inner bailey ditch', in T. Rowley, 'First report on the excavations at Middleton Stoney Castle, Oxfordshire, 1970–71', *Oxoniensia*, 37 (1972), 129–36.

Evans, J. G. 1975. *The environment of early man in the British Isles*. London, 1975.

Evans, J. G. 1978. *An introduction to environmental archaeology*. London, 1978.

Evans, J. G. and Limbrey, S. 1974. 'The experimental earthwork on Morden Bog, Wareham, Dorset, England: 1963 to 1972', *Proc. Prehist. Soc.*, 40 (1974), 170–202.

Eydoux, H. P. 1967. 'Le château de Coudray-Salbart', *Bull. Monumental*, 125 (1967), 247–60.

Eyton, R. W. 1857. *Antiquities of Shropshire*, **5**. London, 1857.

Fairbank, F. R. 1907. 'The last earl of Warenne and Surrey', *Yorkshire Archaeol. J.*, 19 (1907), 193–264.

Faulkner, P. A. 1958. 'Domestic planning from the twelfth to the fourteenth centuries', *Archaeol. J.*, 115 (1958), 150–83.

Faulkner, P. A. 1963. 'Castle planning in the fourteenth century', *Archaeol. J.*, 120 (1963), 215–35.

Fenn, R. W. D. 1962. 'The pre-Norman diocese of Llandaff', in E. T. Davies (ed.), *The story of the church in Glamorgan, 560–1960*, 9–28. London, 1962.

Ferguson, C. W. 1970. 'Concepts and techniques of dendrochronology', in Berger 1970, 183–200.

Fletcher, J. M. (ed.) 1978. *Dendrochronology in Europe: principles, interpretations and applications to archaeology and history*. Oxford, 1978.

Fletcher, J. M. *et al.* 1974. 'Dendrochronology—a reference curve for slow grown oaks, AD 1230 to 1546', *Archaeometry*, 16 (1974), 31–40.

Fryde, E. B. 1962. *The Book of Prests of the king's wardrobe for 1294–5*. Oxford, 1962.

Gardelles, J. 1972. *Les châteaux du moyen âge dans la France du sud-ouest: la Gascogne anglaise de 1216 à 1327*. Geneva, 1972.

Gardner, I. 1915. 'Raglan Castle', *Archaeol. Cambrensis*, 6 ser., 15 (1915), 40–46.

Gardner, W. 1961. 'The mound at Rug, near Corwen', *J. Merioneth Hist. Rec. Soc.*, 4.1 (1961), 3–6.

GCH 1971. *Glamorgan County History. III. The middle ages*, ed. by T. B. Pugh. Cardiff, 1971.

GCH 1974. *Glamorgan County History. IV. Early modern Glamorgan from the Act of Union to the Industrial Revolution*, ed. by G. Williams. Cardiff, 1974.

Gem, R. D. H. 1975. 'A recession in English architecture during the early eleventh century and its effect on the development of the Romanesque style', *J. Brit. Archaeol. Ass.*, 3 ser., 38 (1975), 28–49.

Gilpin, W. 1782. *Observations on the river Wye*. London, 1782.

Gladstone, E. W. 1974. *Hawarden old castle*. Privately published, 1974.

Godfrey, W. H. 1972. *Lewes Castle*. Lewes, 1972.

Grant, A. 1977. 'The animal bones', in B. Cunliffe, *Excavations at Portchester Castle. III. Medieval. The outer bailey and its defences*, 212–33. London, 1977.

Grant, A. 1978. 'Variation in dental attrition in mammals and its relevance to age estimation', in D. R. Brothwell *et al.* (eds.), *Research problems in zooarchaeology*, 103–06. London, 1978.

Gresham, C. A. and Hemp, W. J. 1949. 'Castell Prysor', *Archaeol. Cambrensis*, 100 (1949), 312–13.

Grieg, J. R. A. *et al.* 1982. 'The plant and insect remains', in Barker and Higham 1982, 60–71.

Griffinhoofe, H. G. 1894. *The mediaeval tiles in St Mary's Church, Monmouth*. Monmouth, 1894.

Griffith, N. J. L. *et al.* 1983. 'Faunal remains and economy', in Mayes and Butler 1983, 341–48.

Griffiths, R. A. 1966. 'The revolt of Rhys ap Maredudd, 1287–88', *Welsh Hist. Review*, 3.2 (1966), 121–43.

Griffiths, R. A. 1972. *The Principality of Wales in the later middle ages: the structure and personnel of government. I. South Wales, 1277–1536*. Cardiff, 1972.

Grimes, W. F. 1930. *Holt, Denbighshire: the works depôt of the Twentieth Legion at Castle Lyons*. London, 1930. (*Y Cymmrodor* 41).

Grose, F. 1785. *The antiquities of England and Wales*, new edition, **3**. London, 1785.

Héliot, P. 1947. 'Le château de Boulogne-sur-Mer et les châteaux gothiques de plan polygonal', *Revue Archéologique*, 6 sér., 27 (1947), 41–59.

Héliot, P. 1965. 'La genèse des châteaux de plan quadrangulaire en France et en Angleterre', *Bull. de la Société des Antiquaires de France*, (1965), 238–57.

Héliot, P. 1972. 'Un organe peu connu de la fortification médiévale: la gaine', *Gladius*, 10 (1972), 45–67.

Hemp, W. J. 1935. 'Holt Castle', *Archaeol. Cambrensis*, 90 (1935), 357–58.

Hertz, J. 1973. 'Further excavations at Solvig', *Château Gaillard*, 6 (1973), 97–105.

Hewett, C. A. 1969. *The development of carpentry, 1200–1700: an Essex study*. Newton Abbot, 1969.

Hewett, C. A. 1972. 'The tithe barn at Siddington, Gloucestershire', *Archaeol. J.*, 129 (1972), 145–47.

Higham, R. 1982. 'Dating in medieval archaeology: problems and possibilities', in B. Orme (ed.), *Problems and case studies in archaeological dating*, 83–107. Exeter, 1982.

Hinton, D. A. (ed.) 1983. *25 years of medieval archaeology*. Sheffield, 1983.

Hinz, H. 1975. 'Das mobile Haus. Bemerkungen zur Zeitbestimmung durch die Dendrochronologie', *Château Gaillard*, 7 (1975), 141–45.

Hoare, R. C. 1983. *The journeys of Sir Richard Colt Hoare through Wales and England 1793–1810*, ed. by M. W. Thompson. Gloucester, 1983.

Hogg, A. H. A. and King, D. J. C. 1963. 'Early castles in Wales and the Marches', *Archaeol. Cambrensis*, 112 (1963), 77–124.

Hogg, A. H. A. and King, D. J. C. 1967. 'Masonry castles in Wales and the Marches', *Archaeol. Cambrensis*, 116 (1967), 71–132.

Hogg, A. H. A. and King, D. J. C. 1970. 'Castles in Wales and the Marches: additions and corrections to lists published in 1963 and 1967', *Archaeol. Cambrensis*, 119 (1970), 119–24.

Hooper, W. 1945. *Reigate: its story through the ages.* Guildford, 1945.

Hope, W. H. St J. 1908. 'The castle of Ludlow', *Archaeologia*, 61.1 (1908), 257–328.

Hope, W. H. St J. 1909. 'The ancient topography of the town of Ludlow, in the county of Salop', *Archaeologia*, 61.2 (1909), 383–88.

Horn, W. 1970. 'The potential and limitations of radiocarbon dating in the middle ages: the art historian's view', in Berger 1970, 23–87.

Huber, B. and Giertz, V. 1970. 'Central European dendrochronology for the middle ages', in Berger 1970, 201–12.

Huggins, P. J. 1970. 'Excavation of a medieval bridge at Waltham Abbey, Essex, in 1968', *Medieval Archaeol.*, 14 (1970), 126–47.

Hugol, L. 1966. 'Die Pfalz Karl der Grosser in Aachen', in W. Braunfels and H. Schnitzler (eds.), *Karl der Grosse: Lebenswerk und Nachleben*, **3**, 534–72. Dusseldorf, 1966.

Humbert, D. 1944. 'Le château de Dourdan', *Congrès Archéologique de France*, 103: *Ile-de-France 1944*, 236–45.

Hurst, J. G. 1966. 'Post-Roman archaeological dating and its correlation with archaeo-magnetic results', *Archaeometry*, 9 (1966), 198–99.

International Study Group 1982. 'An inter-laboratory comparison of radiocarbon mea-surements in tree-rings', *Nature*, 298 (1982), 619–23.

James, T. 1980. *Carmarthen: an archaeological and topographical survey.* Carmarthen, 1980.

Janssen, W. 1972. 'Neue Grabungsergebnisse von der frühmittelalterlichen Niederungs-burg bei Haus Meer, Gem. Meerbusch-Büderich, Kr. Grevenbroich', *Château Gaillard*, 5 (1972), 85–99.

Jewell, P. A. and Dimbleby, G. W. (eds.) 1966. 'The experimental earthwork on Over-ton Down, Wiltshire, England: the first four years', *Proc. Prehist. Soc.*, 32 (1966), 313–42.

Johns, C. N. 1984. *Criccieth Castle/Castell Cricieth, Gwynedd*, 2nd edition. Cardiff, 1984.

Johnson, S. 1980. 'Excavations at Conisbrough Castle 1973–1977', *Yorkshire Archaeol. J.*, 52 (1980), 59–88.

Johnstone, H. 1946. *Edward of Caernarvon, 1284–1307.* Manchester, 1946.

Jones, A. 1910. *The history of Gruffydd ap Cynan.* Manchester, 1910.

Jones, F. E. 1955–57. 'Thoughts on the Norman coinage of Wales in the light of two additions to the series', *Brit. Numis. J.*, 28 (1955–57), 192–94.

Jones, G. R. J. 1983. 'The pre-Norman field system and its implications for early territor-ial organisation', in Mayes and Butler 1983, 70–72.

Jones, I. 1919. 'Sir Matthew Cradock and some of his contemporaries', *Archaeol. Cambren-sis*, 6 ser., 19 (1919), 393–458.

Jones, J. E. 1964. 'Tomen Castell, Dolwyddelan', *Archaeol. in Wales*, 4 (1964), 17.

Jones, P. N. and Renn, D. F. 1982. 'The military effectiveness of arrow loops: some experiments at White Castle', *Château Gaillard*, 9–10 (1982), 445–56.

Jope, E. M. 1972. 'Models in medieval studies', in D. L. Clarke (ed.), *Models in archaeology*, 963–90. London, 1972.

Kemp, A. J. 1839. 'Notices of the castle and lordship of Laugharne, Carmarthenshire', *Gentleman's Mag.*, n. ser., 12 (1839), 18–23, 353–59, 599–602.

Kenyon, J. R. 1981. 'Early artillery fortifications in England and Wales: a preliminary survey and reappraisal', *Archaeol. J.*, 138 (1981), 205–40.

Kenyon, J. R. 1982. 'The Civil War earthworks around Raglan Castle, Gwent: an aerial view', *Archaeol. Cambrensis*, 131 (1982), 139–42.

King, D. J. C. 1947. 'Bow and Arrow Castle, Portland', *Proc. Dorset Natur. Hist. Archaeol. Soc.*, 69 (1947), 65–67.

King, D. J. C. 1963. *Llanstephan Castle, Carmarthenshire*. London, 1963.

King, D. J. C. 1972. 'The field archaeology of mottes in England and Wales: eine kurze Ubersicht', *Château Gaillard*, 5 (1972), 101–12.

King, D. J. C. 1974. 'Two castles in northern Powys: Dinas Brân and Caergwrle', *Archaeol. Cambrensis*, 123 (1974), 113–39.

King, D. J. C. 1977. 'Pembroke Castle: derivations and relationships of the domed vault of the donjon, and of the Horseshoe Gate', *Château Gaillard*, 8 (1977), 159–69.

King, D. J. C. 1978. 'Pembroke Castle', *Archaeol. Cambrensis*, 127 (1978), 75–121.

King, D. J. C. 1982. 'The trebuchet and other siege-engines', *Château Gaillard*, 9–10 (1982), 457–70.

King, D. J. C. 1983. *Castellarium Anglicanum: an index and bibliography of the castles in England, Wales and the islands*, 2 vols. New York, 1983.

King, D. J. C. and Alcock, L. 1969. 'Ringworks of England and Wales', *Château Gaillard*, 3 (1969), 90–127.

King, D. J. C. and Perks, J. C. 1950–51. 'Castell Nanhyfer, Nevern (Pemb.)', *Archaeol. Cambrensis*, 101 (1950–51), 123–28.

King, D. J. C. and Perks, J. C. 1962. 'Carew Castle, Pembrokeshire', *Archaeol. J.*, 119 (1962), 270–307.

King, D. J. C. and Perks, J. C. 1970. 'Manorbier Castle, Pembrokeshire', *Archaeol. Cambrensis*, 119 (1970), 83–118.

King, D. J. C. and Spurgeon, C. J. 1965. 'The mottes in the Vale of Montgomery', *Archaeol. Cambrensis*, 114 (1965), 69–86.

Knight, J. K. 1963. 'The keep of Caerleon Castle', *Monmouthshire Antiq.*, 1.3 (1963), 71–72 [misprinted 23–24].

Knight, J. K. 1964. 'The excavation of a mound at Bettws Newydd', *Monmouthshire Antiq.*, 1.4 (1964), 125–26.

Knight, J. K. 1970. 'Caerleon Castle', in *The hundred-and-seventeenth annual meeting in the Vale of Usk, 1970*, Cambrian Archaeological Association, 16–18. [S.l.], 1970.

Knight, J. K. 1970–71. 'St Tatheus of Caerwent: an analysis of the Vespasian Life', *Monmouthshire Antiq.*, 3.1 (1970–71), 29–36.

Knight, J. K. 1977. 'Usk Castle and its affinities', in M. R. Apted *et al.* (eds.), *Ancient monuments and their interpretation: essays presented to A. J. Taylor*, 139–54. Chichester, 1977.

Knight, J. K. 1980. *Grosmont Castle, Gwent/Castell y Grysmwnt*. Cardiff, 1980.

Knight, J. K. and Talbot, E. J. 1968–70. 'The excavation of a castle mound and round barrow at Tre Oda, Whitchurch', *Trans. Cardiff Natur. Soc.*, 95 (1968–70), 9–23.

Knights, B. A. *et al.* 1983. 'Evidence concerning the Roman military diet at Bearsden, Scotland, in the 2nd century AD', *J. Archaeol. Sci.*, 10 (1983), 139–52.

Korf, D. 1963. *Dutch tiles*. London, 1963.

Kreusch, F. 1966. 'Kirche, Atrium und Portches de Aachener Pfalz', in W. Braunfels and H. Schnitzler (eds.), *Karl der Grosse: Lebenswerk und Nachleben*, **3**, 463–533. Dusseldorf, 1966.

Lauwerier, R. C. G. M. 1983. 'Pigs, piglets and determining the season of slaughtering', *J. Archaeol. Sci.*, 10 (1983), 483–88.

Leach, A. L. 1937. *The history of the Civil War (1642–1649) in Pembrokeshire and on its borders*. London, 1937.

Leask, H. G. 1936. 'Irish castles: 1180–1310', *Archaeol. J.*, 93 (1936), 143–99.

Leboutet, L. 1972. 'Problèmes de la dendrochronologie en Normandie', *Château Gaillard*, 5 (1972), 113–20.

Lewis, C. 1985. 'The Norman settlement of Herefordshire under William I', in R. A. Brown (ed.), *Anglo-Norman Studies VII: proceedings of the Battle Conference 1984*, 195–213. Woodbridge, 1985.

Lewis, E. A. 1923. 'The account roll of the chamberlain of west Wales from Michaelmas 1301 to Michaelmas 1302', *Bull. Board Celtic Stud.*, 2.1 (1923), 49–86.

Lewis, J. M. 1975. 'Recent excavations at Loughor Castle (South Wales)', *Château Gaillard*, 7 (1975), 147–57.

Lewis, J. M. 1976. *Welsh medieval paving tiles*. Cardiff, 1976.

Lightfoot, K. W. B. 1979. 'Cae Castell, Rumney', *Annual Rep. 1977–78*, Glamorgan-Gwent Archaeological Trust, 6–9. Swansea, 1979.

Lightfoot, K. W. B. 1981. 'An interim report on the excavation of Cae Castell, Rumney, Cardiff', *Annual Rep. 1979–80*, Glamorgan–Gwent Archaeological Trust, 9–12. Swansea, 1981.

Lightfoot, K. W. B. 1982. 'Cae Castell, Rumney, Cardiff', *Annual Rep. 1980–81*, Glamorgan–Gwent Archaeological Trust, 11–15. Swansea, 1982.

Lightfoot, K. W. B. 1983. 'Cae Castell, Rumney, Cardiff—final interim report', *Annual Rep. 1981–82*, Glamorgan–Gwent Archaeological Trust, 1–7. Swansea, 1983.

Limbrey, S. 1975. *Soil science and archaeology*. London, 1975.

Lloyd, D. J. 1979. *Broad Street: its homes and residents through eight centuries*. Birmingham, 1979. (Ludlow Research Papers 3).

Lloyd, J. D. K. and Knight, J. K. 1981. *Montgomery Castle, Powys/Castell Trefaldwyn*, 2nd edition. Cardiff, 1981.

Lloyd, J. E. 1899–1900. 'Wales and the coming of the Normans (1039–1093)', *Trans. Hon. Soc. Cymmrodorion*, (1899–1900), 122–79.

Lloyd, J. E. 1939. *A history of Wales from the earliest times to the Edwardian conquest*, 3rd edition, 2 vols. London, 1939.

Lloyd, J. Y. W. 1874. 'History of the lordship of Maelor Gymraeg or Bromfield, the lordship of Ial or Yale, and Chirkland, in the principality of Powys Fadog [parts 2, 3 and 4]', *Archaeol. Cambrensis*, 4 ser., 5 (1874), 22–41, 132–46, 185–99.

Lutz, D. 1977. 'Die Wasserburg Eschelbronn bei Heidelberg, ein Niederadelssitz des 13. bis 18. Jahrhunderts', *Château Gaillard*, 8 (1977), 193–222.

McNeill, T. E. 1980. *Anglo-Norman Ulster: the history and archaeology of an Irish barony, 1177–1400*. Edinburgh, 1980.

Maguire, J. B. 1974. 'Seventeenth century plans of Dublin Castle', *J. Roy. Soc. Antiq. Ir.*, 104 (1974), 5–14.

Mahany, C. 1977. 'Excavations at Stamford Castle, 1971–6', *Château Gaillard*, 8 (1977), 223–45.

Marsden, E. W. 1969–71. *Greek and Roman artillery*, 2 vols. Oxford, 1969–71.

Mason, J. F. A. 1963. 'Roger de Montgomery and his sons (1067–1102)', *Trans. Roy. Hist. Soc.*, 5 ser., 13 (1963), 1–28.

Mason, J. F. A. and Barker, P. A. 1961. 'The Norman castle at Quatford', *Trans. Shropshire Archaeol Soc.*, 57.1 (1961), 37–62.

Mayes, P. and Butler, L. 1983. *Sandal Castle excavations, 1964–1973: a detailed archaeological report*. Wakefield, 1983.

Merrick, R. 1983. *Morganiae archaiographia: a book of the antiquities of Glamorganshire*, ed. by B. Ll. James. Barry, 1983.

Moorhouse, S. 1983. 'The medieval pottery', in Mayes and Butler 1983, 83–212.

Morgan, R. 1977. 'Dendrochronological dating of a Yorkshire timber building', *Vernacular Architect.*, 8 (1977), 809–14.

Morgan, R. 1980. 'Tree-ring dating: a reply to D. J. Schove', *Medieval Archaeol.*, 24 (1980), 215–17.

Morley, B. M. 1981. 'Aspects of fourteenth-century castle design', in A. Detsicas (ed.), *Collectanea historica: essays in memory of Stuart Rigold*, 104–13. Maidstone, 1981.

Morley, E. L. 1964. 'A 13th century mystery at Ludlow: Walter de Lacey's moat', *Shropshire Mag.*, December (1964), 27.

Morris, J. E. 1901. *The Welsh wars of Edward I.* Oxford, 1901.

Munby, J. and Renn, D. 1985. 'Description of the castle buildings', in B. Cunliffe and J. Munby, *Excavations at Portchester Castle. IV. Medieval. The inner bailey*, 72–119. London, 1985.

Neaverson, E. 1947. *Mediaeval castles in North Wales: a study of sites, water supply and building stones.* Liverpool, 1947.

Nelson, L. H. 1966. *The Normans in South Wales, 1070–1171.* Austin, 1966.

Nicolaisen, W. F. H. *et al.* 1970. *The names of towns and cities in Britain.* London, 1970.

Noddle, B. A. *et al.* 1977. 'The animal bones', in Charlton *et al.*1977, 63–73.

North, F. J. 1957. *The stones of Llandaff Cathedral.* Cardiff, 1957.

Ogilby, J. 1675. *Britannia, volume the first: or, an illustration of the kingdom of England and dominion of Wales.* London, 1675.

O'Neil, B. H. St J. 1938. *Usk Castle, Monmouthshire.* Privately published, 1938.

O'Neil, B. H. St J. 1942–43. 'Excavations at Fridd Faldwyn camp, Montgomery, 1937–39; *Archaeol. Cambrensis*, 97 (1942–43), 1–57.

O'Neil, B. H. St J. and Foster-Smith, A. H. 1936. 'Excavations at Twyn y Cregen, Llanarth, Monmouthshire', *Archaeol. Cambrensis*, 91 (1936), 247–58.

Orton, C. 1980. *Mathematics in archaeology.* London, 1980.

Owen, G. 1892. *The description of Penbrokshire*, **1**. London, 1892.

Owen, G. 1897. *The description of Penbrokshire*, **2**. London, 1897.

Palmer, A. N. 1903. *A history of the country districts of Wrexham.* Wrexham, 1903.

Palmer, A. N. 1906. 'The town of Holt, in county Denbigh', *Archaeol. Cambrensis*, 6 ser., 6 (1906), 217–40.

Palmer, A. N. 1907. 'The town of Holt, in county Denbigh, (contd.)', *Archaeol. Cambrensis*, 6 ser., 7 (1907), 1–34, 311–34, 384–434.

Palmer, A. N. 1908. 'The town of Holt, in county Denbigh, (contd.)', *Archaeol. Cambrensis*, 6 ser., 8 (1908), 155–82.

Paterson, D. R. 1920. 'Scandinavian influence in the place-names and early personal names of Glamorgan', *Archaeol. Cambrensis*, 6 ser., 20 (1920), 31–89.

Paterson, D. R. 1921. 'The Scandinavian settlement of Cardiff', *Archaeol. Cambrensis*, 76 (1921), 53–83.

Payne, S. 1972a. 'Partial recovery and sample bias: the results of some sieving experiments', in E. S. Higgs (ed.), *Papers in economic prehistory*, 49–64. Cambridge, 1972.

Payne, S. 1972b. 'On the interpretation of bone samples from archaeological sites', in E. S. Higgs (ed.), *Papers in economic prehistory*, 65–81. Cambridge, 1972.

Payne-Gallwey, R. 1903. *The crossbow: medieval and modern, military and sporting.* London, 1903.

Peers, C. R. 1915–16. 'Carnarvon Castle', *Trans. Hon. Soc. Cymmrodorion*, (1915–16), 1–74.

Percy, T. (ed.) 1905. *The regulations and establishment of the household of Henry Algernon Percy, the fifth Earl of Northumberland, 1512.* London, 1905.

Perks, J. C. 1967. *Chepstow Castle, Monmouthshire*, 2nd edition. London, 1967.

Pevsner, N. 1963. *Herefordshire*. Harmondsworth, 1963.

Phillips, J. R. 1874. *Memoirs of the Civil War in Wales and the Marches 1642–49*, 2 vols. London, 1874.

Phillips, J. R. S. 1975. *The justices of the peace in Wales and Monmouthshire 1541–1689*. Cardiff, 1975.

Piboule, P. 1982. 'Les souterrains médiévaux et leur place dans l'histoire des structures de défense', *Château Gaillard*, 9–10 (1982), 237–53.

Powell, J. R. 1962. *The navy in the English Civil War*. London, 1962.

Powicke, M. 1913. *The loss of Normandy*. Manchester, 1913.

Pratt, D. 1963. 'Wrexham militia in the 14th century', *Trans. Denbighshire Hist. Soc.*, 12 (1963), 26–40.

Pratt, D. 1965. 'The medieval borough of Holt', *Trans. Denbighshire Hist. Soc.*, 14 (1965), 9–74.

Pré, M. 1961. 'Le château de Laval', *Congrès Archéologique de France*, 119: *Maine 1961*, 353–72.

Probert, L. A. 1967. 'Deepweir Tump', *Archaeol. in Wales*, 7 (1967), 22.

Proudfoot, B. 1959. 'Report on soil samples from Lismahon', in D. M. Waterman, 'Excavations at Lismahon, Co. Down', *Medieval Archaeol.*, 3 (1959), 171–73.

Pugh, T. B. (ed.) 1963. *The marcher lordships of South Wales 1415–1536: selected documents*. Cardiff, 1963.

Rackham, D. J. 1977. 'The faunal remains', in P. V. Addyman and J. Priestley, 'Baile Hill, York: a report on the Institute's excavations', *Archaeol. J.*, 134 (1977), 146–52.

Rahtz, P. A. *et al.* 1982. 'Architectural reconstruction of timber buildings from archaeological evidence', *Vernacular Architect.*, 13 (1982), 39–47.

Rawlinson, R. (ed.) 1728. *The history of Sir John Perrott*. London, 1728.

RCAM 1914. *An inventory of the ancient monuments in Wales and Monmouthshire. IV. County of Denbigh*, Royal Commission on the Ancient and Historical Monuments and Constructions in Wales and Monmouthshire. London, 1914.

RCAM 1917. *An inventory of the ancient monuments in Wales and Monmouthshire. V. County of Carmarthen*. Royal Commission on the Ancient and Historical Monuments and Constructions in Wales and Monmouthshire. London, 1917.

RCAM 1937. *An inventory of the ancient monuments in Anglesey*, Royal Commission on Ancient and Historical Monuments (Wales). London, 1937.

RCAM 1956. *An inventory of the ancient monuments in Caernarvonshire. I. East*, Royal Commission on Ancient and Historical Monuments in Wales and Monmouthshire. London, 1956.

RCAM 1960. *An inventory of the ancient monuments in Caernarvonshire. II. Central*, Royal Commission on Ancient and Historical Monuments in Wales and Monmouthshire. London, 1960.

RCAM 1981. *An inventory of the ancient monuments in Glamorgan. IV. Domestic architecture from the Reformation to the Industrial Revolution: I. The greater houses*, Royal Commission on Ancient and Historical Monuments in Wales. Cardiff, 1981.

RCAM 1982. *An inventory of the ancient monuments in Glamorgan. III. Medieval secular monuments: II. Non-defensive*, Royal Commission on Ancient and Historical Monuments in Wales. Cardiff, 1982.

RCHM 1934. *An inventory of the historical monuments in Herefordshire. III. North-west*, Royal Commission on Historical Monuments. London, 1934.

RCHM 1972. *An inventory of the historical monuments in the city of York. II. The defences*, Royal Commission on Historical Monuments (England). London, 1972.

Rees, A. and Bartley, D. 1983a. 'Plant remains in peat from the outer moat', in Mayes and Butler 1983, 350–52.

Rees, A. and Bartley, D. 1983b. 'Pollen analysis of soil samples', in Mayes and Butler 1983, 353.

Rees, W. 1933. *South Wales and the border in the XIV century.* Southampton, 1933.

Rees, W. 1951. *An historical atlas of Wales from early to modern times.* Cardiff, 1951.

Renn, D. F. 1961. 'The round keeps of the Brecon region', *Archaeol. Cambrensis,* 110 (1961), 129–43.

Renn, D. F. 1964. 'The first Norman castles in England (1051–1071)', *Château Gaillard,* 1 (1964), 125–32.

Renn, D. F. 1967–68. 'The donjon at Pembroke Castle', *Trans. Ancient Monuments Soc.,* n. ser., 15 (1967–68), 35–47.

Renn, D. F. 1969. 'The Avranches traverse at Dover Castle', *Archaeol. Cantiana,* 84 (1969), 79–92.

Renn, D. F. 1971. 'The *Turris de Penuesel:* a reappraisal and a theory', *Sussex Archaeol. Collect.,* 109 (1971), 55–64.

Renn, D. F. 1973a. *Norman castles in Britain,* 2nd edition. London, 1973.

Renn, D. F. 1973b. 'Defending Framlingham Castle', *Proc. Suffolk Inst. Archaeol.,* 33.1 (1973), 58–67.

Renn, D. F. 1975. 'An Angevin gatehouse at Skipton Castle (Yorkshire, West Riding)', *Château Gaillard,* 7 (1975), 173–82.

Richard, A. J. 1927. 'Kenfig Castle', *Archaeol. Cambrensis,* 82 (1927), 161–82.

Rigold, S. E. 1969. 'Recent investigations into the earliest defences of Carisbrooke Castle, Isle of Wight', *Château Gaillard,* 3 (1969), 128–38.

Rigold, S. E. 1973. 'Timber bridges at English castles and moated sites', *Château Gaillard,* 6 (1973), 183–93.

Rigold, S. E. 1975. 'Structural aspects of medieval timber bridges', *Medieval Archaeol.,* 19 (1975), 48–91.

Robinson, W. R. B. 1977. 'Sir George Herbert of Swansea (d. 1570)', *Bull. Board Celtic Stud.,* 27.2 (1977), 303–09.

Roesdahl, E. 1982. 'The building activities of king Harald Bluetooth: notes after the dendrochronological dating of the Viking fortress of Trelleborg', *Château Gaillard,* 9–10 (1982), 543–45.

Rose-Troup, F. 1913. *The western rebellion of 1549.* London, 1913.

Rowley, T. 1972. *The Shropshire landscape.* London, 1972.

Rushforth, G. M. N. 1924. 'Medieval tiles in the church of Llangattock-nigh-Usk', *Antiq. J.,* 4 (1924), 382–87.

Sailhan, P. 1978. 'Typologie des archères et cannonières', *Bull. de la Société de l'Ouest et des Musées de Poitiers,* 14 (1978), 511–41.

Salch, Ch.-L. 1979. *Dictionnaire des châteaux et les fortifications du moyen âge en France.* Strasbourg, 1979.

Salzman, L. F. 1953. 'The property of the Earl of Arundel, 1397', *Sussex Archaeol. Collect.,* 91 (1953), 32–52.

Saunders, A. D. 1980. 'Lydford Castle, Devon', *Medieval Archaeol.,* 24 (1980), 123–86.

Schiffer, M. B. 1972. 'Archaeological context and systemic context', *American Antiquity,* 37 (1972), 156–65.

Schove, D. J. and Lowther, A. W. G. 1957. 'Tree-rings and medieval archaeology', *Medieval Archaeol.,* 1 (1957), 78–95.

Schramm, E. 1980. *Die antiken Geschütze der Saalburg.* Bad Homburg, 1980.

Shaw, H. 1858. *Specimens of tile pavements drawn from existing authorities.* London, 1858.

Simpson, W. D. 1978. *Bothwell Castle*, 2nd edition. Edinburgh, 1978.

Smith, J. B. 1965. 'The origins of the revolt of Rhys ap Maredudd', *Bull. Board Celtic Stud.*, 21.2 (1965), 151–63.

Smith, M. J. *et al.* 1983a. 'An investigation of the garderobe deposits', in Mayes and Butler 1983, 354–55.

Smith, M. J. *et al.* 1983b. 'An investigation of the charcoal samples', in Mayes and Butler 1983, 356–57.

Solomon, A. 1982. *The last siege of Dryslwyn Castle*. Carmarthen, 1982.

Sorrell, A. 1981. *Reconstructing the past*, ed. by M. Sorrell. London, 1981.

Soulsby, I. 1983. *The towns of medieval Wales: a study of their history, archaeology and early topography*. Chichester, 1983.

South, S. 1977. *Method and theory in historical archaeology*. New York, 1977.

Spurgeon, C. J. 1965–66. 'The castles of Montgomeryshire', *Montgomeryshire Collect.*, 59 (1965–66), 1–59.

Spurgeon, C. J. 1975. *The castle and borough of Aberystwyth*. [2nd edition]. Aberystwyth, 1975.

Spurgeon, C. J. 1981. 'Moated sites in Wales', in F. A. Aberg and A. E. Brown (eds.), *Medieval moated sites in north-west Europe*, 19–70. Oxford, 1981.

Statham, E. P. 1917–20. *History of the family of Maunsell (Mansell, Mansel)*, 3 vols. London, 1917–20.

Stiesdal, H. 1982. 'Eriksvolde', *Château Gaillard*, 9–10 (1982), 255–64.

Stuiver, M. 1982. 'A high-precision calibration of the AD radiocarbon time scale'. *Radiocarbon*, 24 (1982), 1–26.

Sturdy, D. M. 1979. 'Nine hundred years of the Tower of London', *London Archaeol.*, 3.10 (1979), 270–73.

Taylor, A. J. 1950. 'The birth of Edward of Caernarvon and the beginnings of Caernarvon Castle', *History*, n. ser., 35 (1950), 256–61.

Taylor, A. J. 1976. 'Who was 'John Pennardd, leader of the men of Gwynedd'?', *Eng. Hist. Rev.*, 91 (1976), 79–97.

Taylor, A. J. 1977. 'Castle-building in thirteenth-century Wales and Savoy', *Proc. Brit. Acad.*, 63 (1977), 265–92.

Taylor, A. J. 1979. *Raglan Castle, Gwent/Castell Rhaglan*, 14th impression. Cardiff, 1979.

Taylor, A. J. 1983. *Four great castles: Caernarfon, Conwy, Harlech, Beaumaris*. Newtown, 1983.

Thompson, M. W. 1966. 'The origins of Bolingbroke Castle, Lincolnshire', *Medieval Archaeol.*, 10 (1966), 152–58.

Thompson, M. W. forthcoming. *The end of the castle*. Cambridge, forthcoming.

Turner, H. L. 1971. *Town defences in England and Wales: an architectural and documentary study AD 900–1500*. London, 1971.

Vallery-Radot, J. 1967. 'Le donjon de Philippe-Auguste à Villeneuve-sur-Yonne et son devis', *Château Gaillard*, 2 (1967), 106–12.

VCH 1908. *[Victoria] History of Shropshire*, **1**. London, 1908.

VCH 1969. *[Victoria] History of the county of Warwick*, **8**. London, 1969.

Vince, A. G. 1980. 'A Monmouth-type floor tile from Llanthony Priory, Gwent', in D. H. Evans, 'Excavations at Llanthony Priory, Gwent, 1978', *Monmouthshire Antiq.*, 4.1&2 (1980), 21–22.

Vis, E. and De Geus, C. 1978. *Alt holländische Fliesen*. Stuttgart, 1978.

Wakeman, T. 1862. 'On the priory of Monmouth', *Collectanea Archaeologica*, 1 (1862), 285–94.

Walker, R. P. 1972. 'Hubert de Burgh and Wales, 1218–1232', *Eng. Hist. Rev.*, 87 (1972), 465–94.

Ward-Perkins, J. B. 1941. 'A late thirteenth-century tile-pavement at Cleeve Abbey', *Proc. Somersetshire Archaeol. Natur. Hist. Soc.*, 87 (1941), 39–55.

Waterman, D. 1970. 'Somersetshire and other foreign building stone in medieval Ireland, c. 1175–1400', *Ulster J. Archaeol.*, 3 ser., 33 (1970), 63–75.

Watson, J. P. N. 1978. 'The interpretation of epiphyseal fusion data', in D. R. Brothwell *et al.* (eds.), *Research problems in zooarchaeology*, 97–101. London, 1978.

Webster, G. 1975. *The Cornovii*. London, 1975.

Webster, P. 1981. 'Dryslwyn Castle 1980', in R. Avent and P. Webster, *Interim reports of excavations at Laugharne Castle, Dyfed, 1976–1980, and Dryslwyn Castle, Dyfed, 1980*, 34–54. Cardiff, 1981.

Webster, P. 1983. 'Dryslwyn Castle 1981–2', in C. Arnold *et al.*, *Interim reports on excavations at three castles in Wales 1981–1982*, 12–22. Cardiff, 1983.

Weyman, H. T. 1914–17. 'Ludlow Castle and church', *Trans. Woolhope Natur. Fld. Club*, (1914–17), 126–36.

Wightman, W. E. 1966. *The Lacy family in England and Normandy 1066–1194*. Oxford, 1966.

Wilcox, R. 1972. 'Timber reinforcement in medieval castles', *Château Gaillard*, 5 (1972), 193–202.

Williams, A. H. 1948. *An introduction to the history of Wales II. The middle ages, part I, 1063–1284*. Cardiff, 1948.

Williams, G. 1962. 'Rice Mansell of Oxwich and Margam (1487–1559)', *Morgannwg*, 6 (1962), 33–51.

Williams, G. 1981. 'The Herberts of Swansea and Sir John Herbert', *Glamorgan Hist.*, 12 (1981), 47–58.

Williams, J. P. G. 1922–23. 'Laugharnshire miscellanea', *Trans. Carmarthenshire Antiq. Soc. Fld. Club*, 16 (1922–23), 2–3.

Wilson, D. M. and Hurst, D. G. 1965. 'Medieval Britain in 1964', *Medieval Archaeol.*, 9 (1965), 170–220.

Index

Index